For Glen, my equestrian sibling,
for Ruth, my artist sibling,
and for my sons, Ben and Paul.

Contents

Foreword

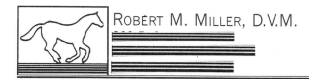

ROBERT M. MILLER, D.V.M.

6-19-19

Jean Abernethy's cartoon horse, Fergus, very popular with horse lovers, inspired several books. This book, Fergus's 20th anniversary cartoon publication will, I am sure, convince readers that the author is more than a cartoonist. She is a very talented artist. Her serious art confirms that.

Because I am also a cartoonist, a veterinarian specializing in equine medicine, and a book author, I am an admirer of Jean Abernethy. Other horselovers will agree. (providing that they have a good sense of humor.)

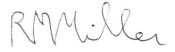

Acknowledgments

Let me first extend my gratitude to my publisher Trafalgar Square Books, and Martha, Rebecca, Caroline...for what is our fifth Fergus book. Your investment in me, and this character we call Fergus, has been a blessing.

Thanks to my family for encouragement and support over the years.

To the editors, journalists, equestrians, bloggers, Santa Clauses, friends, and writers who have boosted Fergus and me along on our merry canter over the past 20 years, thank you. One never travels alone, and I'm grateful to each and every one of you for your support on this journey.

Thank you, Facebook, for a platform that allowed Fergus to reach beyond a few print publications, a medium through which, finally, I could give Fergus to the world. Moreover, thank you to all the social media viewers who have helped Fergus grow by commenting, "liking," and sharing Fergus around the globe. And now, those of you who follow on Instagram, thank you, too. You cannot know how much it means to me, to see your names come up again and again—friends I've met, and friends I've never met. I know that if you showed up at my fireside, the stories would be rich.

Thank you to all the dear folk who have welcomed me into their barns and with whom I have ridden and driven horses.

Thank you to all the horses who have touched my life
and been my inspiration.

Thank *you* for holding this book in your hands.

No animals were harmed in the creation of this book.

Warning
Not to be taken seriously. Keep within reach of children.

Recommended Dosage
Read all these comics immediately, or a bit at a time, as you like. For committed equestrians, especially before lessons or clinics, take two or more comics lightly with a grain of salt. For equestrians under intense emotional/mental/competitive pressure, these comics can be used in lieu of an illegal substance or topical ointment.

Ingredients
Experience, silliness.

BEST BEFORE
You go to the barn.

Other Information:
Keep at room temperature (for personal comfort while you read).

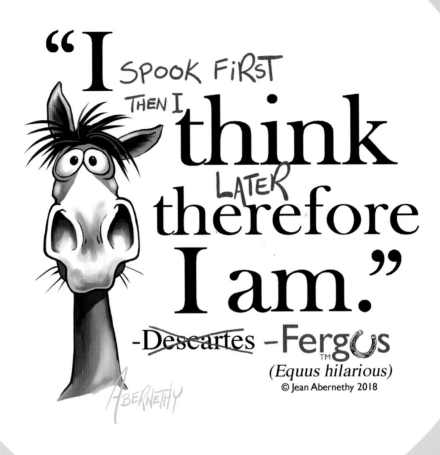

"I *spook first then I* **think** *later* **therefore** **I am.**"

-~~Descartes~~ –Fergus™
(Equus hilarious)
© Jean Abernethy 2018

Part One:

Introduction

Prologue

Dear Fergus,

It's hard to believe it's been 20 years since I scribbled you onto a page and stuffed you into a fax machine. As I continued to sketch, your personality developed.

As a published cartoonist, I wondered if I was taking some kind of risk by branching away from the generic horse characters I had been drawing for over a decade.

You see, I didn't want my equine cartoons to be narrowed into any particular breed, sport, or niche in the horse industry, which is *already* a niche market.

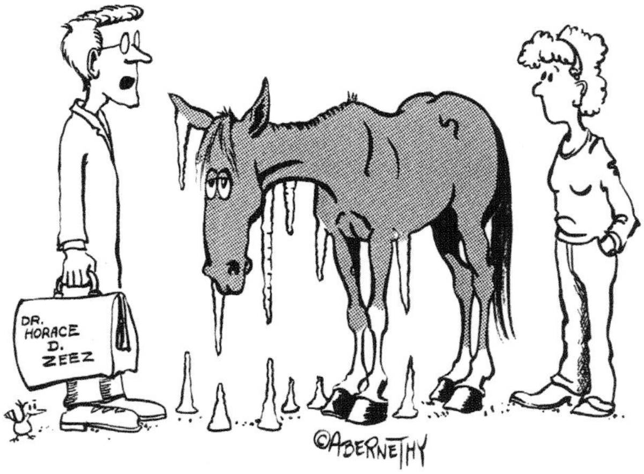
DR. HORACE D. ZEEZ
©ABERNETHY

He's developing stalactites. Try decreasing the mineral in his diet.

In those old comics, the generic horses stood with absent expressions while the human characters captioned the jokes.

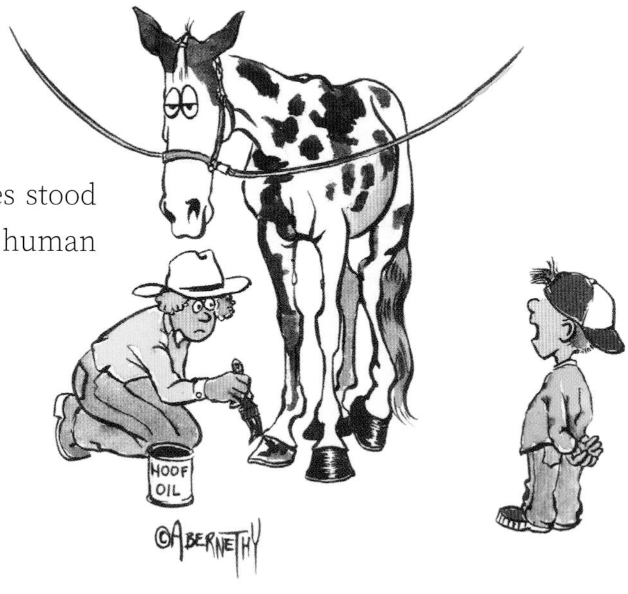
HOOF OIL
©ABERNETHY

Radical design, Ma'am. When you paint your horses, do you always paint the feet last?

But when I drew you, Fergus, something magical happened.
You came to life beneath me!

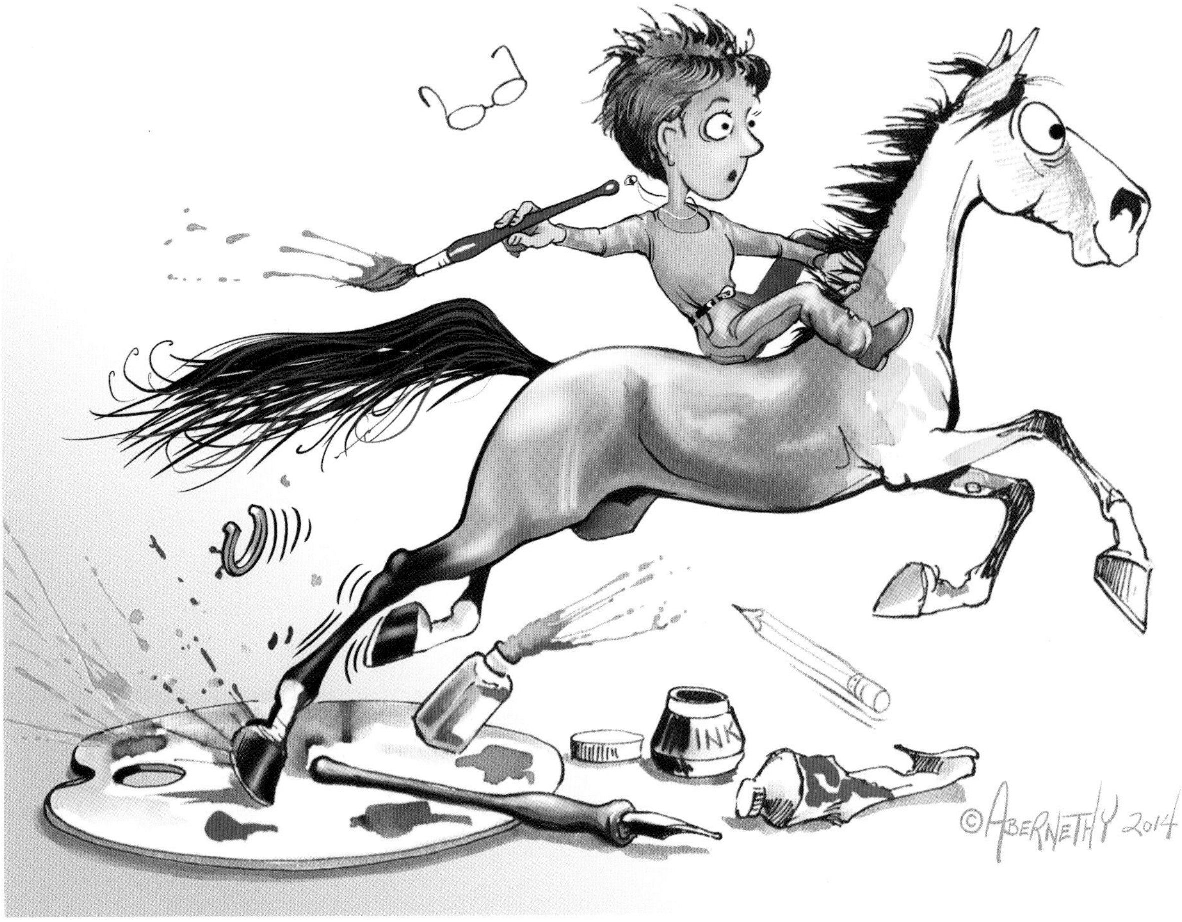
INK
©ABERNETHY 2014

Our first few gigs were in equestrian print magazines. I was working with inks and brushes on paper back then. Here, you appeared in Monty Roberts' *Join-Up Journal,* teaching readers about adrenaline.

What's Adrenaline?

BY JEAN ABERNETHY

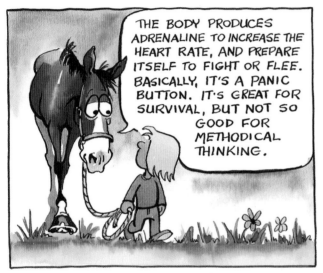

THE BODY PRODUCES ADRENALINE TO INCREASE THE HEART RATE, AND PREPARE ITSELF TO FIGHT OR FLEE. BASICALLY, IT'S A PANIC BUTTON. IT'S GREAT FOR SURVIVAL, BUT NOT SO GOOD FOR METHODICAL THINKING.

FOR EXAMPLE, LOOK AT THAT LITTLE BEE. IF SHE WAS IN A PANIC, SHE COULDN'T LEARN WHICH FLOWERS WERE THE BEST...

©ABERNETHY '06

LIKE THE MAN SAYS: ADRENALINE UP, LEARNING DOWN.

A BEE! AAUUGGHH!!

Most horses that spook dangerously are less likely to be employed. But not you. Your talent for spooking and bolting seemed to get you even more work.

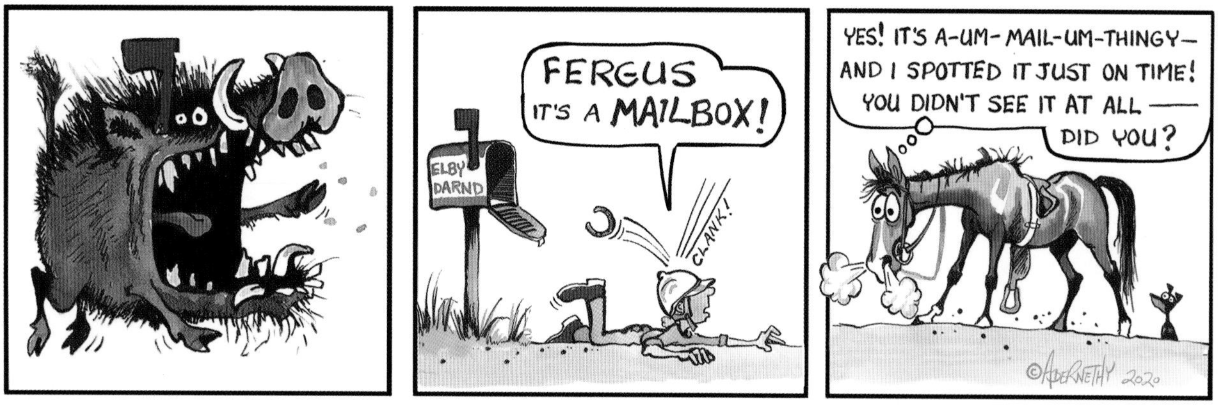
ELBY DARND
FERGUS IT'S A MAILBOX!
CLANK!
YES! IT'S A-UM-MAIL-UM-THINGY— AND I SPOTTED IT JUST ON TIME! YOU DIDN'T SEE IT AT ALL —— DID YOU?

Then we branched into the panel comics. Oh, you were needy, Fergus! You have been the neediest creature I've ever known! Being a versatile horse, you needed tack of every kind. You needed trucks and trailers, even though you refused to load. You needed shoes, even though they wouldn't stay on. You needed carts, carriages, and jumps, whether or not you might choose to pull or jump them. You needed pastures, fences, barns, dogs, cats, goats, turkeys, cows, armadillos, beavers, flies, gophers, a talking pasture rock... sometimes you even needed spaceships and aliens to make an appearance. What a lot of work *that* was!

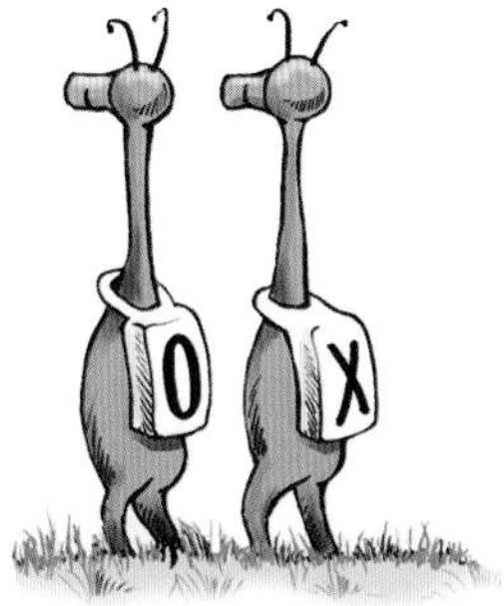
O
X

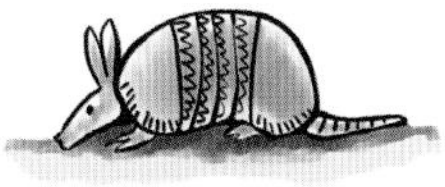

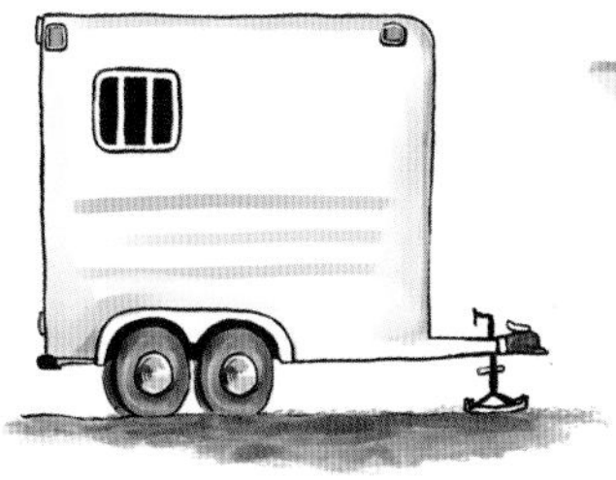

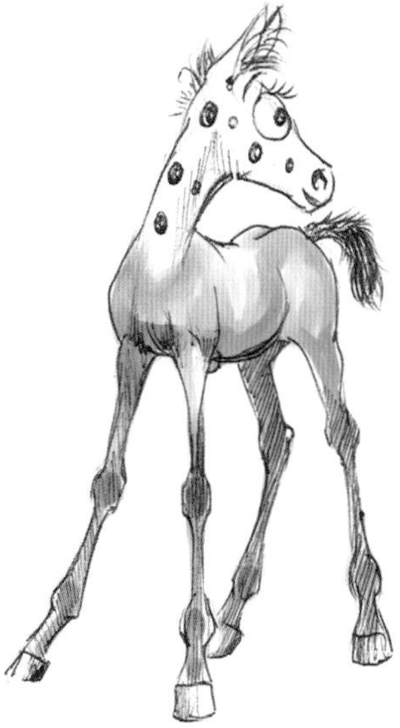
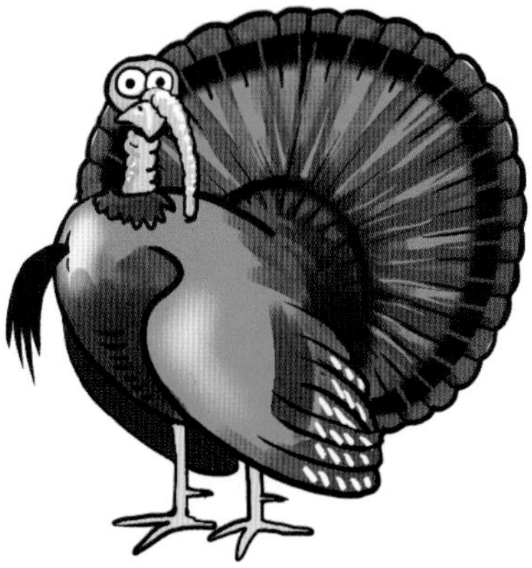
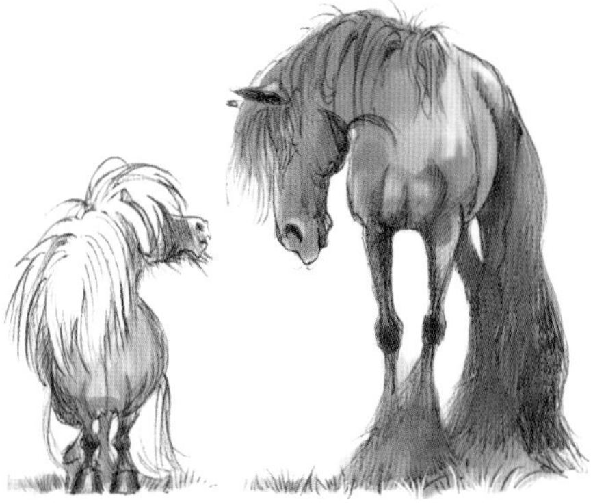
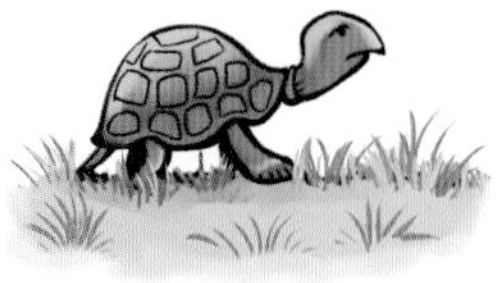

Most significantly, you needed friends with whom to play out your stories. Together, our skills expanded, and our stable grew. You needed a large friend, I gave you Hughie the Clydesdale. You needed a small friend, I gave you Grace the pony. You needed an intellectually superior friend, I gave you Clevis the mule. I gave you humans to work with, so that you would have employment, and a link to the hearts of our readers.

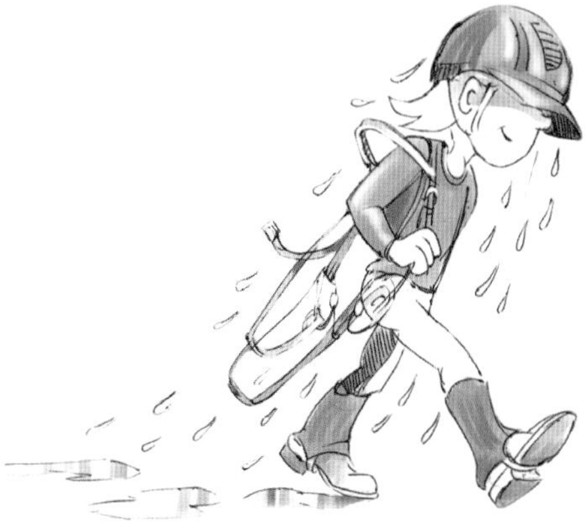
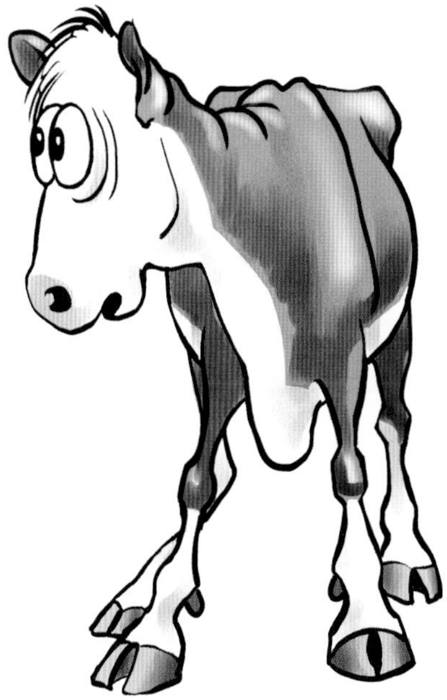

As our community of characters grew, a transformation unfolded. It was subtle at first, but I eventually realized that the humor had reversed. Now it was the *horses* who told the jokes.

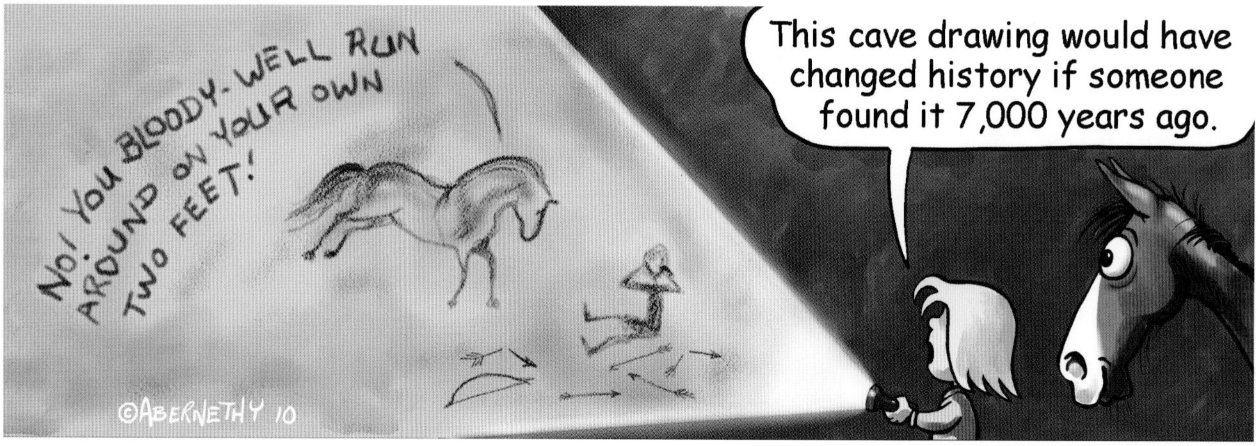
NO! YOU BLOODY-WELL RUN AROUND ON YOUR OWN TWO FEET!
This cave drawing would have changed history if someone found it 7,000 years ago.
©ABERNETHY 10

I find it fascinating that this 20-year transformation happened parallel with and perhaps because of the gentle "natural" horsemanship that was spreading around the world. The equestrian conscience was evolving to a new and different level. Terminology changed among horse folk. Colts were no longer "broken," they were "started." Trainers and competitors strove to communicate rather than dominate. And globally, in that same span of time, Fergus, horse people have come to appreciate that the intellect within you, and your kith and kin, is much more sophisticated than we humans have understood in centuries past.

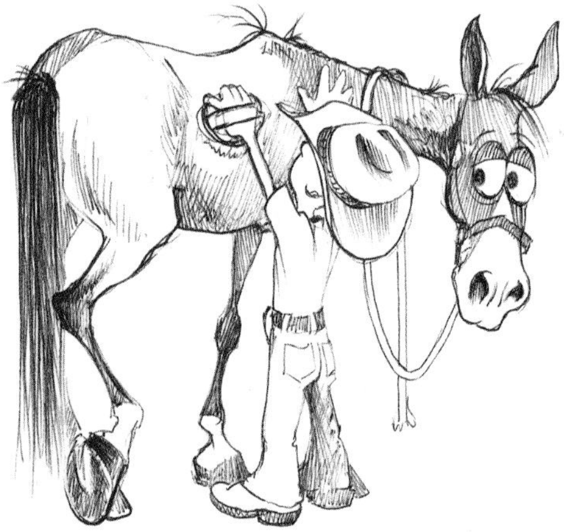

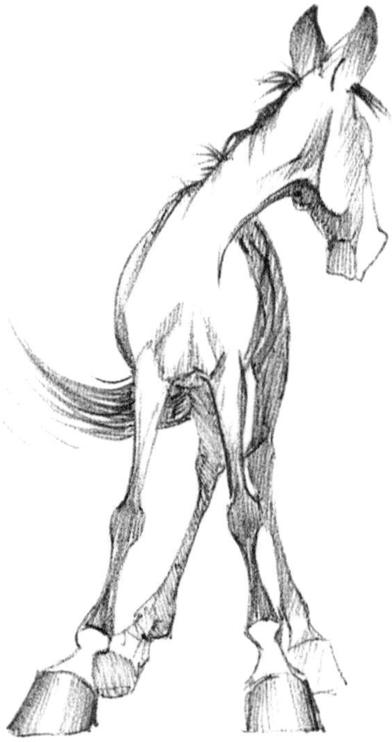

Oh yes, you've been a needy creature, Fergus. You demanded uncounted hours of my time in training, trying to get you to wherever you're going. Most of your successes in humor happened when you didn't really do what your humans wanted you to. Exposure was lean in the old days of print publications, but those in the horse industry who loved you kept asking for more. So, I kept you fed and shod (well, kind of).

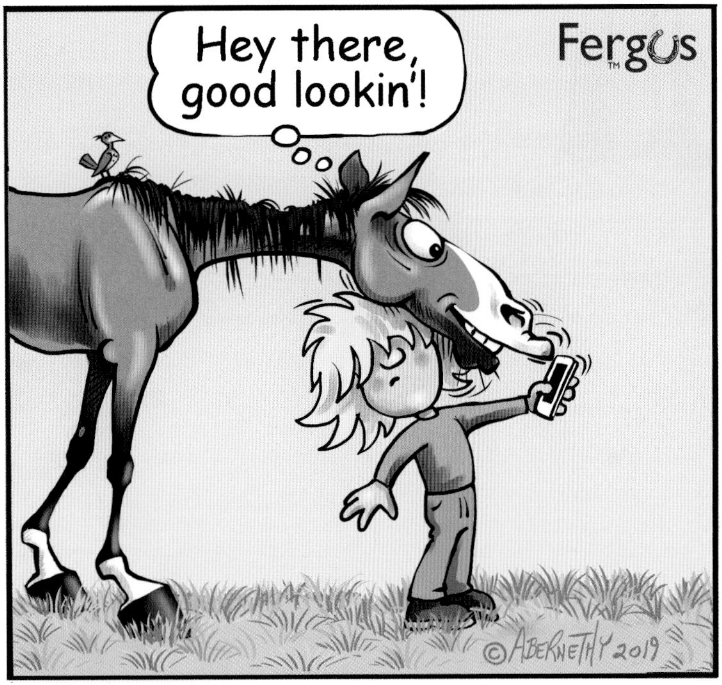
Hey there, good lookin'!
Fergus™
©ABERNETHY 2019

Then when we learned to use social media in 2012, you showed me that you had some talent! Turned loose in cyberspace, you zoomed around the world, shared through the hearts of equestrians. Over 300,000 followers and our first book by 2015! Pretty amazing for a horse with such a "sketchy" pedigree!

Through your adventures, Fergus, you have taught me that the humans who cracked the jokes in the "old" cartoons had no capacity to train you—or any other horse. So in 2015 I hired a clever lad to work with you in our book *Fergus: A Horse to be Reckoned With*.

He had a great smile.

As any savvy trainer would say, "I let the horse be the teacher." You weren't easy on the lad, Fergus, because you assumed that *you* were the trainer. But that lad got to riding you, and by the end of the book, you'd become who you were always meant to be: a working partner who maintained his authority over his own heart and soul.

After that lad got you going, you were hungry for more—I mean *really* hungry. Fergus, it was enough to drive an artist to madness trying to fence you in!

For our third book, *Fergus and the Greener Grass*, I spent hours building barriers of boards, wire, logs, stones, rails...but none could contain you. I suppose I should have known that if I put wings on you, you'd fly.

In any career, that of horse or human, success is never achieved
without help from friends.

Fergus' friends, left to right: Monique, Hugh, Clevis, Dottie, Grace, Russell,
Cleveland Ray, Case, Bjorn, Art, Fergus, Cow, 'nother Cow.

Fergus, I hope you're as grateful for your friends as I am for mine.

Once I understood your capacity to fly, I set you up with your friends to accomplish the outrageous: a cruise with St. Nicholas. Oh, it was precarious! Though our sleigh was a masterpiece, hitching eleven horses in tandem was an endeavor beyond anything I'd yet undertaken: I couldn't get Grace's harness to fit. Russell, the cowhorse, was constantly distracted by the cows. Clevis and Dottie were rather too close in the hitch (they don't like each other much). And, doggone it, none of you would fly straight! But, by golly, we did it: Our third book, *Fergus and The Night Before Christmas,* was born. With your friends, you gave Santa quite a ride.

Fergus, the greatest lesson you've taught me, emerged through numerous comments from fans through social media that read something like this: "I've been going through a rough time lately, thanks for the laugh."

Or this:

This is just the giggle I needed this morning...

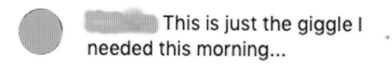

Reading words like these, I realize that you're not just about me finding a way to make a living as an artist. You're about something much bigger, perhaps, than either of us.

So, dear Fergus, I look back over our 20-year journey with great pride, and with even greater gratitude. Like any horse I've worked with, you've taught me a great deal during our time together...

...and I'm quite certain you're not finished training me.

Quote of the Day

Fergus, for a while now we have created calendars to help people smile as they track their days and weeks. For each month, I include a quote and a sketch, as well as a comic. In some instances, the quotes I choose are more about the comic than the accompanying sketch...but nevertheless, there are some musings here that are perhaps worth sharing again. (And I invite our readers to mix and match as they see fit!)

"In my experience, horses who are extraordinarily beautiful seem to know they are."

"Horses who understand children are one of our loveliest mysteries."

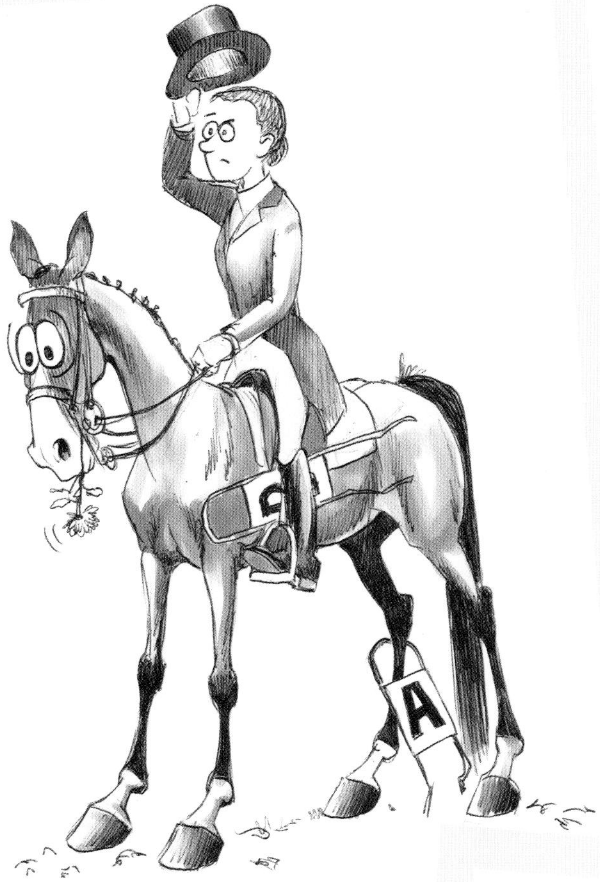
A

"How is it that some horses can come up with an idea that leaves you scratching your head and wondering: 'How did you think that up?'"

"When I hear people say that a horse 'had a mind of his own,' I wonder whose mind they expected him to have."

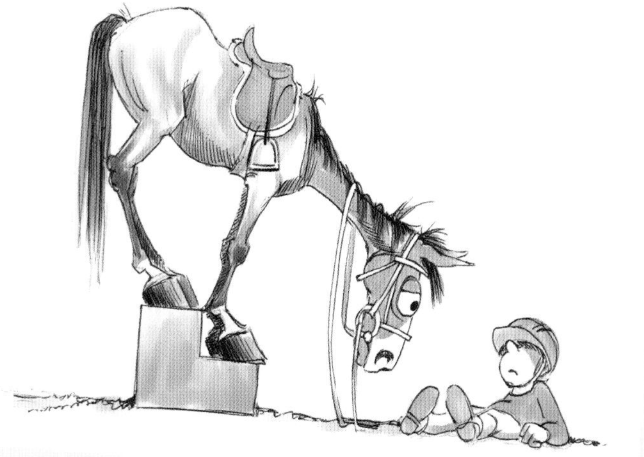

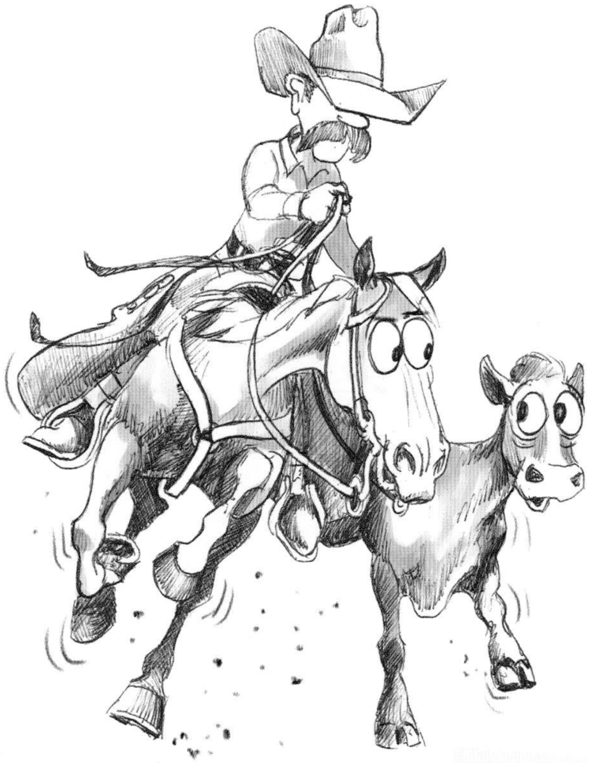

"It is a joy to observe horses who seem to know intrinsically what their job is."

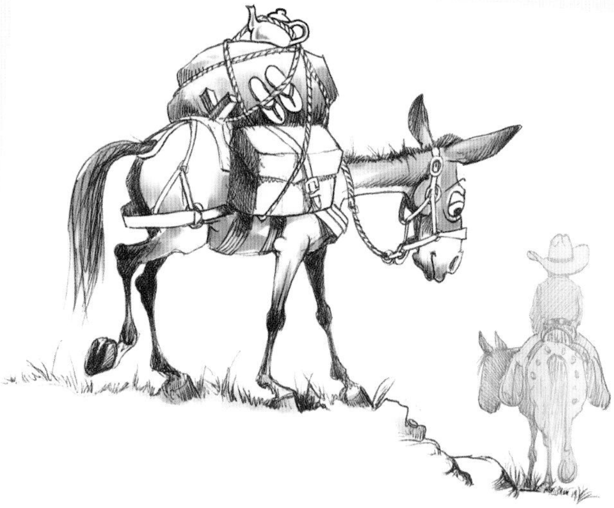

"Do good work. It's the best job security you'll ever have."

"One of a horse's most
important jobs is to teach...

...patience."

"I've heard it said that a horse has
no agenda. Yet when I show up
at the barn for morning chores,
I beg to differ."

"Some horses really do want to please us and will try in earnest to do so."

"Who are more dear to our hearts than the 'lesson horses'? Short-term they teach us determination. Long-term, they teach us forgiveness."

"A horse's mental simplification of any scenario can plow up our established human way of thinking...which is usually a good thing."

"Perhaps we underestimate what transpires between our horses and the other creatures they live with."

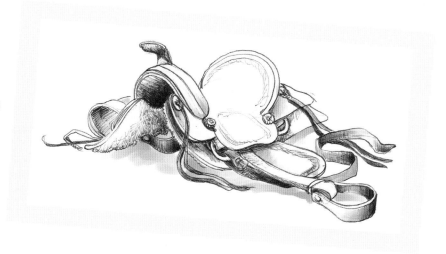

"To a horse, every day is
'Earth Day.'"

"Humans are champions at
making simple things complicated.
Horses are champions at
undoing that for us."

"When I watch horses respond to weather conditions I am reminded how much energy people spend worrying about it!"

"Oh, the trials we put ourselves through to learn patience from these noble creatures!"

"The concept of wearing clothes is completely beyond the imagination of the beast who grows his own coat."

"Blessed is the horse who tries to please you. Even if he doesn't get it right, it's still a good laugh!"

"I've often wondered if horses think about their training sessions during their idle hours. After all, they have a lot of idle hours to think about *something!*"

"It's awful what we go through to get the good stories..."

"Perhaps we shouldn't underestimate an equine's capacity for abstract thought."

"I suppose we'd be foolish to think that we humans are the only species who can joke with one another."

"The best horse in the
world will embarrass you
at some point. That's why
a sense of humor is
so important."

"Only two kinds of things will
spook a horse: things that move,
and things that don't move."

"Horses have a simple
philosophy about exercise:
'If it ain't fun, don't do it.'"

"Humans seem to live under the
illusion that life should make sense.
Horses know better."

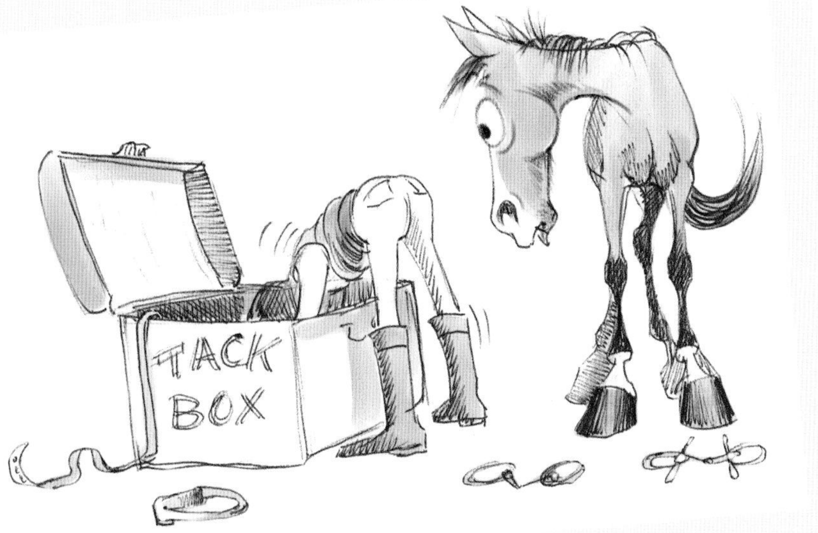
TACK
BOX

"I've often wished that horses could answer my questions. But I wouldn't want to have to answer theirs!"

"Excellence is something to strive for. Perfection is simply a monster."

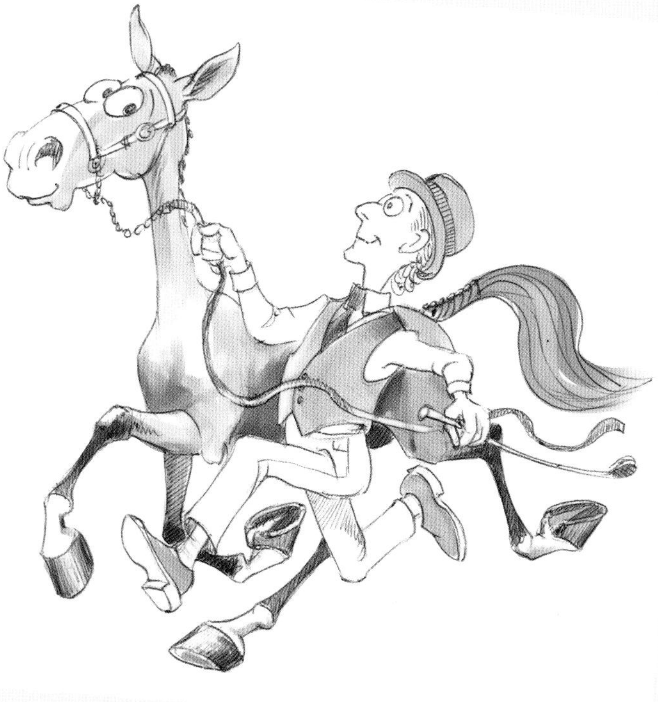

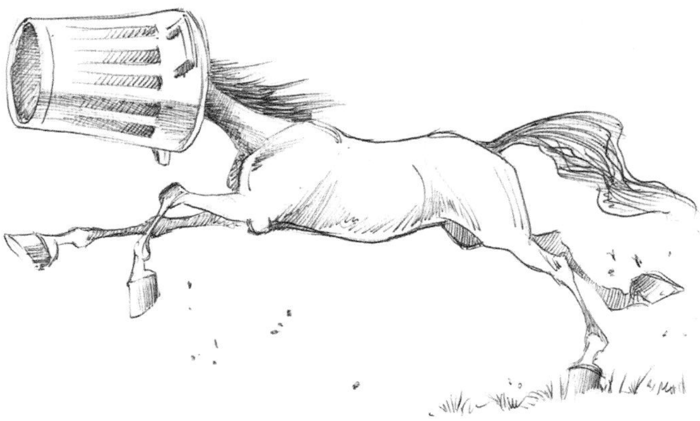

"Curiosity might kill the cat,
but it usually just trains
a horse."

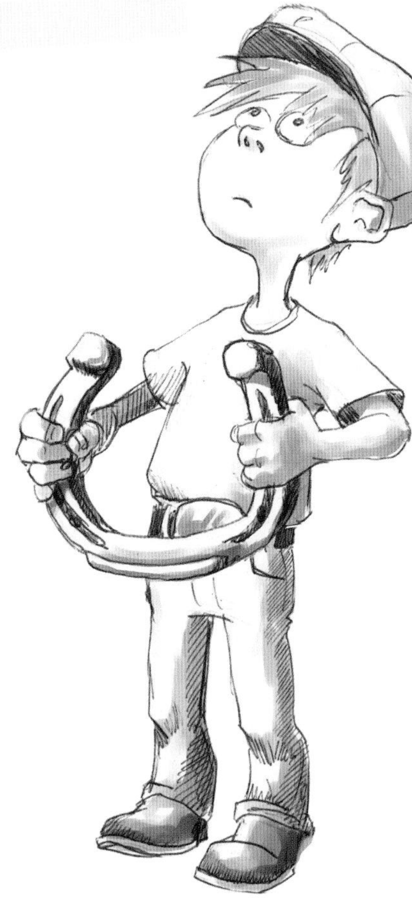

"A child who spends time
with horses will forge stories
to carry for life."

"Be patient. It takes ten years to make a good ten-year-old horse."

"The most valuable lessons are learned outside of your comfort zone."

©ABERNETHY 2011

Fergus Photobombs

You've always been a little bit unpredictable, Fergus. Maybe that's what endears you to so many horse people. The next time I got on your back (not since p. 5), we both looked a lot different. I was learning to do more and more with photographs and digital art. Though I enjoyed my expanding skills, this ride made me nervous. I couldn't tell if you were going to go straight or blow up! But like the brave horse you are, you carried me along to the next chapter...

Fergus, my friend...after that very first time I got on your back, I kept practicing at the drawing board. As the years progressed, I took you with me when I traveled. While it may be true that you've gained a reputation for being sometimes being difficult, when it comes to exploring new places and new tasks, I couldn't ask for a more willing partner.

Algonquin Provincial Park (Ontario, Canada): A trail ride along the old logging roads.

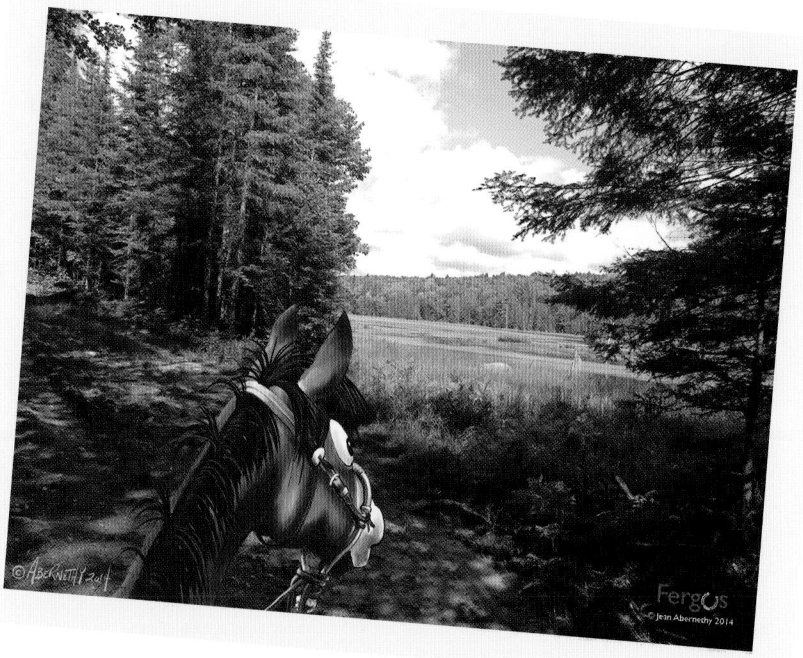
©ABERNETHY 2014
Fergus
©Jean Abernethy 2014

Exploding down the course on
Epsom Downs (Surrey, England).
The first time Fergus ever ran
on turf. (Threw a shoe...)

Sampling the grass at
Stonehenge.

Outside the saloon at Eaves Movie Ranch (near Santa Fe, New Mexico) where many Westerns have been filmed.

Trying out the old stables in the depths of Dunster Castle (near Somerset, England).

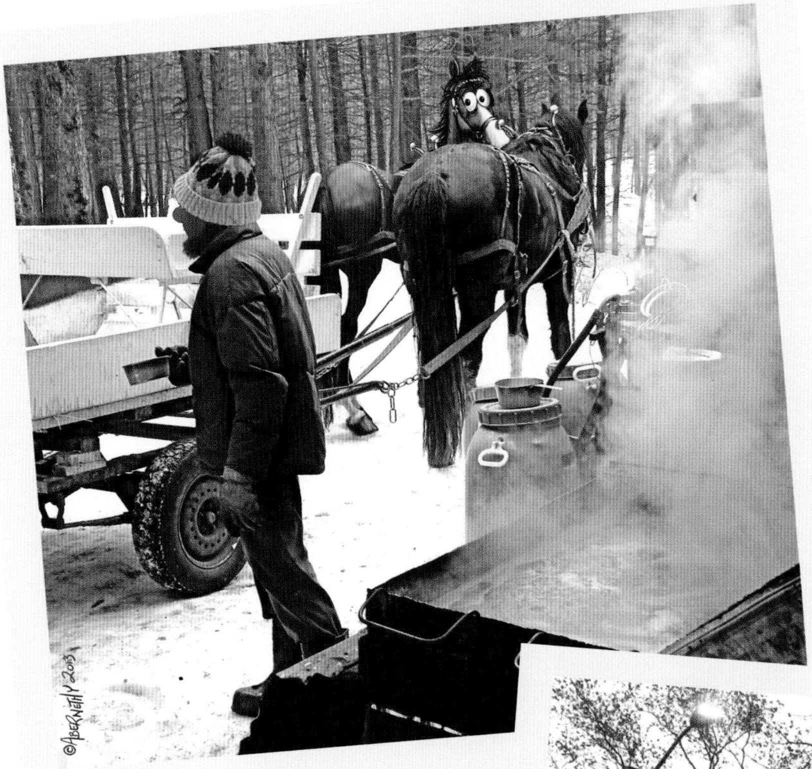
©Abernethy 2015

Pitching in to help haul sap barrels and firewood to the boiler during maple syrup season (Ontario, Canada).

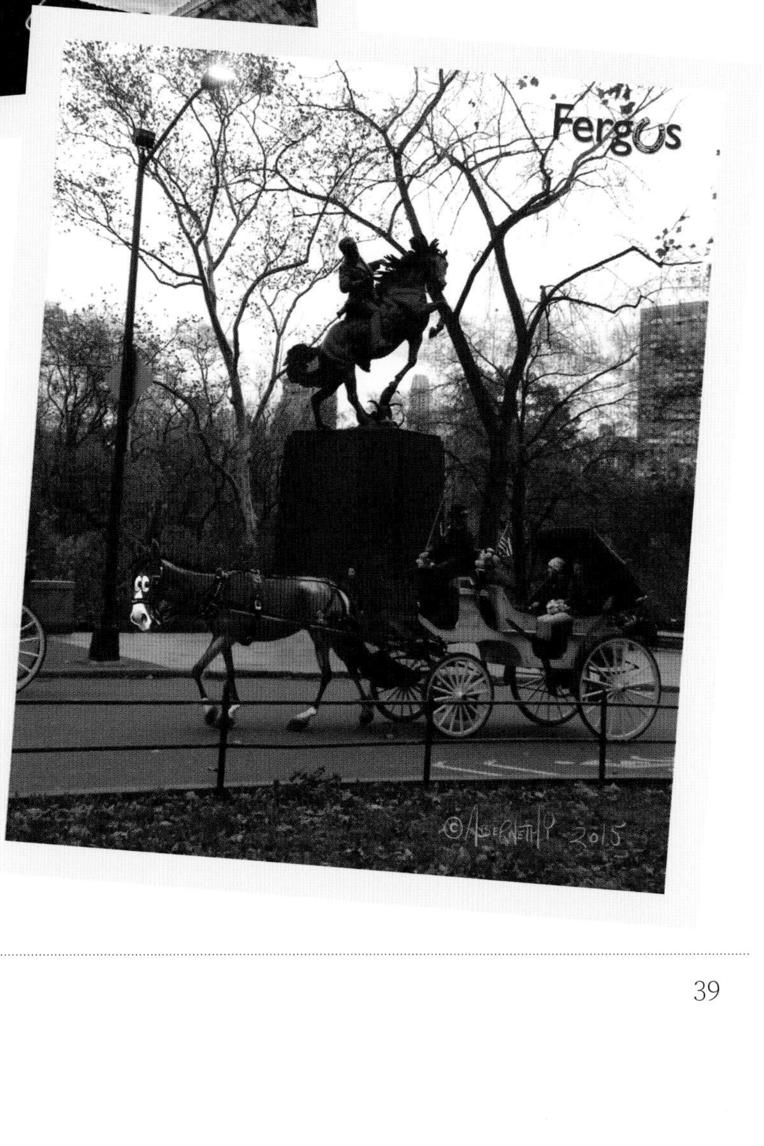
Fergus
©Abernethy 2015

Taking a carriage around Central Park, New York City.

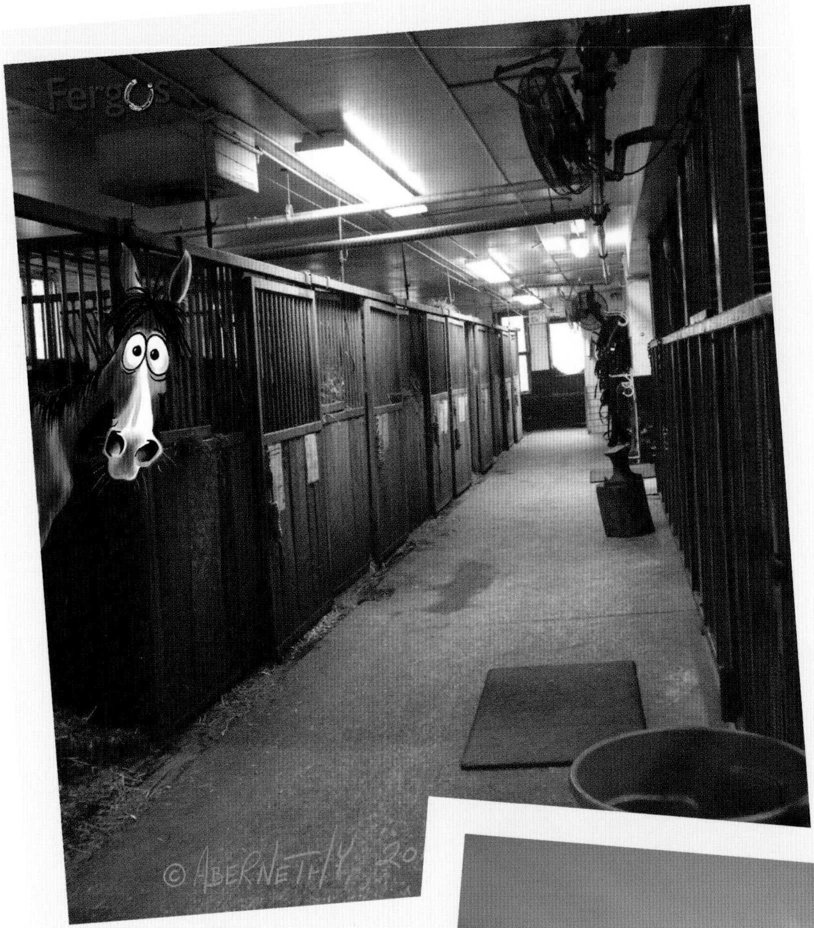
Fergus
© ABERNETHY

There doesn't seem to be
a barn anywhere where Fergus
doesn't feel at home (Clinton Park
Stable, New York City).

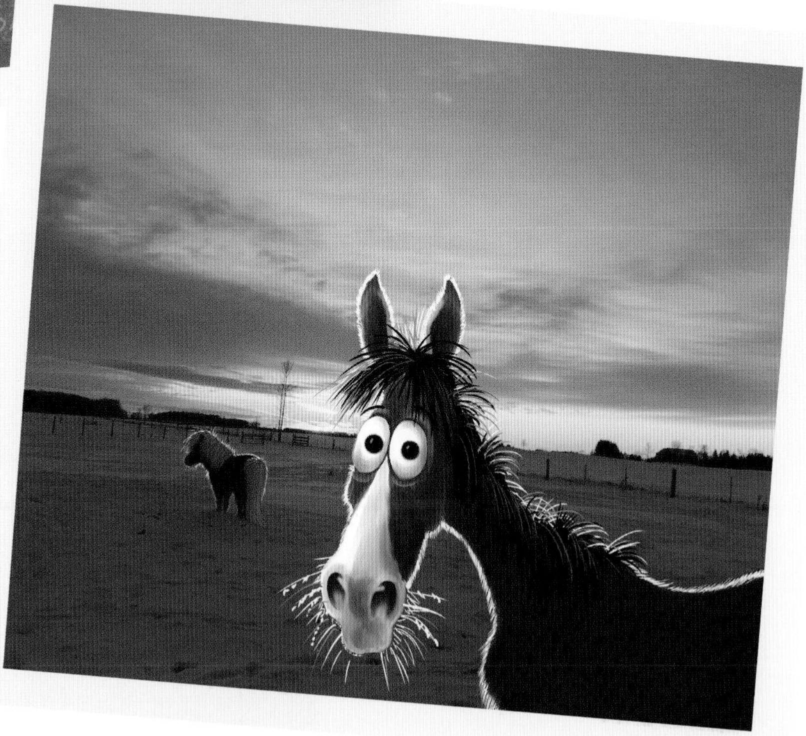

With Grace in the frosty twilight
of Winter Solstice in Canada.

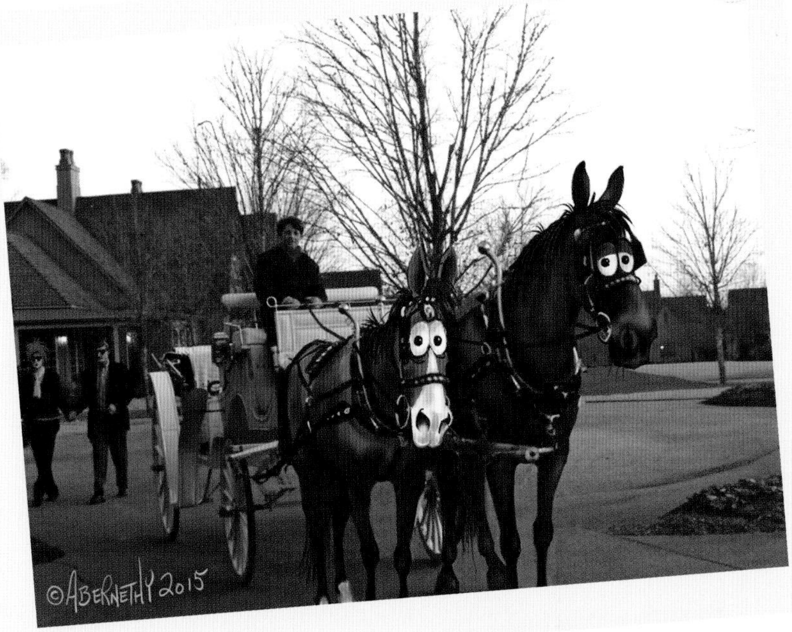
©ABERNETHY 2015

Fergus and Cleveland Ray in a beautiful vis-à-vis carriage (with me driving!) in northern Georgia (USA).

Fergus loves a snowy Canadian winter.

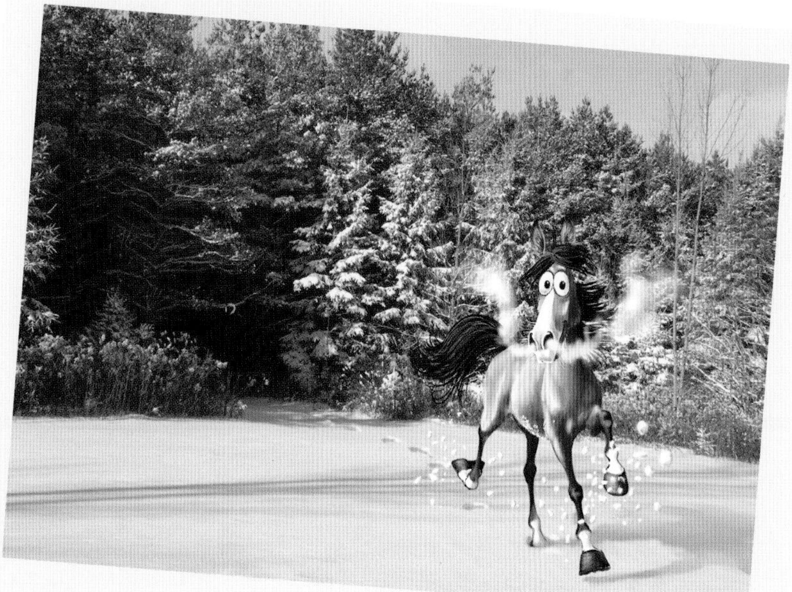

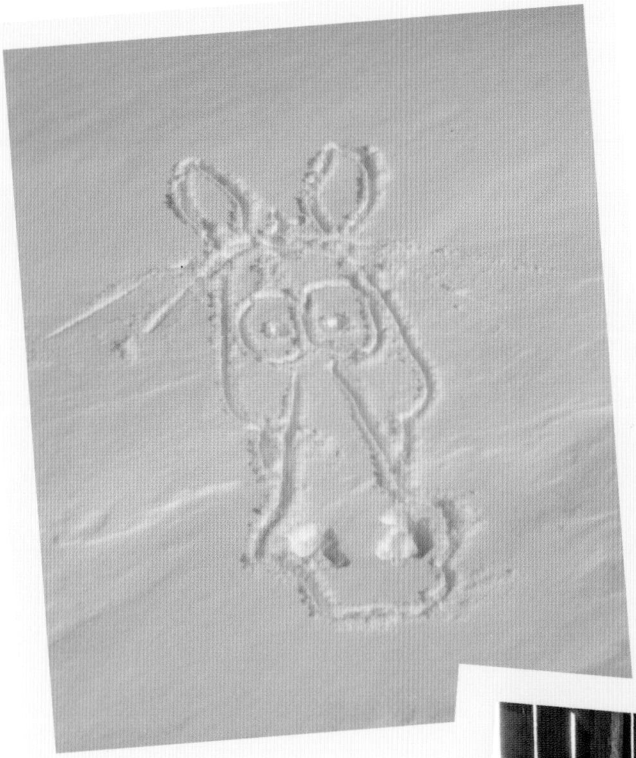

Fresh snow is a fresh page.

Pondering the innumerable stories of his ancestors that an old barn and an old cutter silently keep.

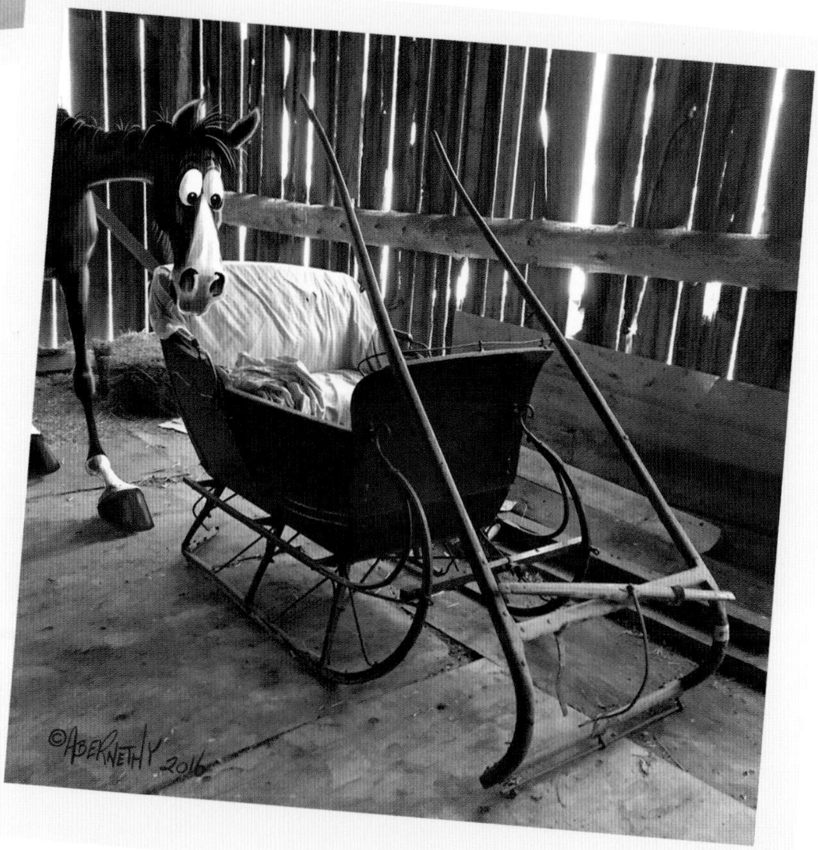
©ABERNETHY 2016

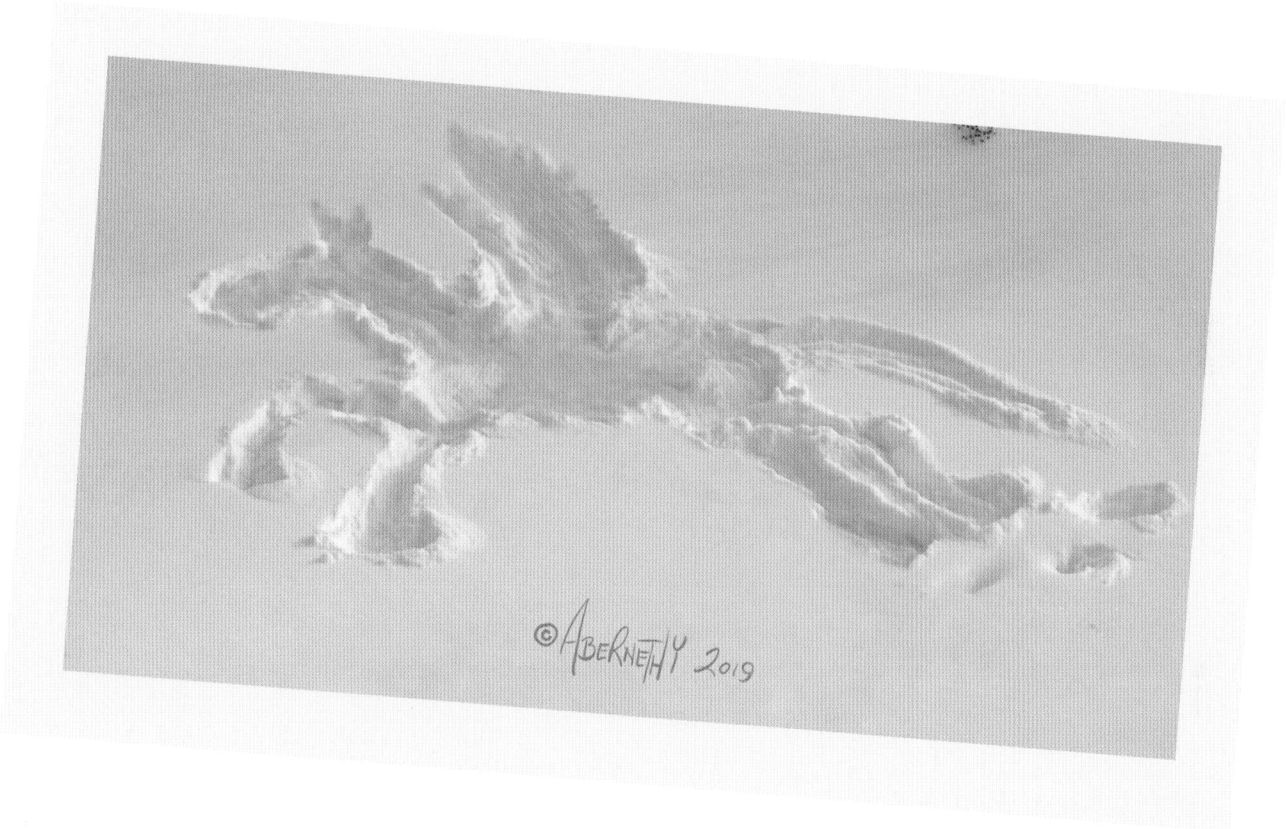
©ABERNETHY 2019

It's impossible to predict where Fergus might appear,
or what kind of magic he might bring with him.

What a Character

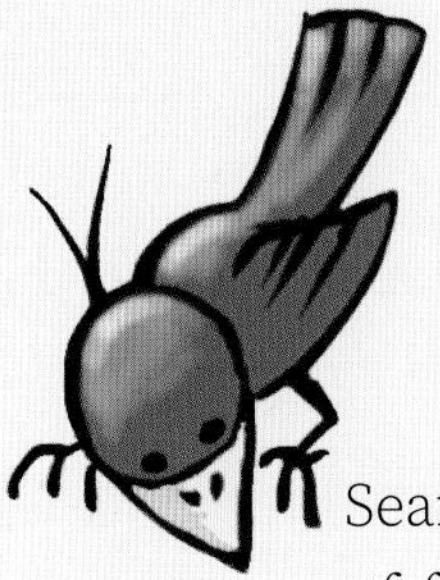

Searching for support characters, for you, Fergus, has been a grand source of fun. I learned early on the wisdom in creating humor that appeals to a general audience rather than specifically to horse people. Though there are often nuances in our comic stories that the layman might miss while the horseman chuckles, I suspect you'll agree, dear Fergus, that we want our punch lines to be available to everyone.

Besides our equine friends—Hughie the Gentle Giant, Monique the Melancholy, Dottie the Nervous, Ditto the Child, Clevis the Intellect—the quest over these 20 years has been to suss out the bizarre and ridiculous, to expect the unexpected. Various creatures who cross your pasture have provided good conversation in the realm of the ridiculous: a turtle, armadillo, llama...and why not throw a unicorn into the mix?

We humans cannot open a history book without finding horses right there with us. Our ancestors drew horses on their cave walls. Horses helped Rome rise...and maybe fall, too.

The Roman

History gives us a very big playground, and it was on that playground that this Roman was inspired back in 2008.

HEY THERE, MISTER... UM... ROMAN SOLDIER GUY. WHERE DID YOU GET THAT COOL THING ON YOUR HELMET?
©ABERNETHY '08

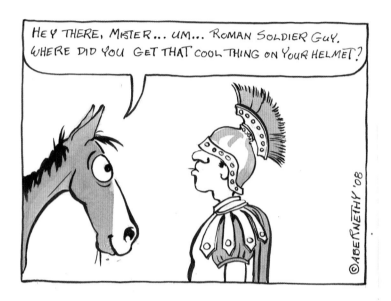

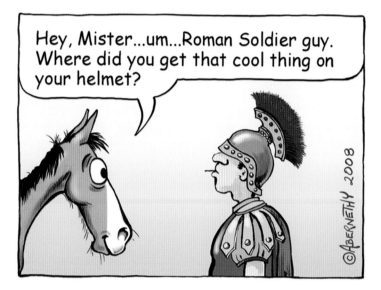

He was a formidable character at first, an officer you wouldn't want to mess with, so you were very polite. This is the first frame of the original two-frame comic strip, drawing with pen, brush, and ink, and later I made a digital, colored version.

Hey, Mister...um...Roman Soldier guy. Where did you get that cool thing on your helmet?
©ABERNETHY 2008

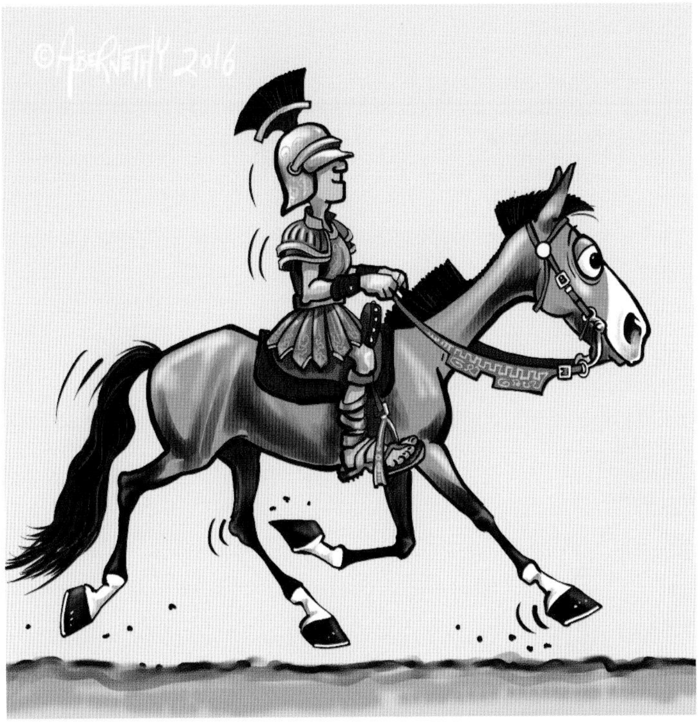
©ABERNETHY 2016

A year or so later, I further explored the concept with a single captionless drawing. When it eventually went out onto social media, this Roman soldier put a lot of folk into stitches of laughter, especially me, because it seemed, many people would look at the drawing for some time before they would see the joke. Or they would not see the punchline at all!

A lot of social media comments were: “I don’t get it!” But without fail, I would be educated by someone: “The Romans did not use stirrups!” I had done a bit of homework prior to drawing this whimsical chap and concluded that the Roman cavalry may or may not have had stirrups nearing the end of the Roman era. Most of my research indicated that they didn’t. But since my humor is greatly influenced by the animated character Bugs Bunny, I wasn’t terribly concerned with this detail. I gave my Roman stirrups, and they obviously enhanced his self-esteem.

As I reposted this comic occasionally over a span of about 10 years, viewers continued to not see the punchline on this fellow's helmet, but continued to remind me that Romans did not have stirrups! So I finally gave in and redrew the cartoon once more, removing the stirrups, to satisfy historical accuracy...

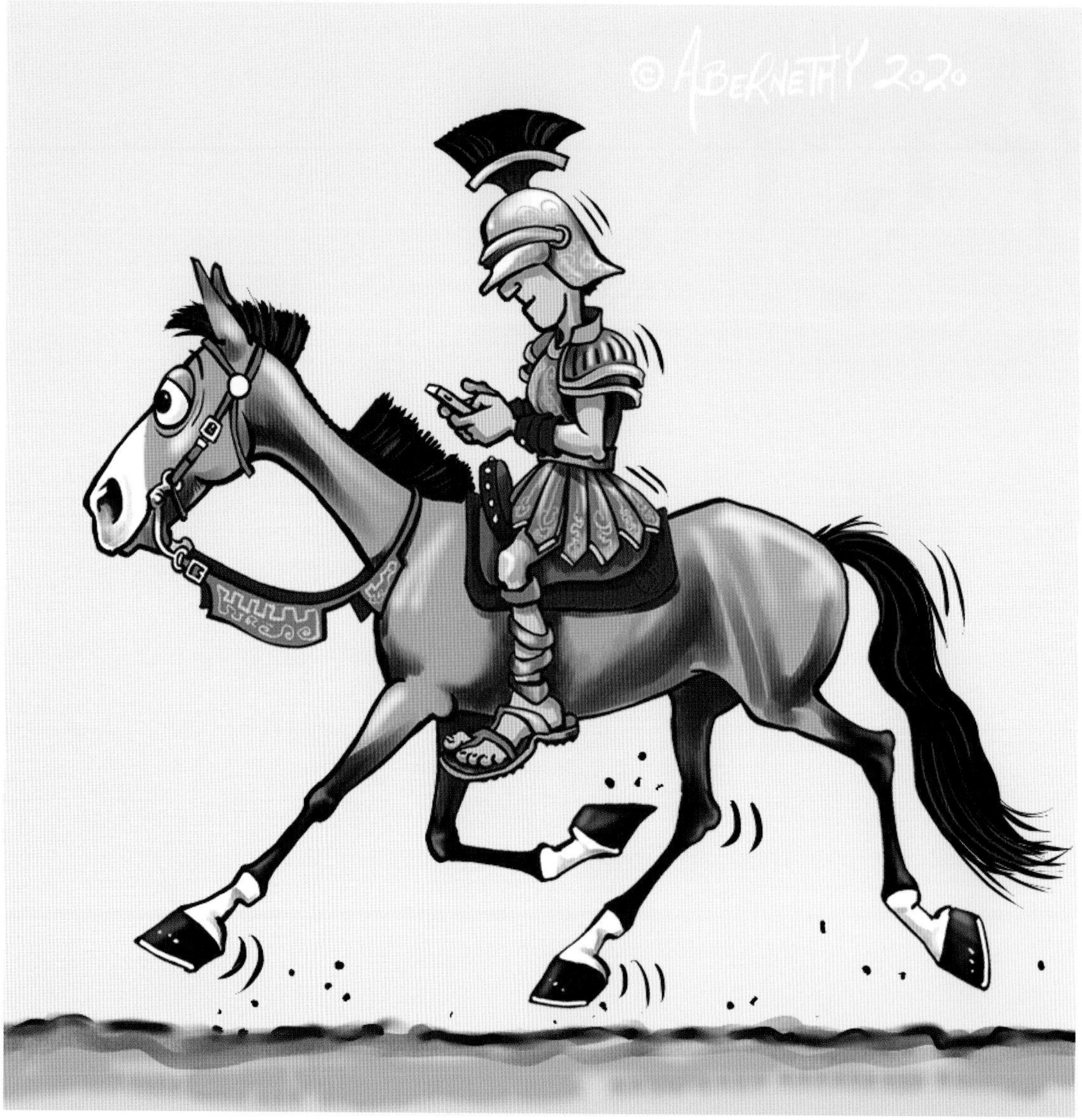
©ABERNETHY 2020

The Armadillo

And then, Fergus, we had some fun with Armadillo.

Fergus BY JEAN ABERNETHY
How long have you been playing the piano?
35 years
©ABERNETHY '12
Gosh! I didn't think armadillos lived that long!
Playing piano keeps me off the road.

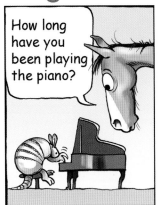

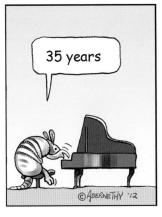

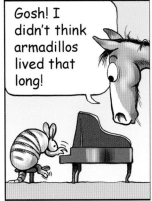

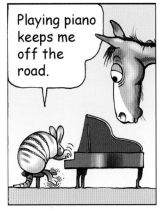

Armadillo's survival, due to his piano-playing skill, ushered him into a long and productive life—something of a phenom among armadillos, I suspect. Fergus, you boosted Armadillo to become something of a "Superdillo"! He was born back in the day when I was drawing with pencils, brush and inks. I drew every comic frame then—no digital cut-and-paste repeating of characters. Not then.

Fergus
...ASK ME LATER, FERGUS, I'M GOING TO THE GYM.
WHAT FOR?
BENCH PRESS. I'M UP TO 625 lbs. I'LL SEE YOU WHEN I GET HOME.
OK-UM, WHICH ROCK DO YOU LIVE UNDER?
ANY ROCK I WANT TO.
©ABERNETHY·05

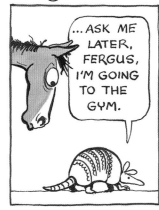

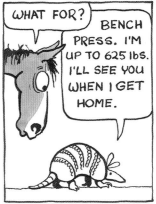

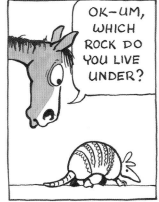

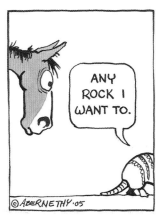

Our readers might notice if they look closely that each character in each frame is drawn fresh.

Fergus

WHAT ARE YOU DOING IN MY WATER TROUGH?

©ABERNETHY 05

SWIMMING.

BUT YOU'RE WALKING ON THE BOTTOM!

275 LAPS, AND YOU'RE QUESTIONING MY TECHNIQUE?

©ABERNETHY 2014

Thanks, Fergus. You inspired both Armadillo and me to develop our talent with new skills.

Executing a sidepass over Armadillo (a move inspired by horseman Guy McLean).

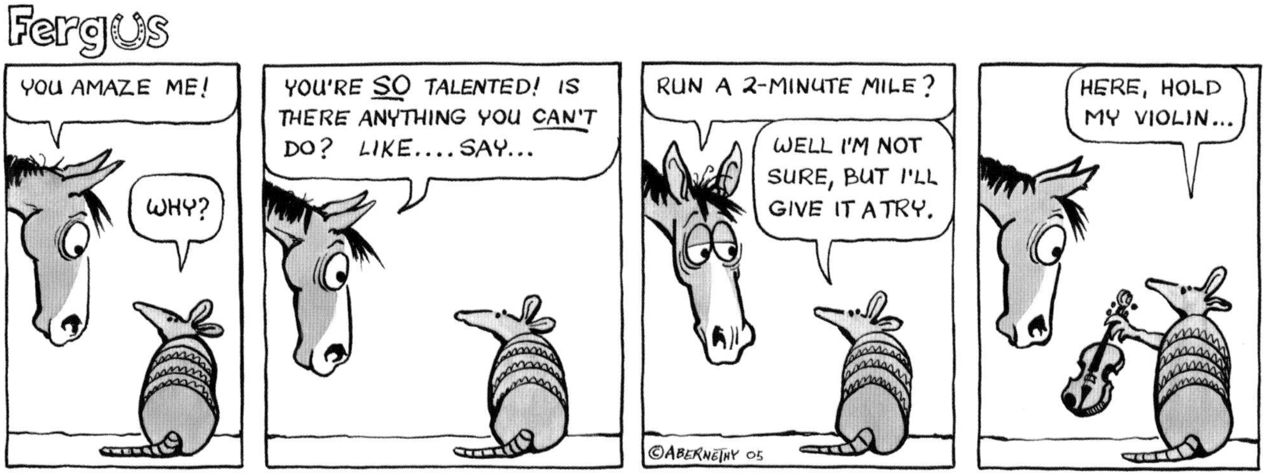
Fergus
YOU AMAZE ME!
WHY?
YOU'RE SO TALENTED! IS THERE ANYTHING YOU CAN'T DO? LIKE.... SAY...
RUN A 2-MINUTE MILE?
WELL I'M NOT SURE, BUT I'LL GIVE IT A TRY.
©ABERNETHY 05
HERE, HOLD MY VIOLIN...

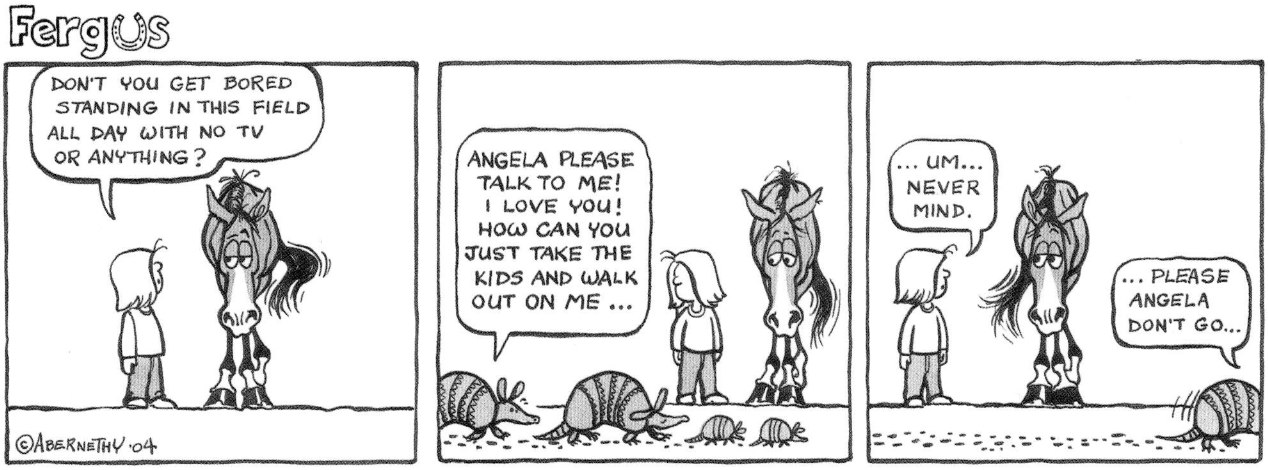
Fergus
DON'T YOU GET BORED STANDING IN THIS FIELD ALL DAY WITH NO TV OR ANYTHING?
©ABERNETHY ·04
ANGELA PLEASE TALK TO ME! I LOVE YOU! HOW CAN YOU JUST TAKE THE KIDS AND WALK OUT ON ME ...
... UM... NEVER MIND.
... PLEASE ANGELA DON'T GO...

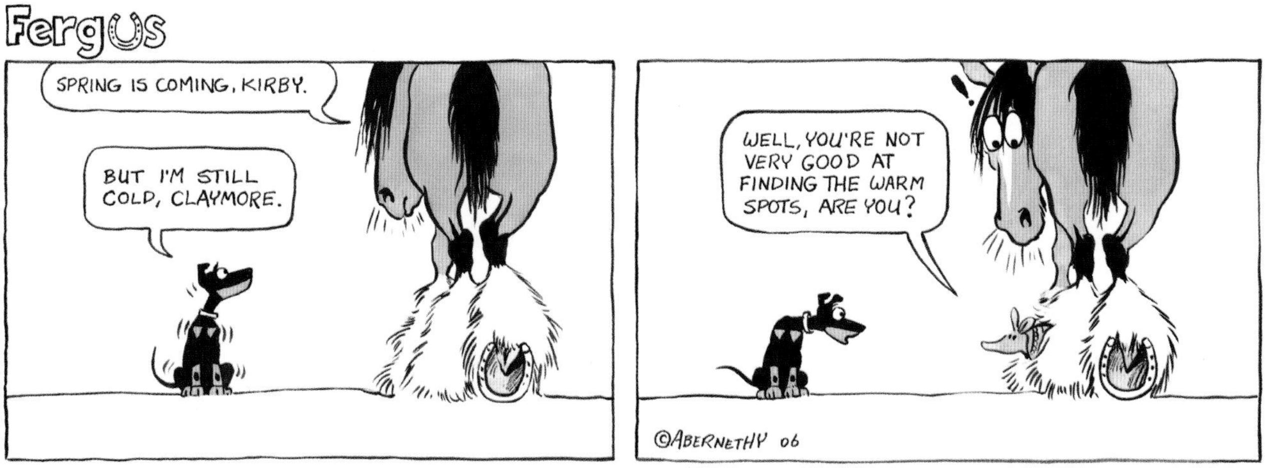
Fergus
SPRING IS COMING, KIRBY.
BUT I'M STILL COLD, CLAYMORE.
!
WELL, YOU'RE NOT VERY GOOD AT FINDING THE WARM SPOTS, ARE YOU?
©ABERNETHY 06

And now, just for this 20th anniversary celebration, we've given our multi-talented Armadillo a name. Fergus, you have a knack for bringing out the best in everyone around you.

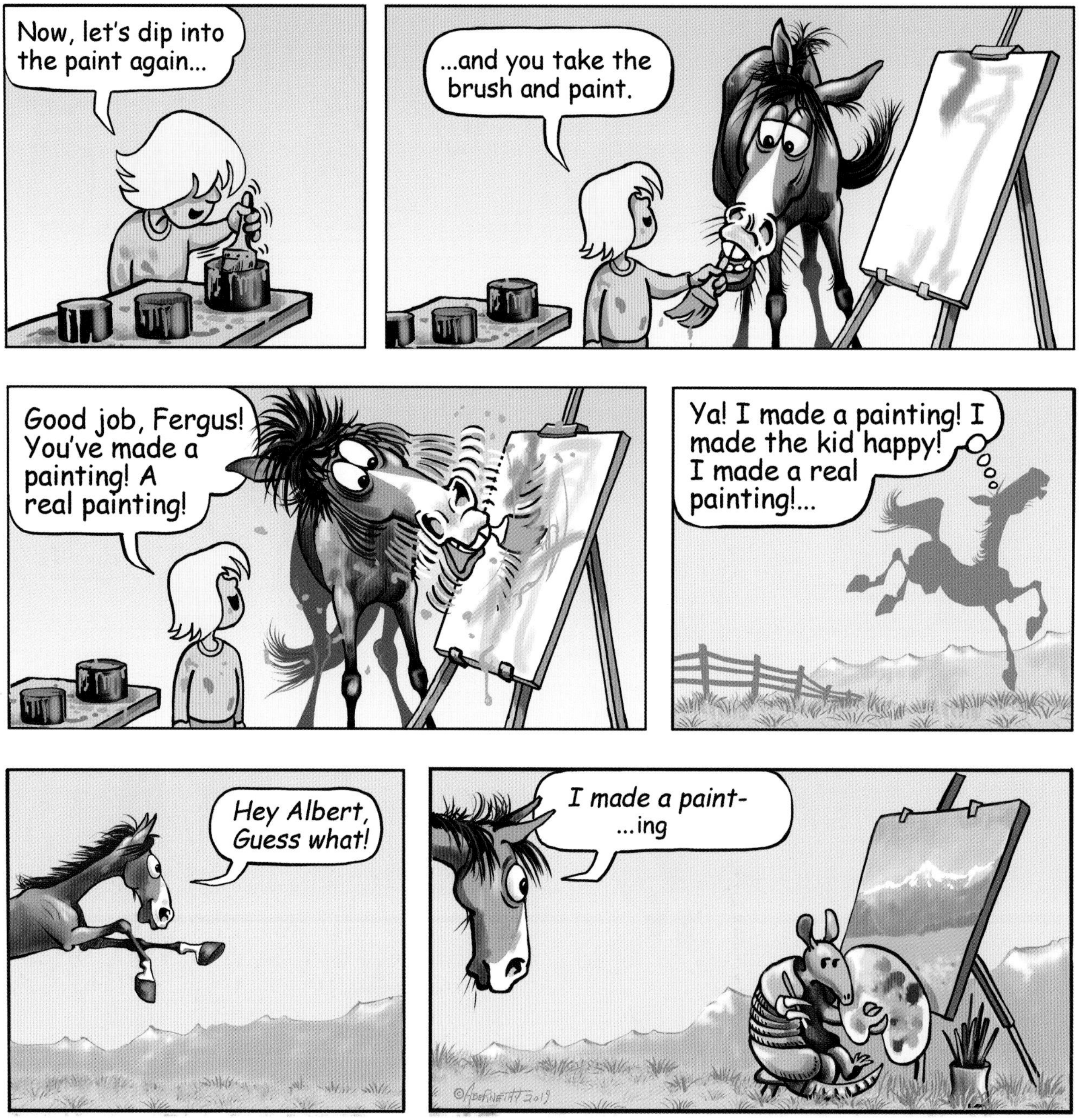
Now, let's dip into the paint again...
...and you take the brush and paint.
Good job, Fergus! You've made a painting! A real painting!
Ya! I made a painting! I made the kid happy! I made a real painting!...
Hey Albert, Guess what!
I made a paint- ...ing
©ABERNETHY 2019

The Turtle

Then there was the summer of 2009, Fergus, when we discovered a turtle in your pasture. Countless social media folk corrected me that this was, in fact, a *tortoise*, but no one seemed to notice that when you asked the turtle a question, the sun was in a different place by the time you got an answer. Even more perplexing was the fact that the turtle's answer was always another question. We might never know if all turtles do this, or if it's a tendency unique to this one...

Hello, wise old turtle. Tell me, can turtles get fat?
Can horses' feet swell?
©ABERNETHY 2009
Why do you always answer a question with another question?
Why not?
©ABERNETHY 2009

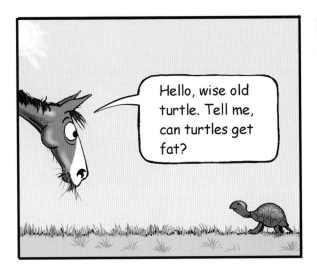

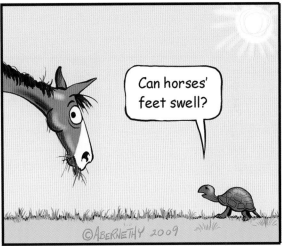

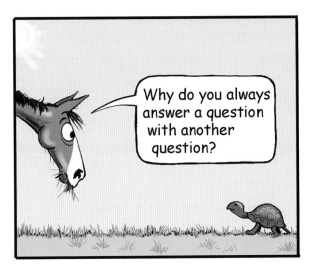

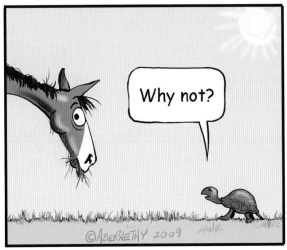

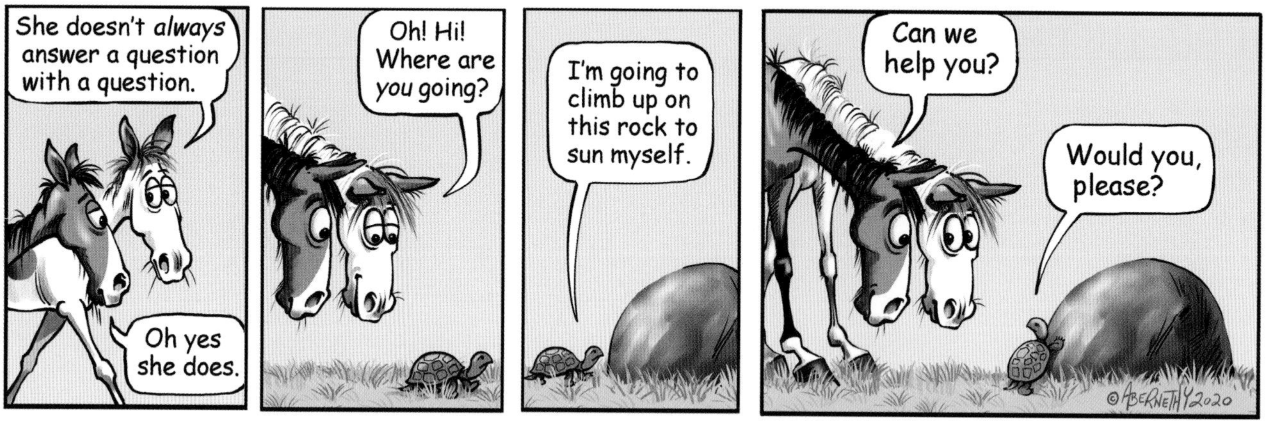
She doesn't *always* answer a question with a question.
Oh yes she does.
Oh! Hi! Where are *you* going?
I'm going to climb up on this rock to sun myself.
Can we help you?
Would you, please?
©ABERNETHY2020

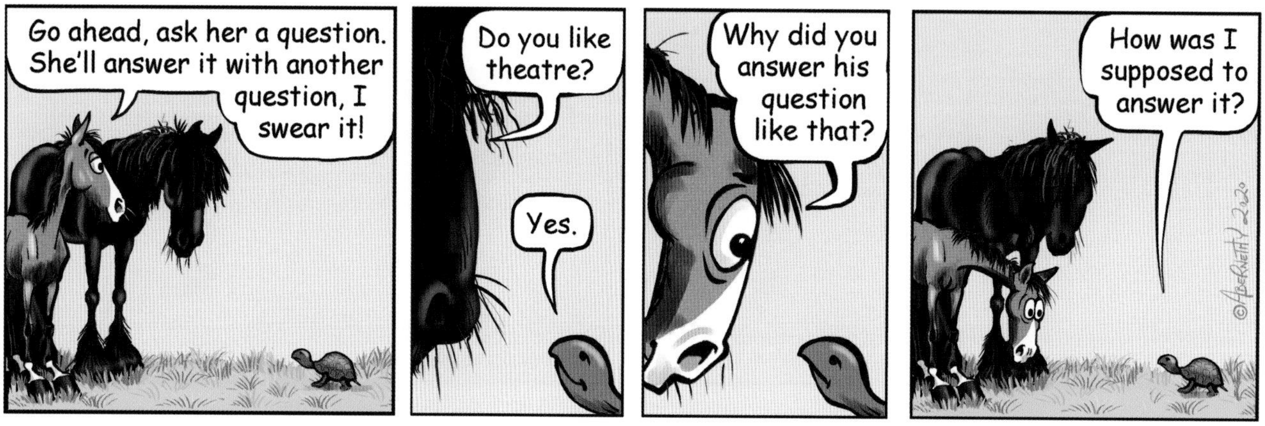
Go ahead, ask her a question. She'll answer it with another question, I swear it!
Do you like theatre?
Yes.
Why did you answer his question like that?
How was I supposed to answer it?
©ABERNETHY2020

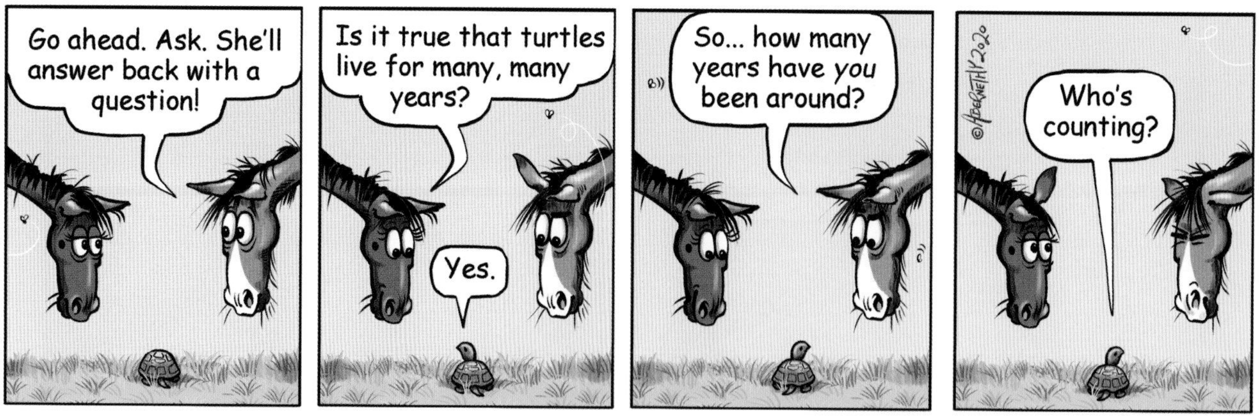
Go ahead. Ask. She'll answer back with a question!
Is it true that turtles live for many, many years?
Yes.
So... how many years have *you* been around?
©ABERNETHY2020
Who's counting?

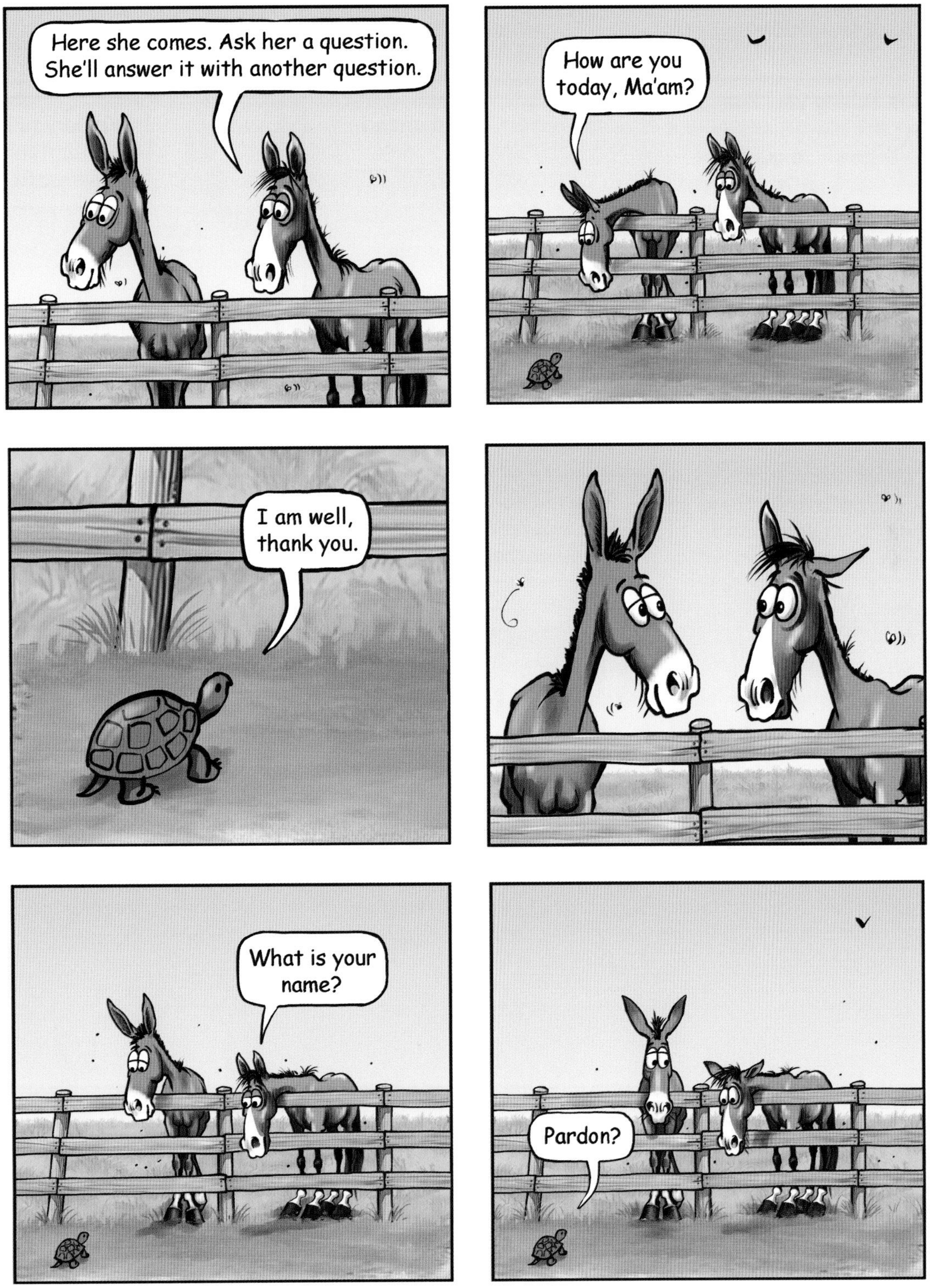
Here she comes. Ask her a question. She'll answer it with another question.
How are you today, Ma'am?
I am well, thank you.
What is your name?
Pardon?

...I'm telling you, Pierce, she always answers a question with another question.

Go ahead. Ask.

Would you like to start our conversation?

What's that thing on your head?

What thing?

There! Did you notice that you answered his question with another question?

Did you notice that Pierce did it too?

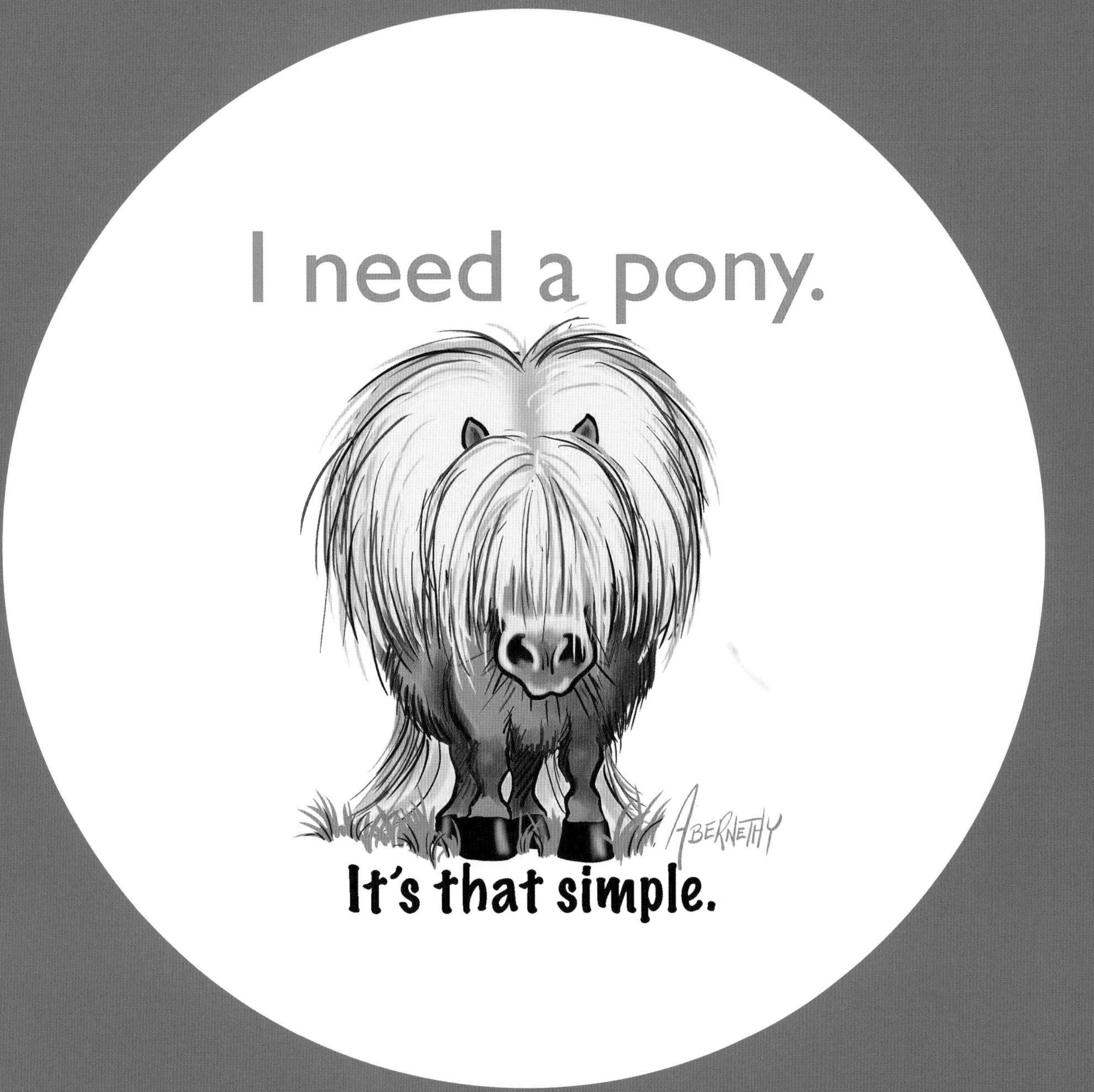
I need a pony.
ABERNETHY
It's that simple.

Part Two:

The Comics

2015-2020

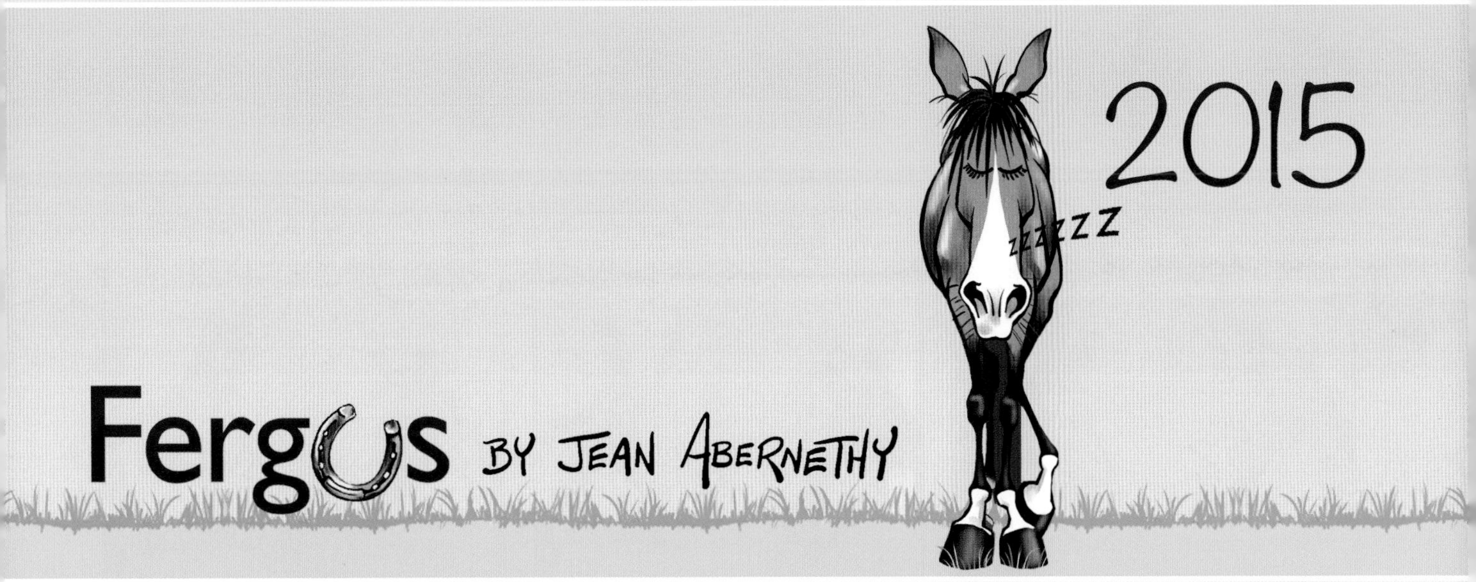
2015
zzzzzz
Fergus BY JEAN ABERNETHY

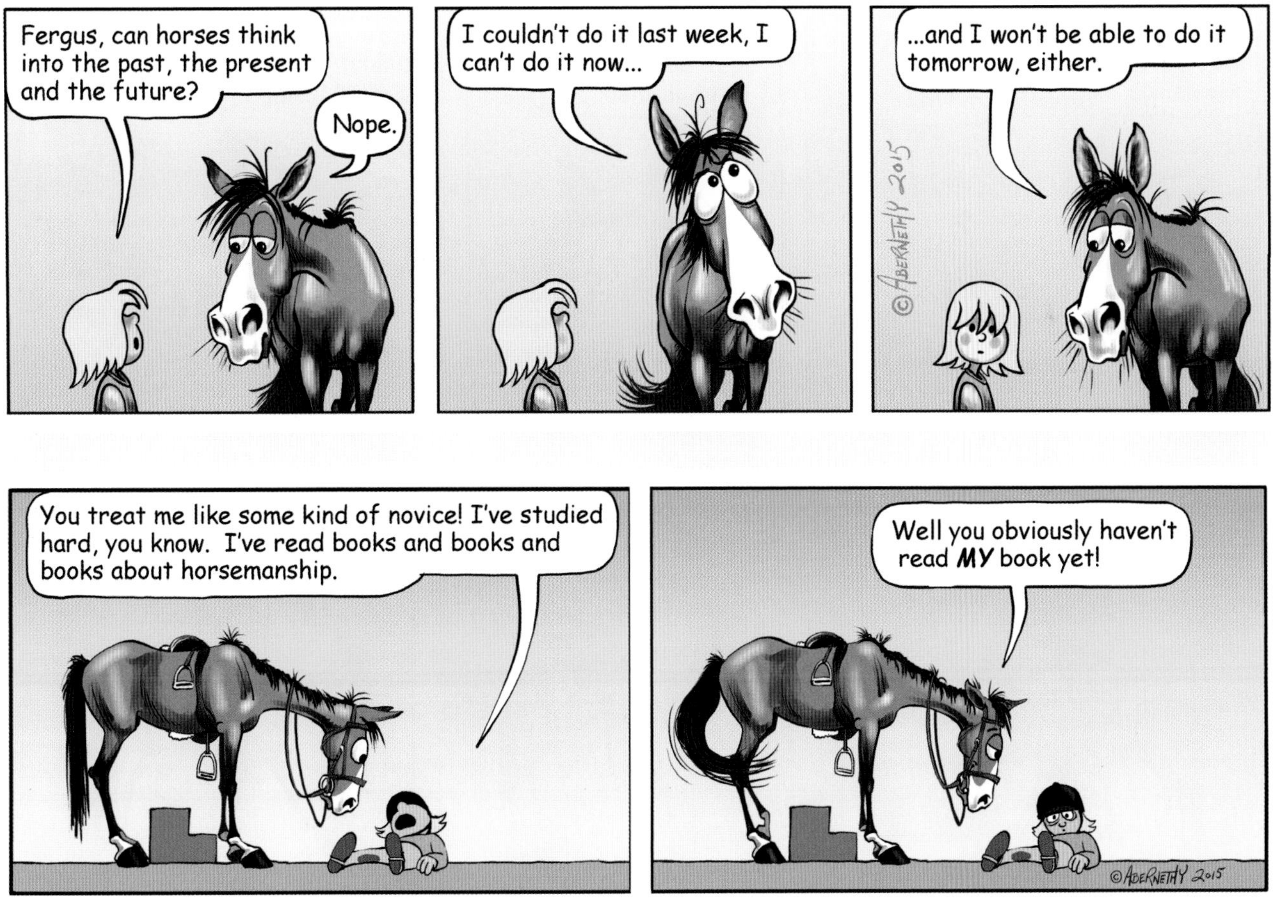
Fergus, can horses think into the past, the present and the future?
Nope.
I couldn't do it last week, I can't do it now...
©Abernethy 2015
...and I won't be able to do it tomorrow, either.
You treat me like some kind of novice! I've studied hard, you know. I've read books and books and books about horsemanship.
Well you obviously haven't read MY book yet!
©Abernethy 2015

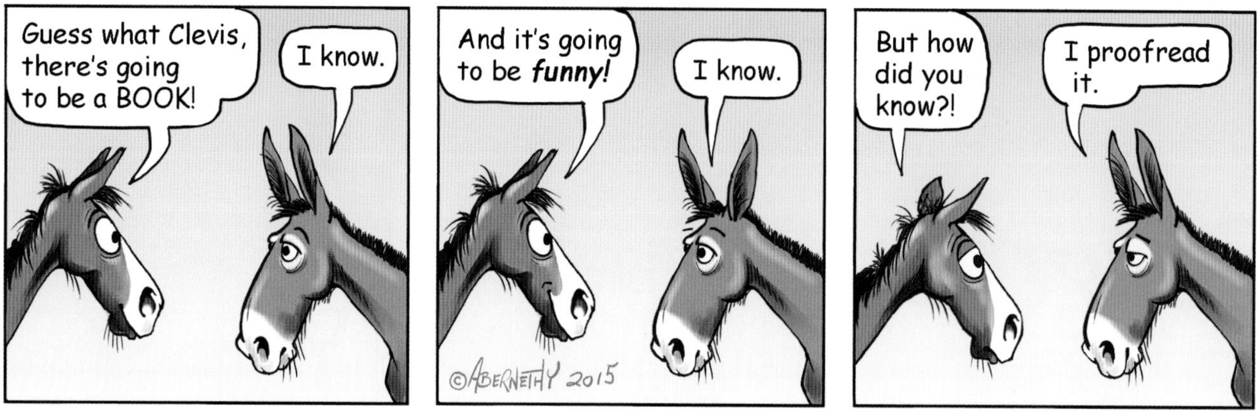
Guess what Clevis, there's going to be a BOOK!
I know.
And it's going to be *funny!*
I know.
©ABERNETHY 2015
But how did you know?!
I proofread it.

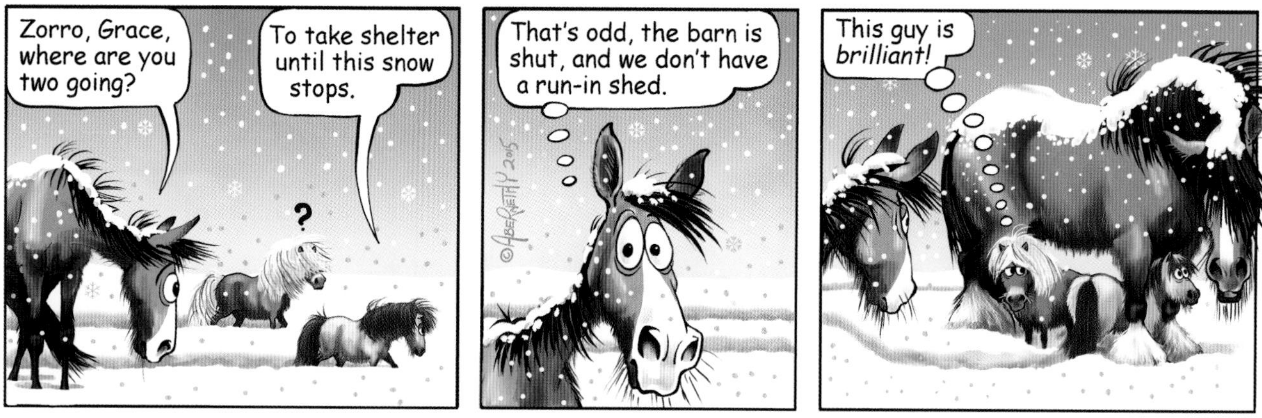
Zorro, Grace, where are you two going?
To take shelter until this snow stops.
?
That's odd, the barn is shut, and we don't have a run-in shed.
©ABERNETHY 2015
This guy is *brilliant!*

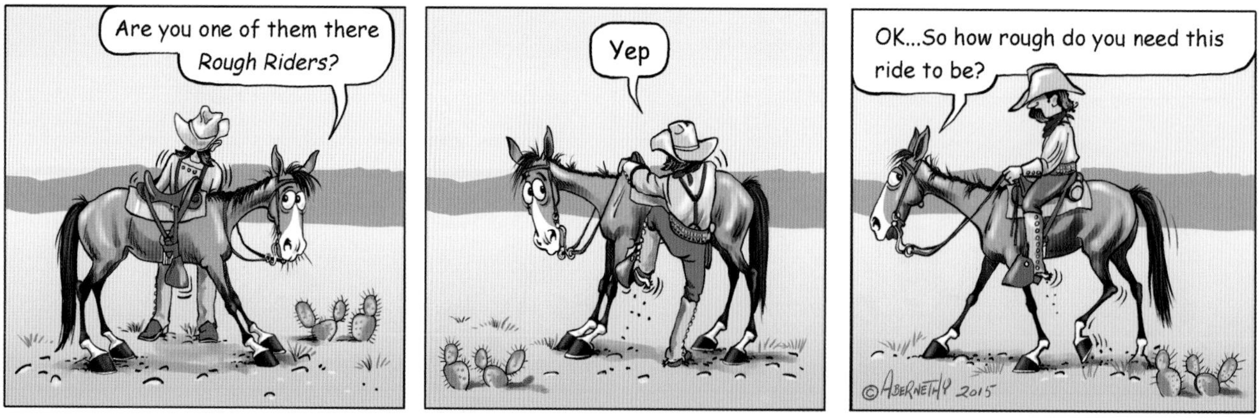
Are you one of them there *Rough Riders?*
Yep
OK...So how rough do you need this ride to be?
©ABERNETHY 2015

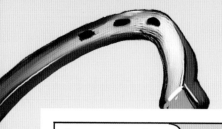

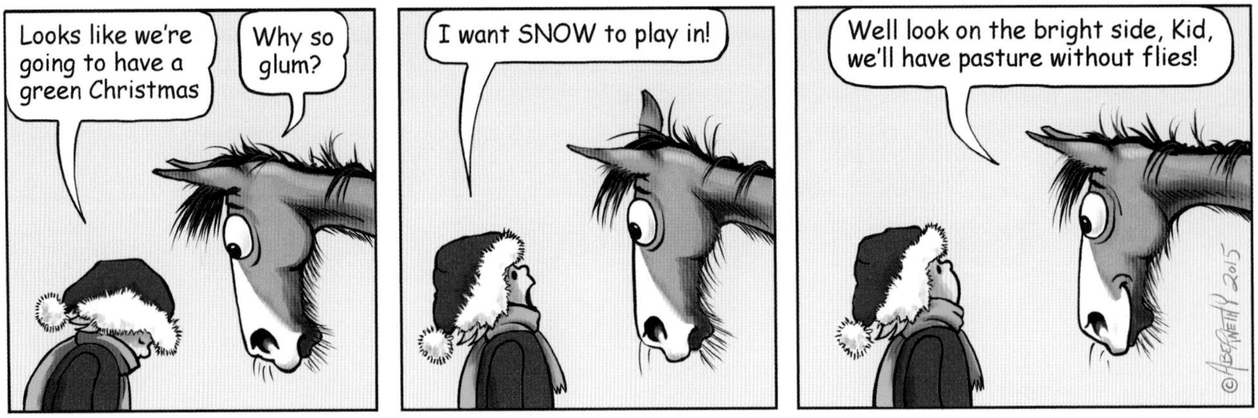
Looks like we're going to have a green Christmas
Why so glum?
I want SNOW to play in!
Well look on the bright side, Kid, we'll have pasture without flies!
©ABERNETHY 2015

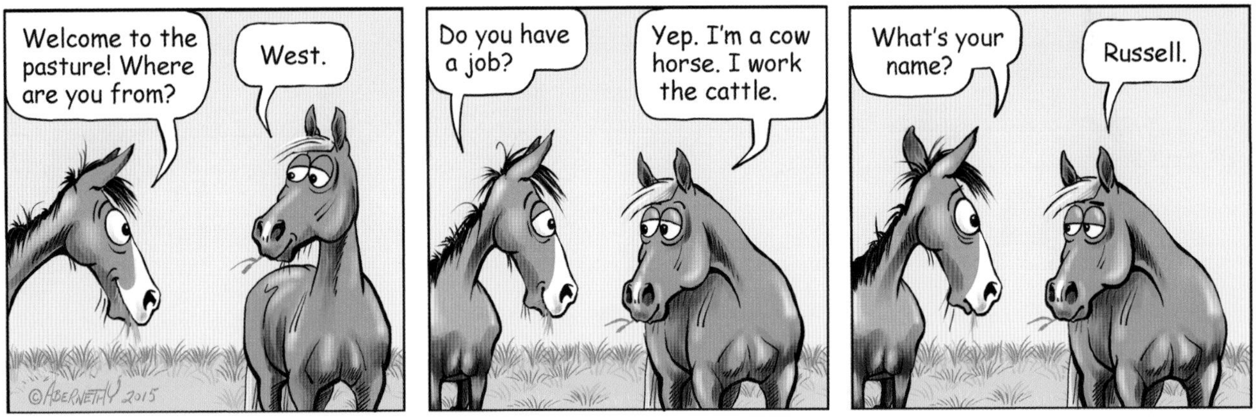
Welcome to the pasture! Where are you from?
West.
Do you have a job?
Yep. I'm a cow horse. I work the cattle.
What's your name?
Russell.
©ABERNETHY 2015

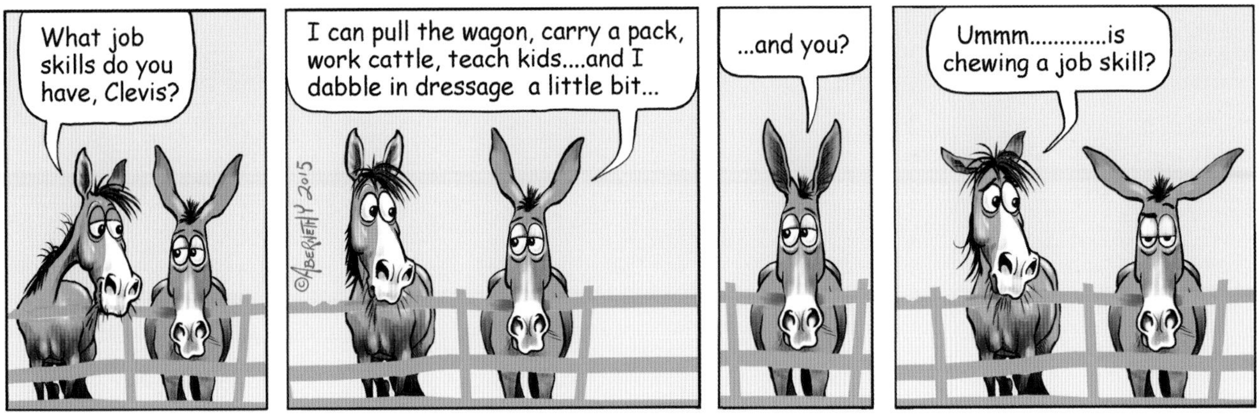
What job skills do you have, Clevis?
I can pull the wagon, carry a pack, work cattle, teach kids....and I dabble in dressage a little bit...
...and you?
Ummm............is chewing a job skill?
©ABERNETHY 2015

...Because I'm a cowhorse, that's why. Now git on back to the herd, Ma'am.

Hmph! A *cowhorse!* Is that anything like a *Catfish,* or a *Turtledove?*

When I took this job I was not prepared for the sting of bovine sarcasm!

Fergus BY JEAN ABERNETHY

2016

Oops! She got past me!

Sorry, Russell. I know we've got cows to gather and sort. I'm trying my best, but I just don't think these cows are taking me seriously.

What makes you think *I'm* taking you seriously?!

I got you a new blanket, Fergus! I got it 50% off!

...next day...

FERGUS!

Oh dear! She was so excited yesterday, I thought getting it 50% off was a *good* thing!

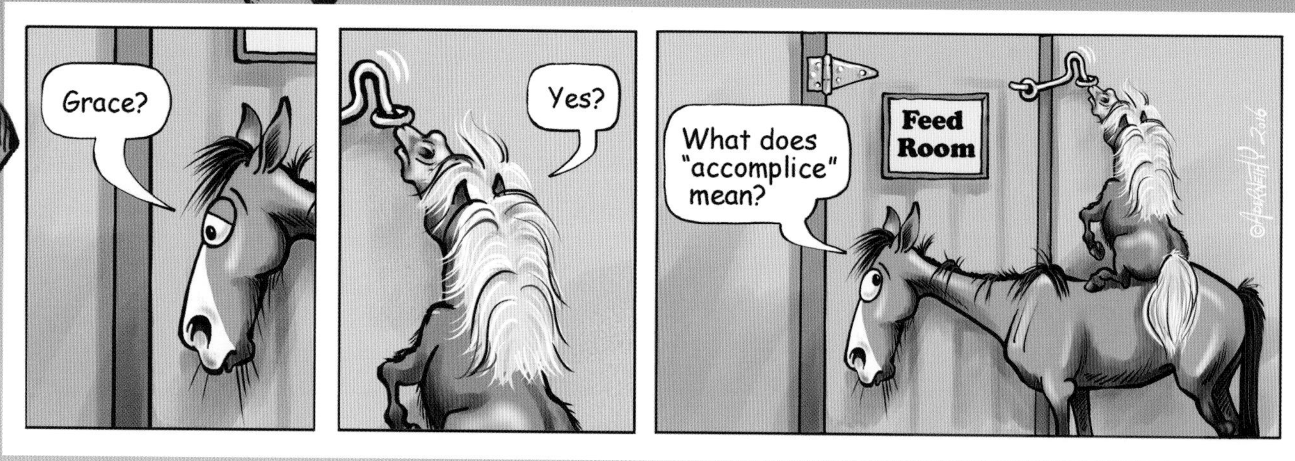
Grace?
Yes?
Feed Room
What does "accomplice" mean?
©ABERNETHY 2016

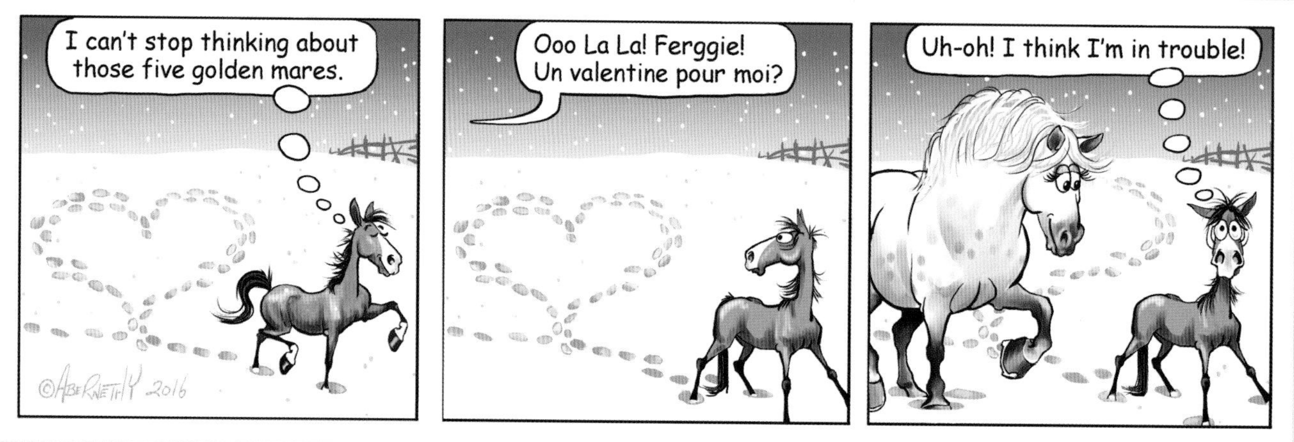
I can't stop thinking about those five golden mares.
Ooo La La! Ferggie! Un valentine pour moi?
Uh-oh! I think I'm in trouble!
©ABERNETHY 2016

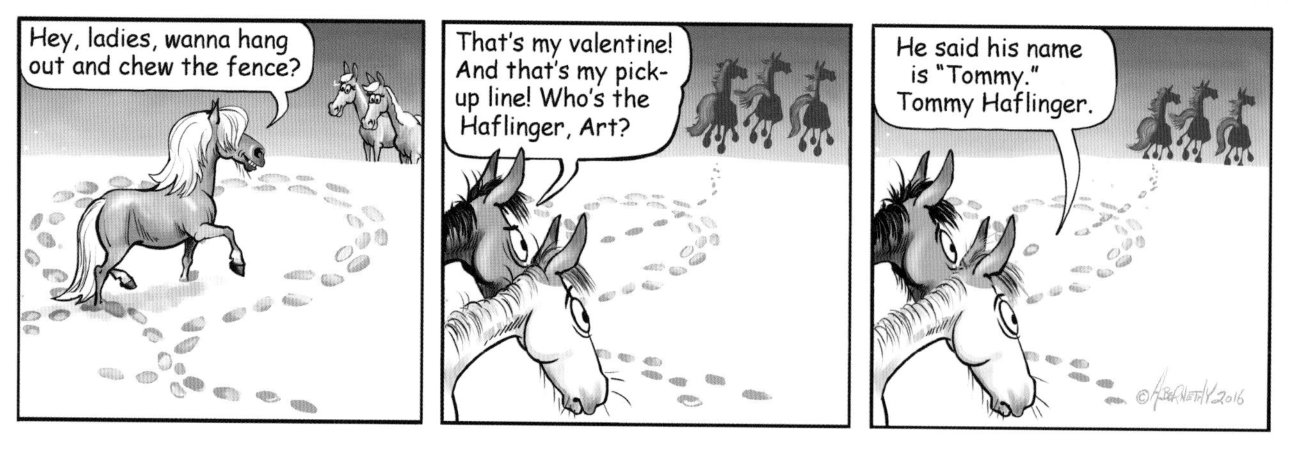
Hey, ladies, wanna hang out and chew the fence?
That's my valentine! And that's my pick-up line! Who's the Haflinger, Art?
He said his name is "Tommy." Tommy Haflinger.
©ABERNETHY 2016

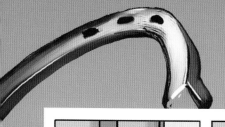

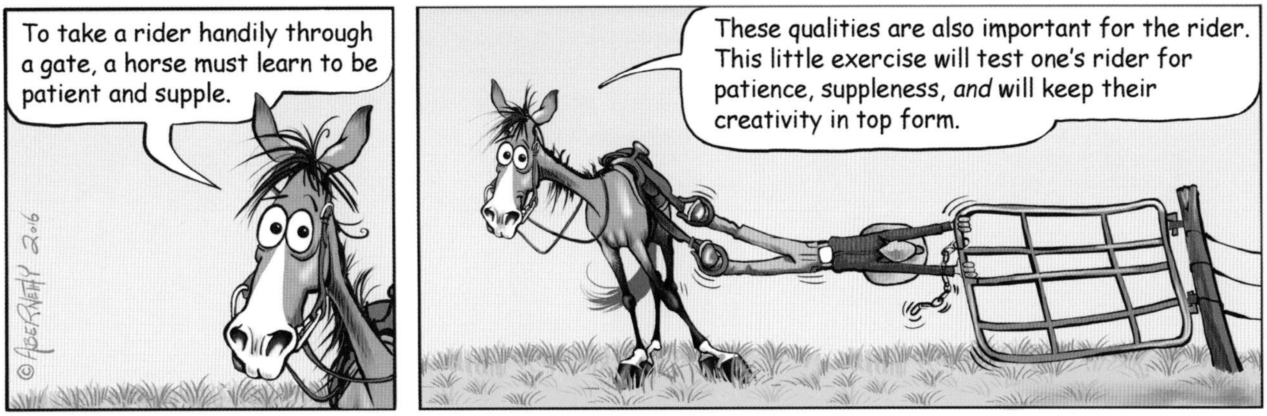
To take a rider handily through a gate, a horse must learn to be patient and supple.
©ABERNETHY 2016
These qualities are also important for the rider. This little exercise will test one's rider for patience, suppleness, *and* will keep their creativity in top form.

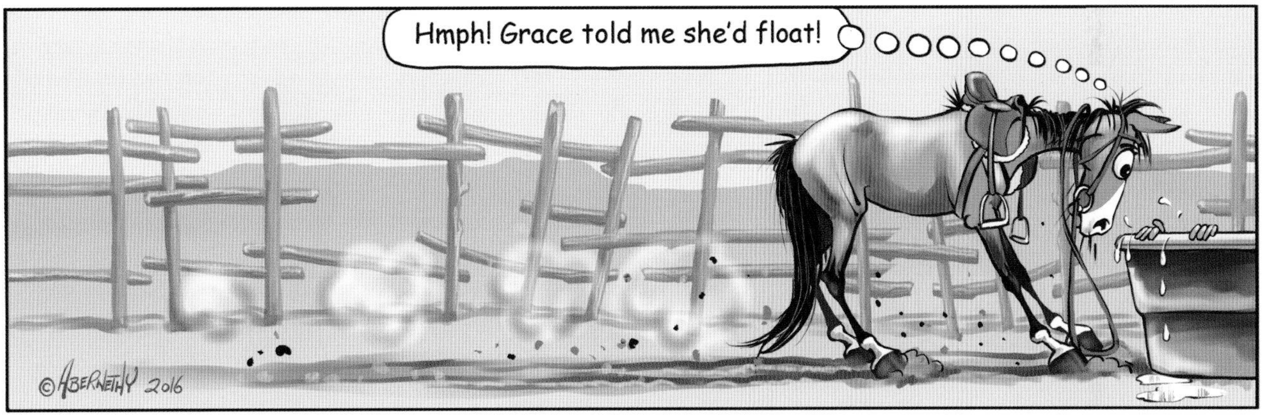
Hmph! Grace told me she'd float!
©ABERNETHY 2016

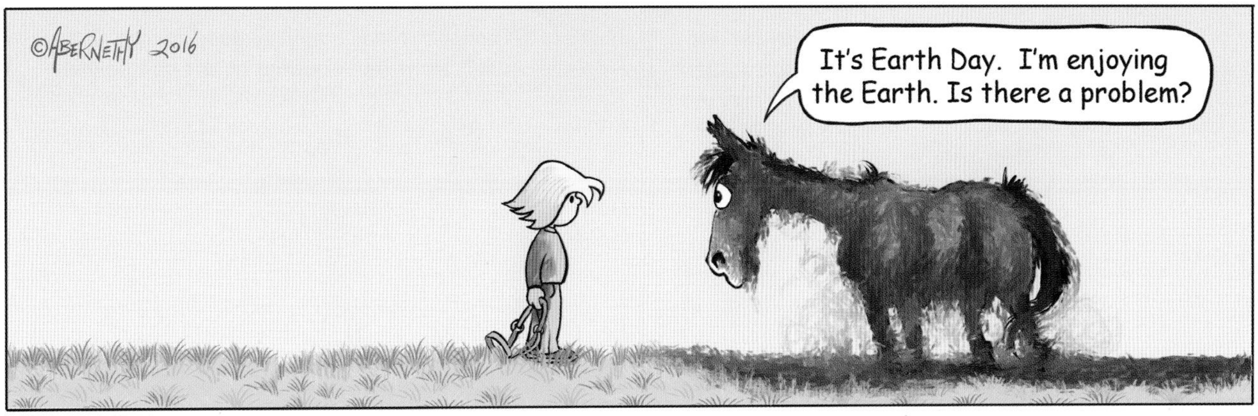
©ABERNETHY 2016
It's Earth Day. I'm enjoying the Earth. Is there a problem?

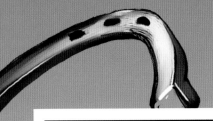

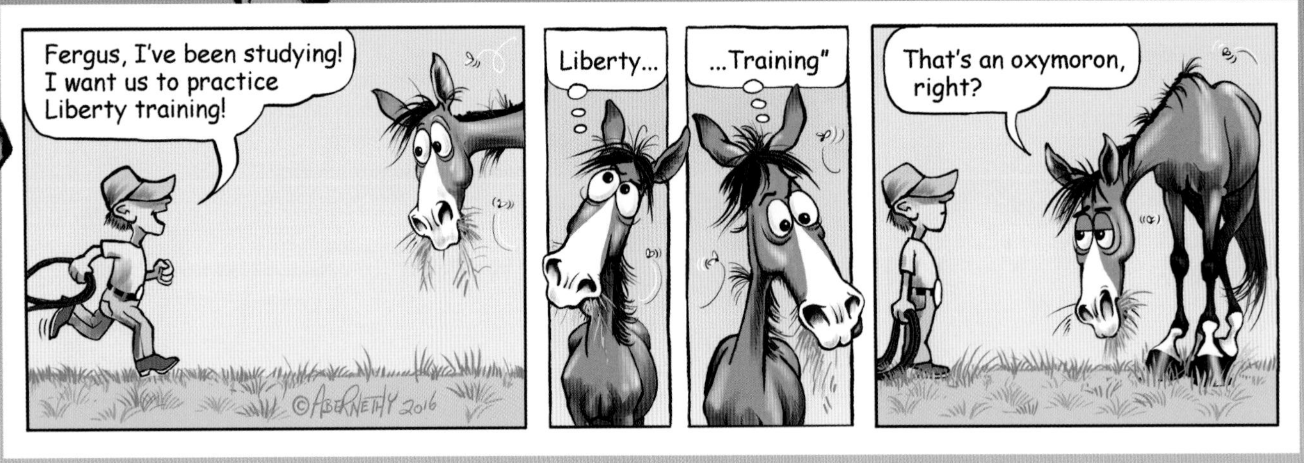
Fergus, I've been studying! I want us to practice Liberty training!
Liberty...
...Training"
That's an oxymoron, right?
©ABERNETHY 2016

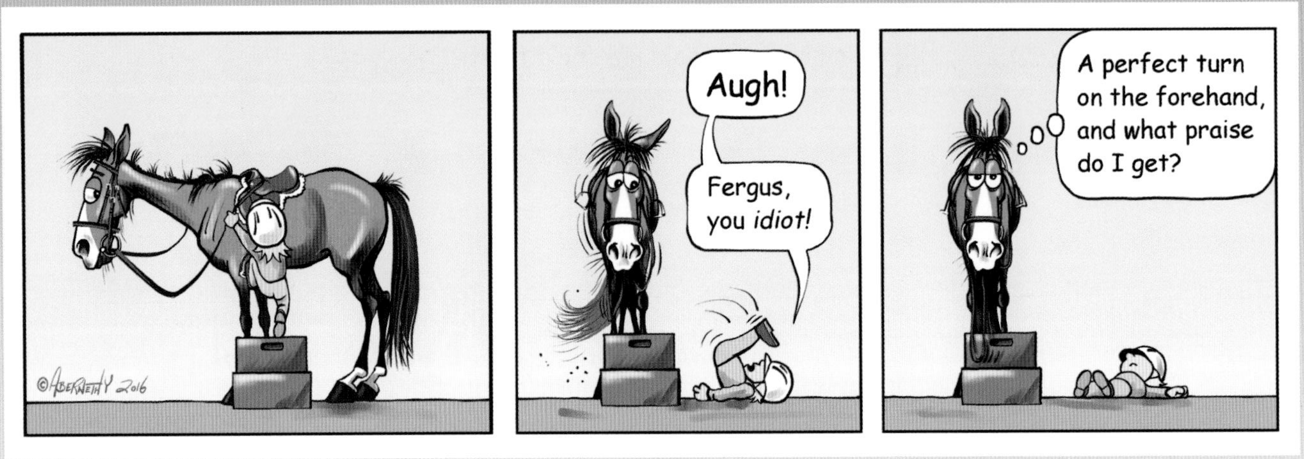
©ABERNETHY 2016
Augh!
Fergus, you *idiot!*
A perfect turn on the forehand, and what praise do I get?

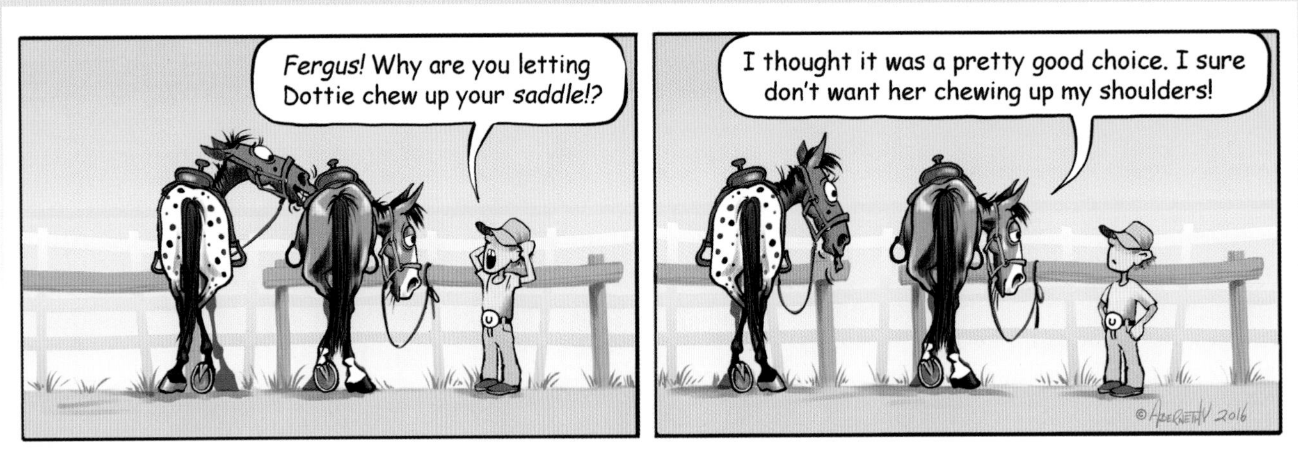
Fergus! Why are you letting Dottie chew up your *saddle!?*
I thought it was a pretty good choice. I sure don't want her chewing up my shoulders!
©ABERNETHY 2016

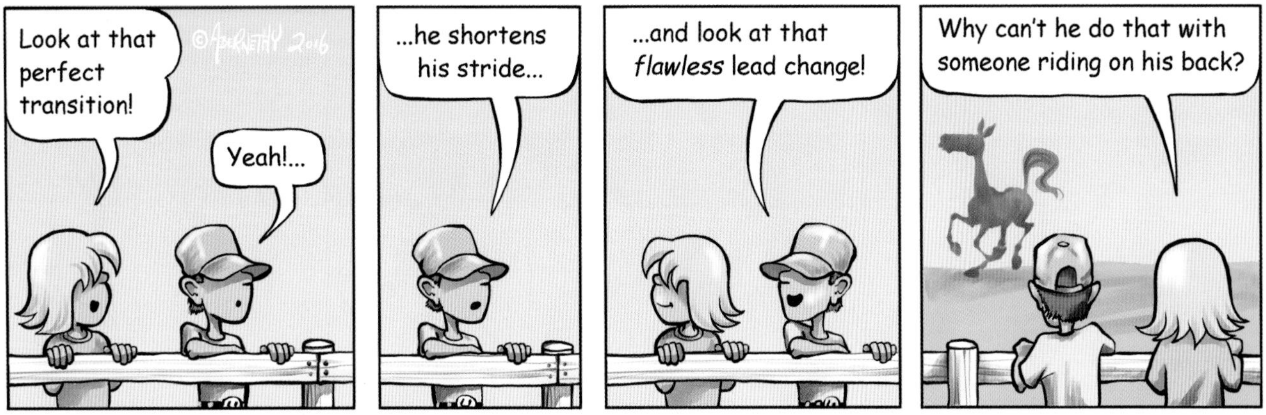
Look at that perfect transition!
©ABERNETHY 2016
Yeah!...
...he shortens his stride...
...and look at that *flawless* lead change!
Why can't he do that with someone riding on his back?

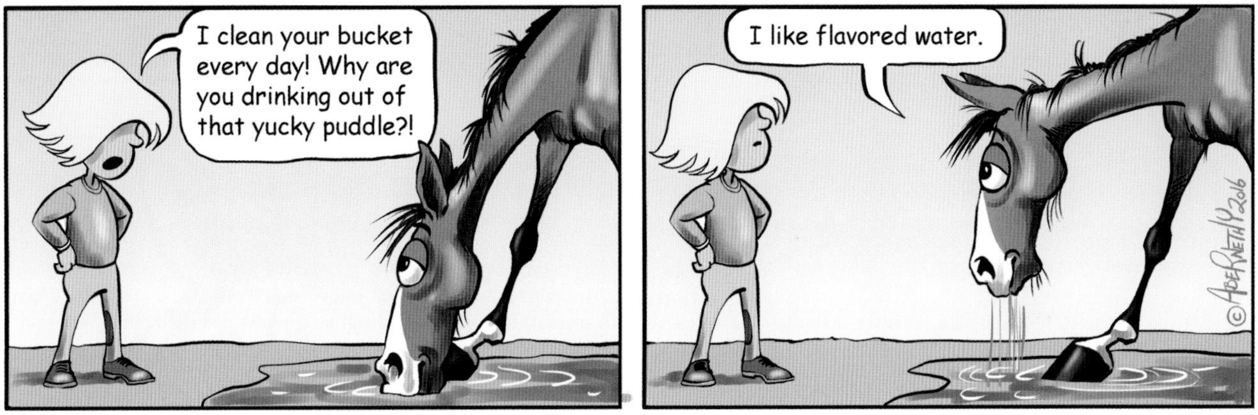
I clean your bucket every day! Why are you drinking out of that yucky puddle?!
I like flavored water.
©ABERNETHY 2016

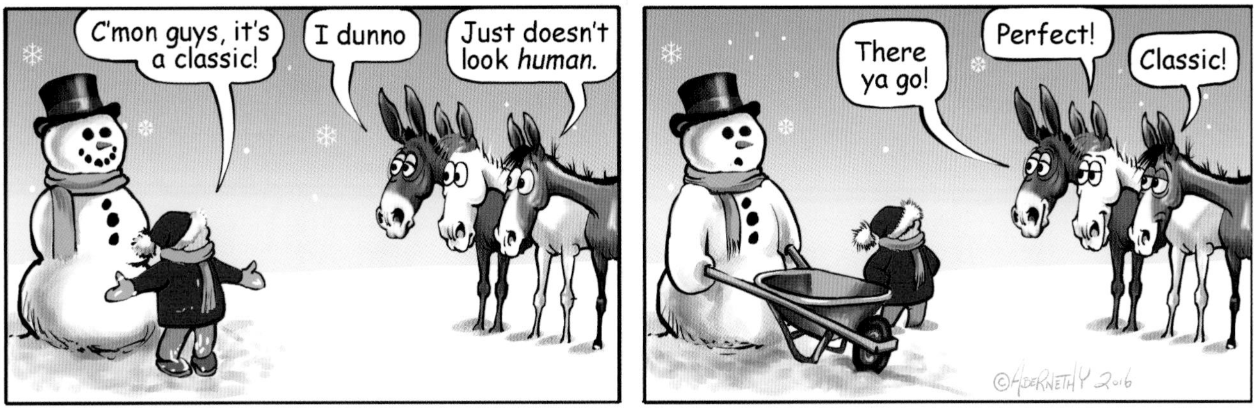
C'mon guys, it's a classic!
I dunno
Just doesn't look *human.*
There ya go!
Perfect!
Classic!
©ABERNETHY 2016

Humans? Well, they follow...
their own instincts...
...not stubborn exactly, but strong-willed...
...quirky...
...and hard to figure out...
I've been working with humans all my life, and I tell you what, some of them sure have a mind of their own!
©ABERNETHY 2016

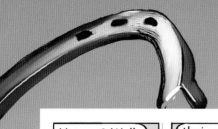

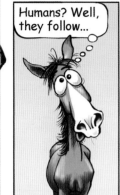

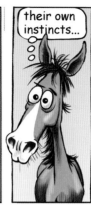

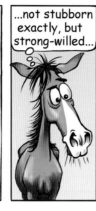

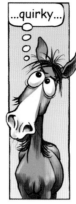

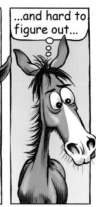

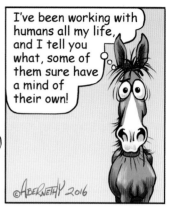

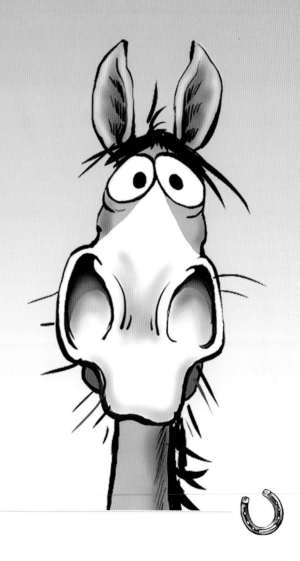

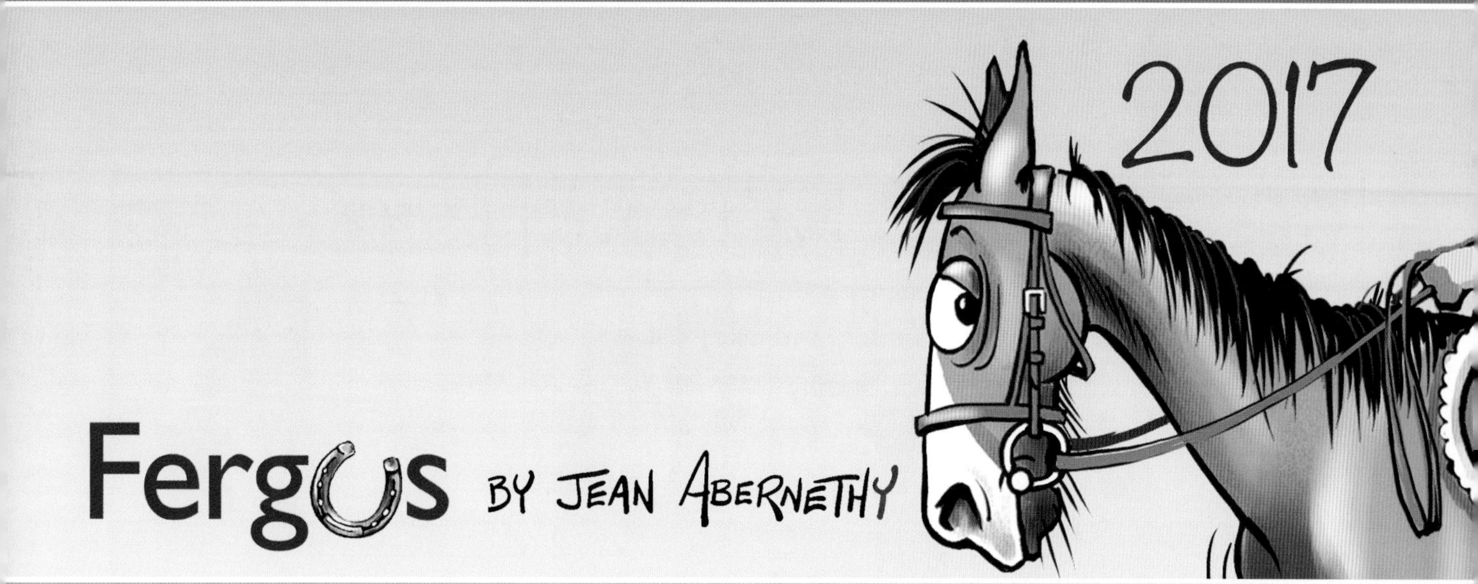
2017
Fergus BY JEAN ABERNETHY

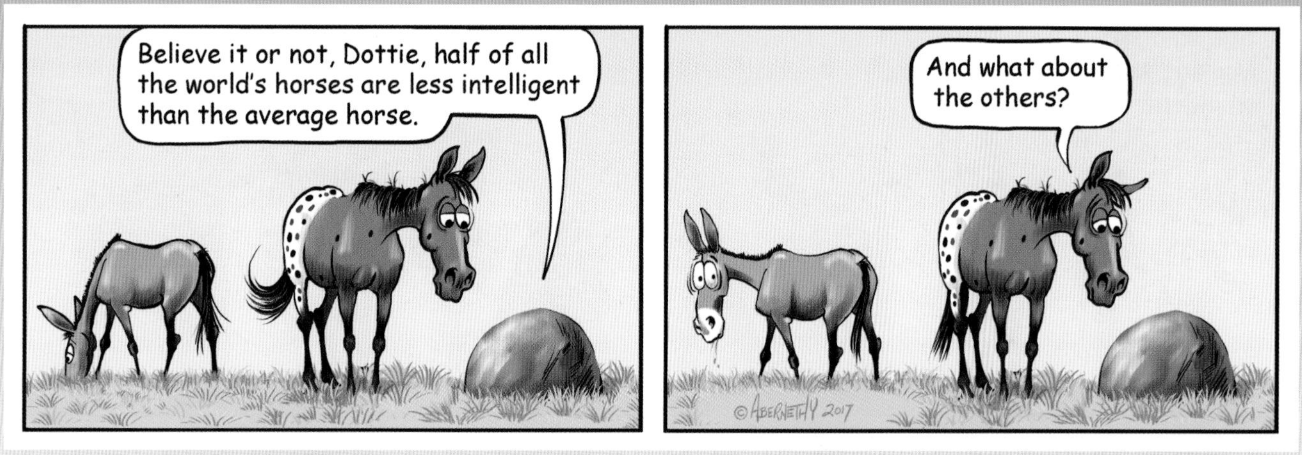
Believe it or not, Dottie, half of all the world's horses are less intelligent than the average horse.
And what about the others?
© ABERNETHY 2017

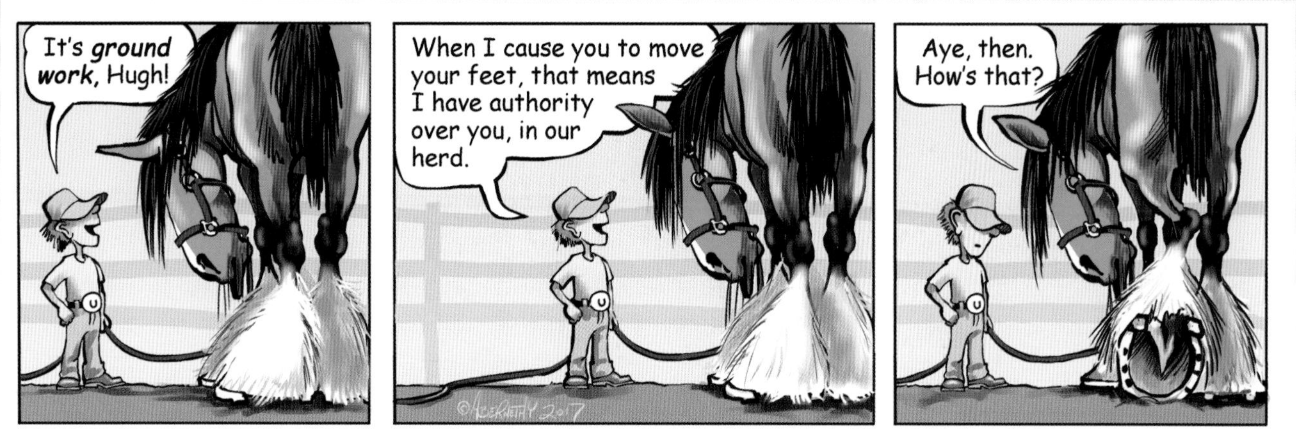
It's *ground work*, Hugh!
When I cause you to move your feet, that means I have authority over you, in our herd.
©ABERNETHY 2017
Aye, then. How's that?

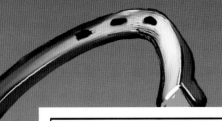

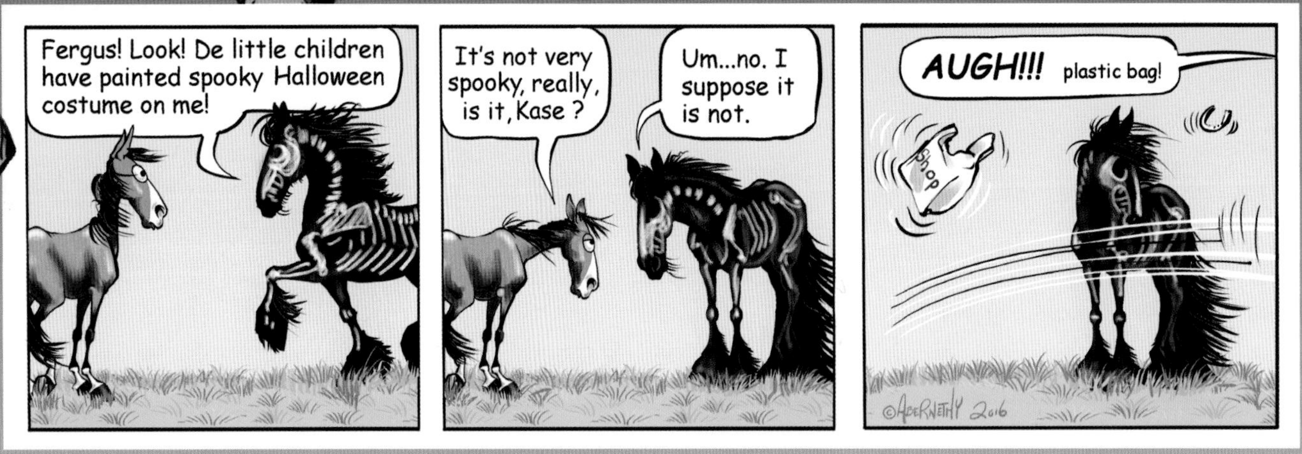
Fergus! Look! De little children have painted spooky Halloween costume on me!
It's not very spooky, really, is it, Kase ?
Um...no. I suppose it is not.
AUGH!!! plastic bag!
Shop
©ABERNETHY 2016

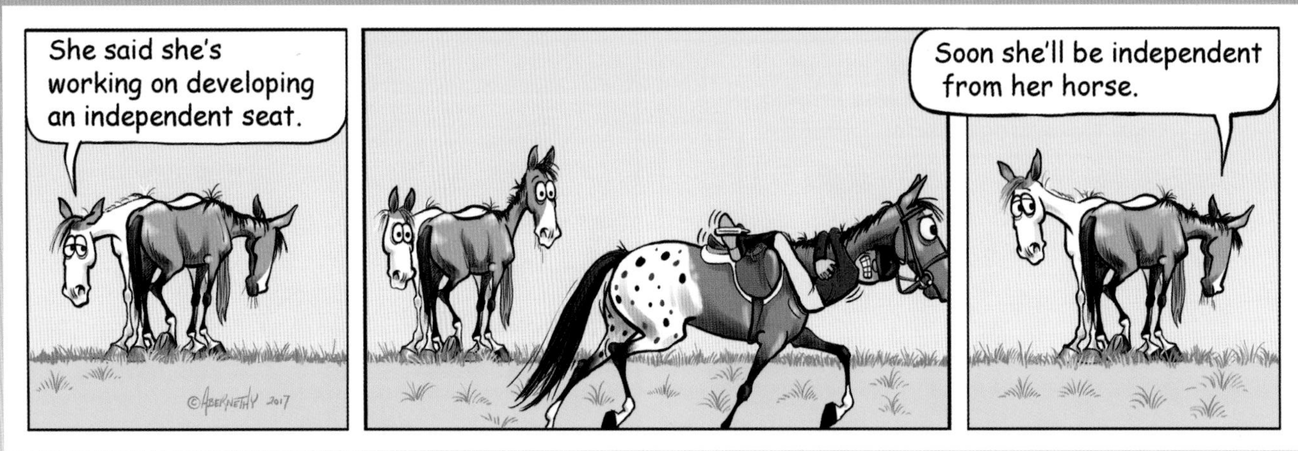
She said she's working on developing an independent seat.
©ABERNETHY 2017
Soon she'll be independent from her horse.

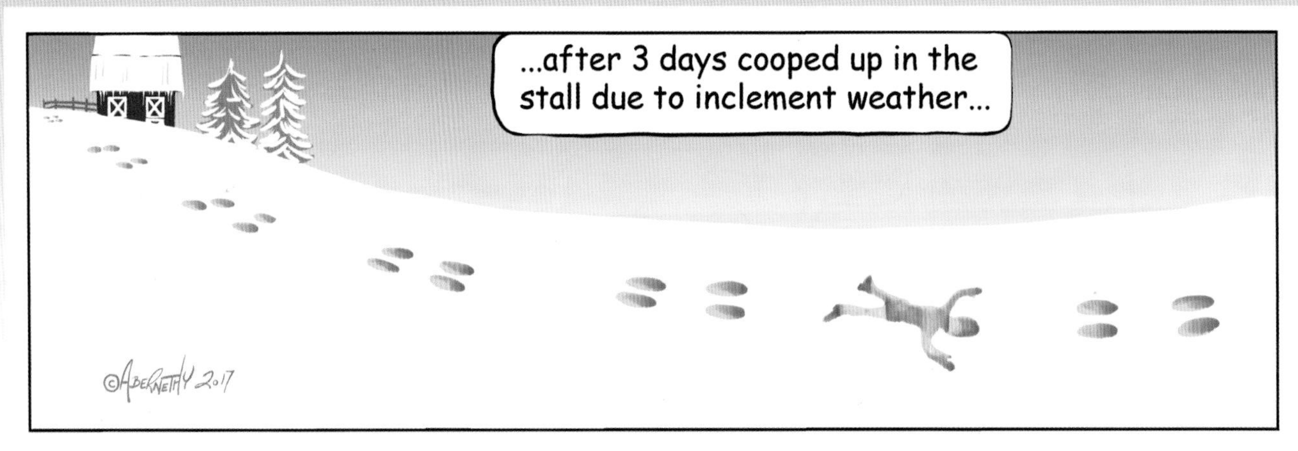
...after 3 days cooped up in the stall due to inclement weather...
©ABERNETHY 2017

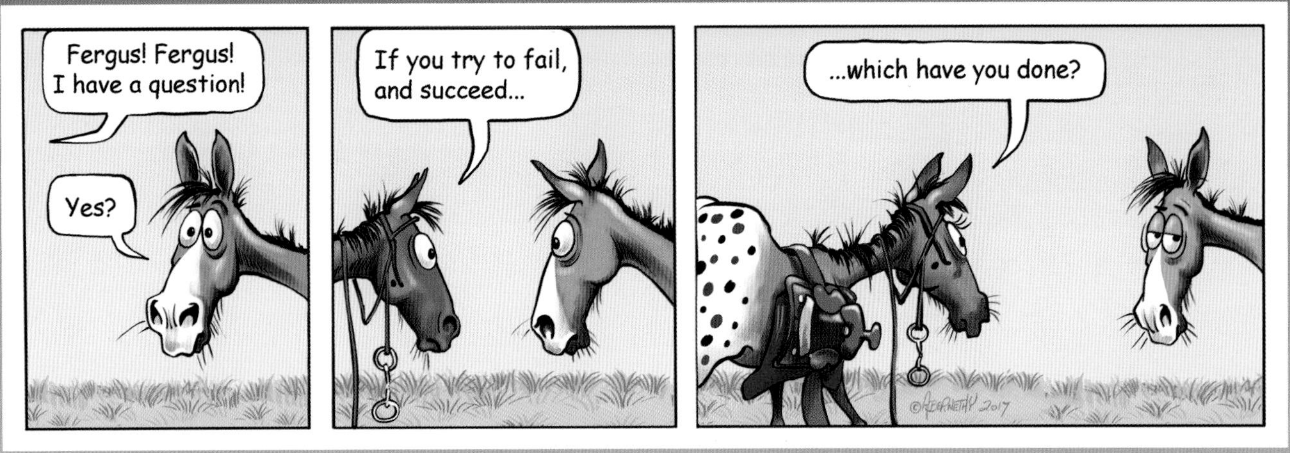
Fergus! Fergus! I have a question!
Yes?
If you try to fail, and succeed...
...which have you done?

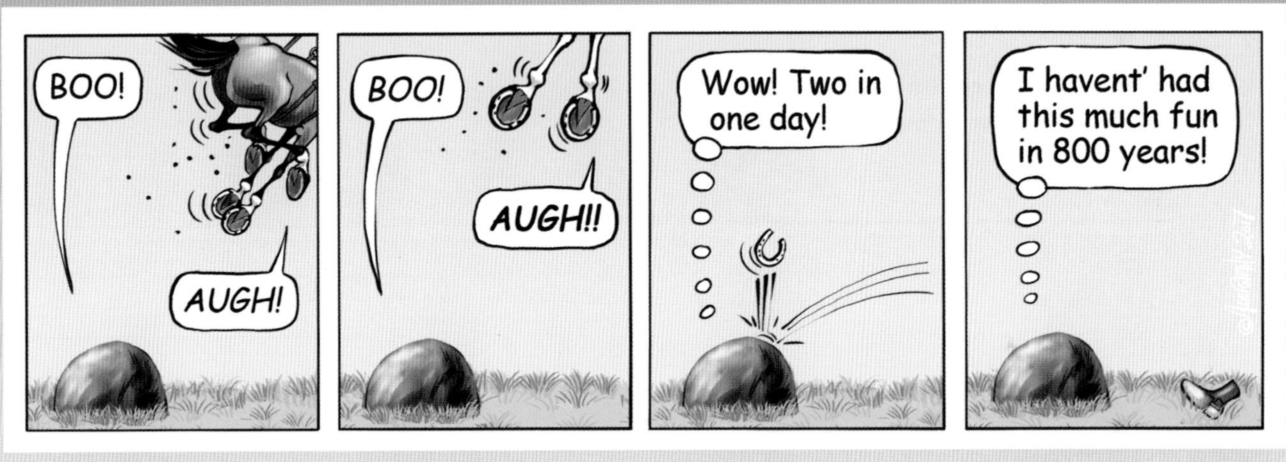
BOO!
AUGH!
BOO!
AUGH!!
Wow! Two in one day!
I havent' had this much fun in 800 years!

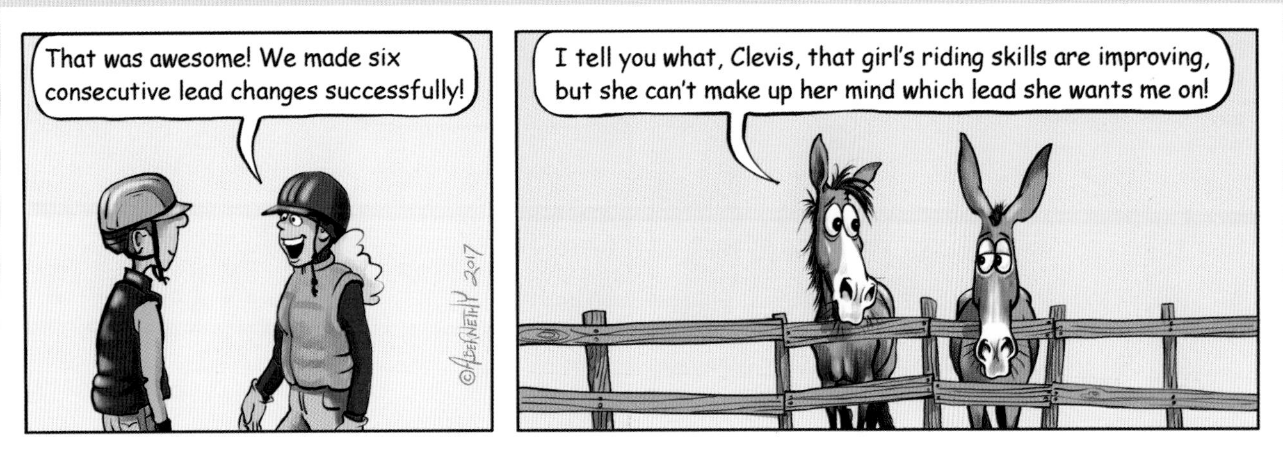
That was awesome! We made six consecutive lead changes successfully!
I tell you what, Clevis, that girl's riding skills are improving, but she can't make up her mind which lead she wants me on!

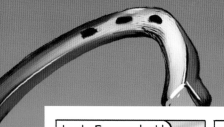

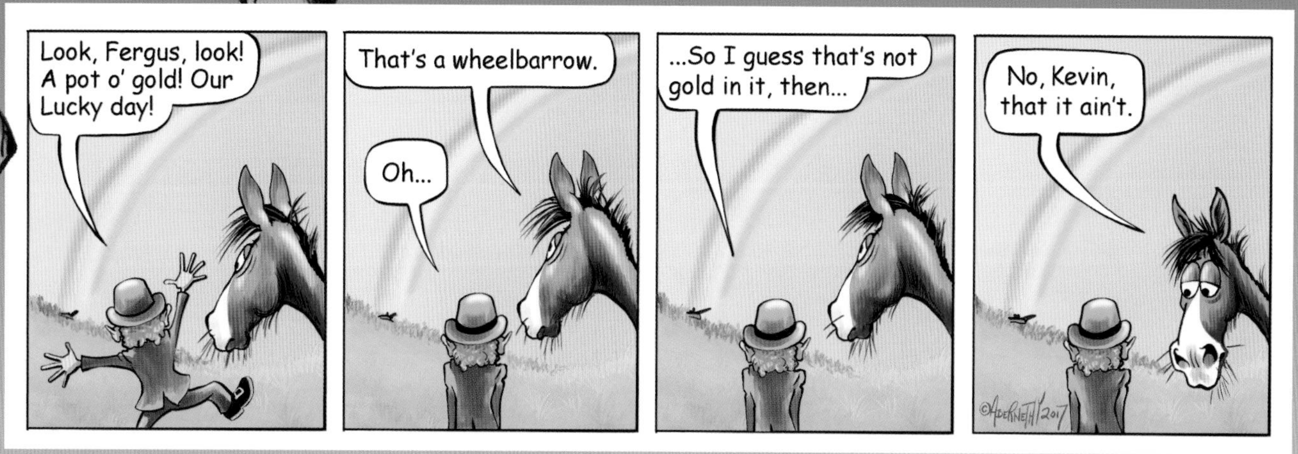
Look, Fergus, look! A pot o' gold! Our Lucky day!
That's a wheelbarrow.
Oh...
...So I guess that's not gold in it, then...
No, Kevin, that it ain't.
©ABERNETHY 2017

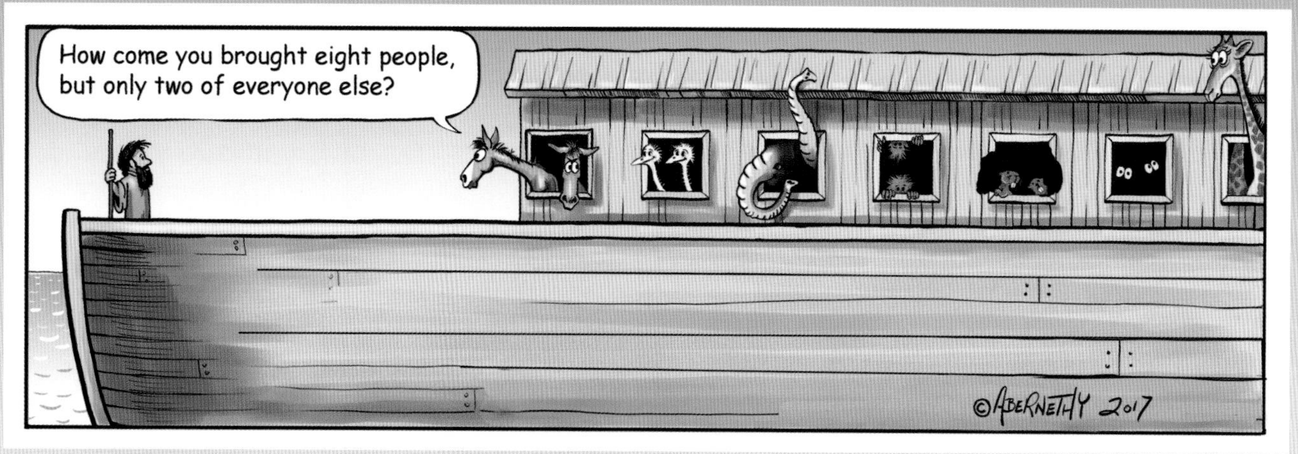
How come you brought eight people, but only two of everyone else?
©ABERNETHY 2017

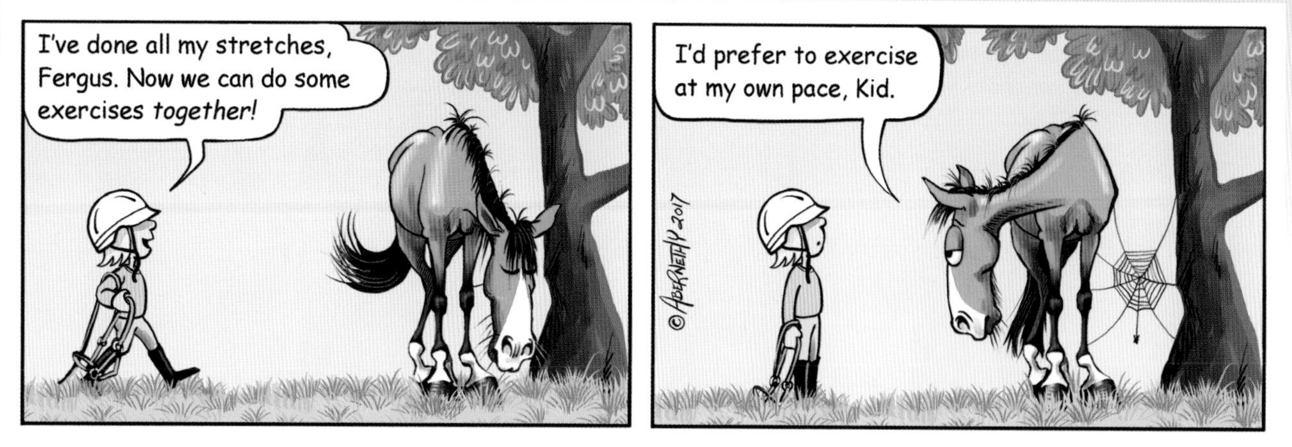
I've done all my stretches, Fergus. Now we can do some exercises *together!*
I'd prefer to exercise at my own pace, Kid.
©ABERNETHY 2017

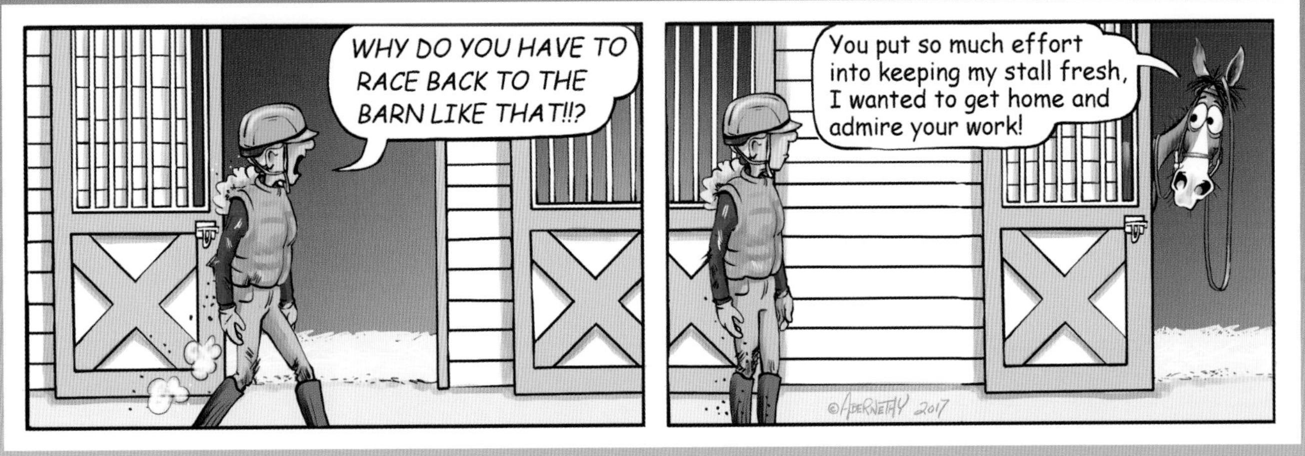
WHY DO YOU HAVE TO RACE BACK TO THE BARN LIKE THAT!!?
You put so much effort into keeping my stall fresh, I wanted to get home and admire your work!

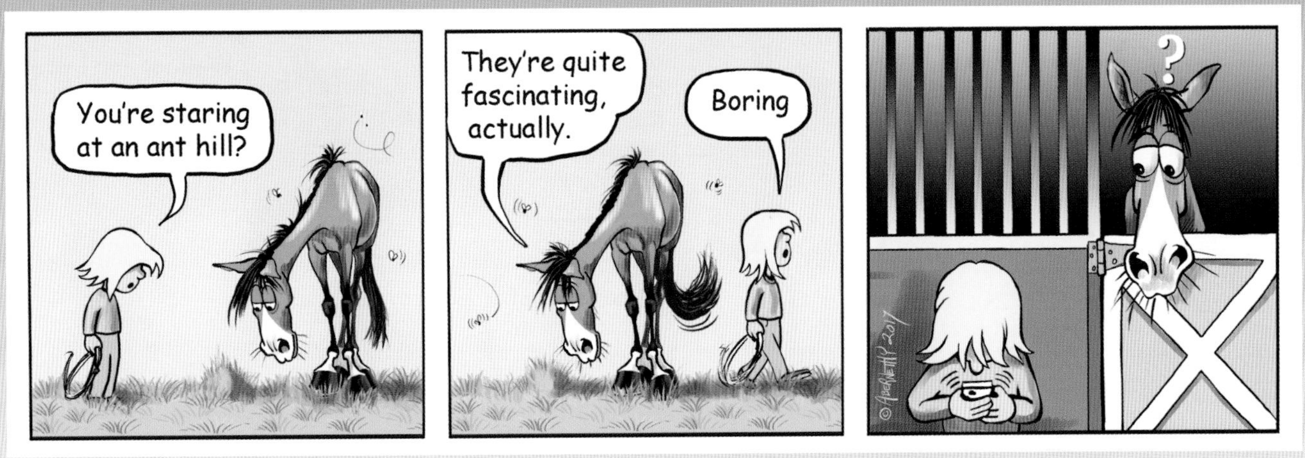
You're staring at an ant hill?
They're quite fascinating, actually.
Boring
?

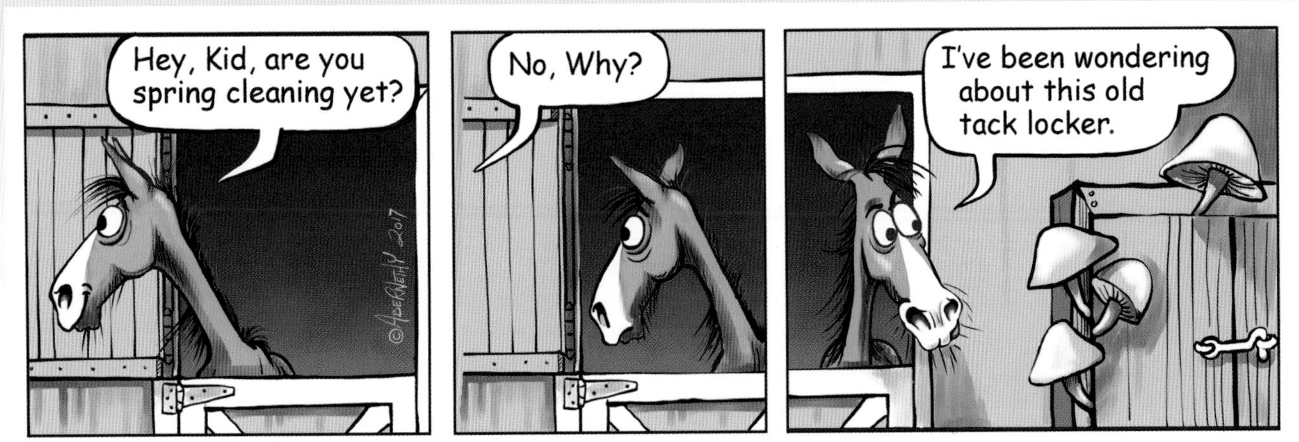
Hey, Kid, are you spring cleaning yet?
No, Why?
I've been wondering about this old tack locker.

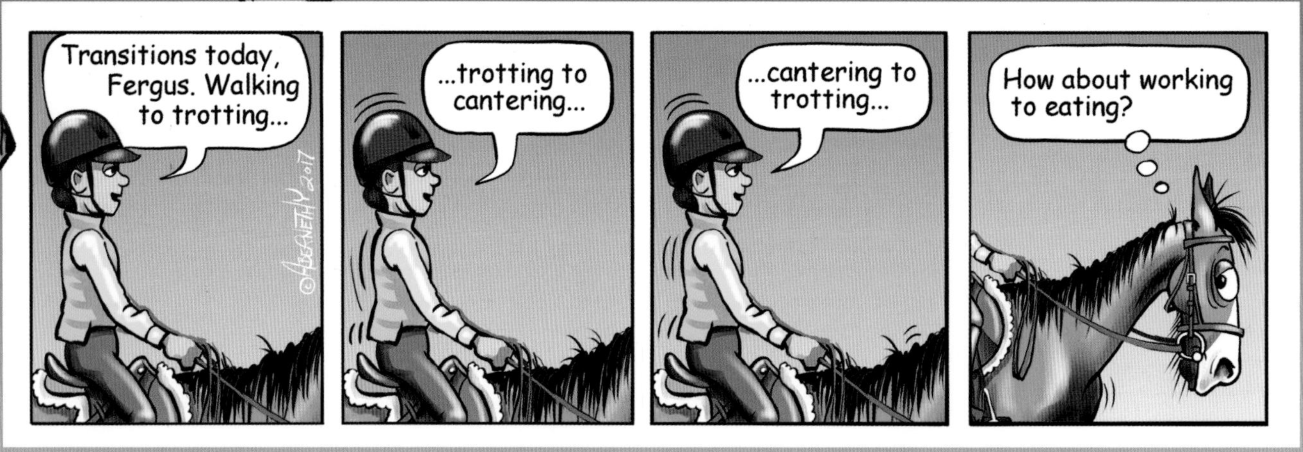
Transitions today, Fergus. Walking to trotting...
©ABERNETHY 2017
...trotting to cantering...
...cantering to trotting...
How about working to eating?

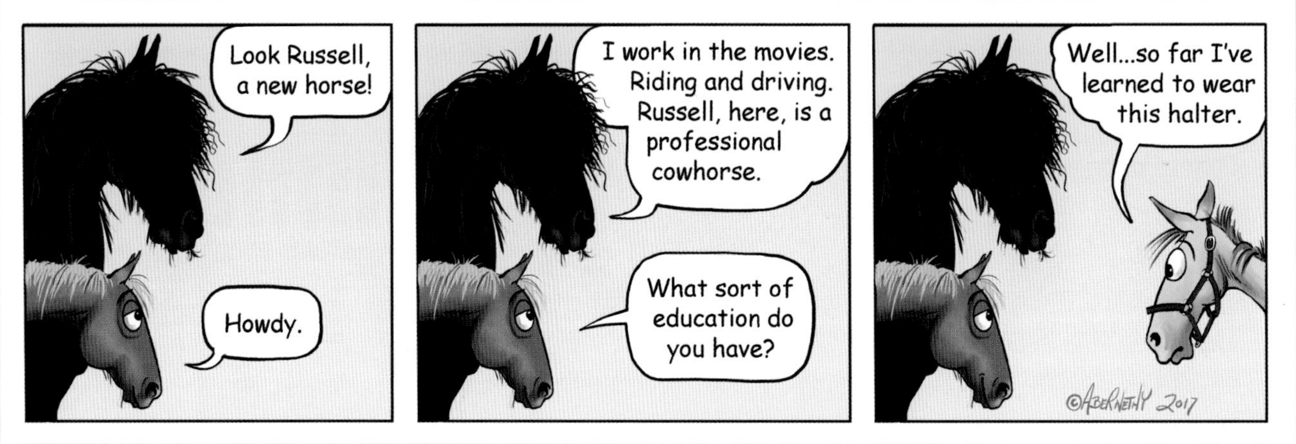
Look Russell, a new horse!
Howdy.
I work in the movies. Riding and driving. Russell, here, is a professional cowhorse.
What sort of education do you have?
Well...so far I've learned to wear this halter.
©ABERNETHY 2017

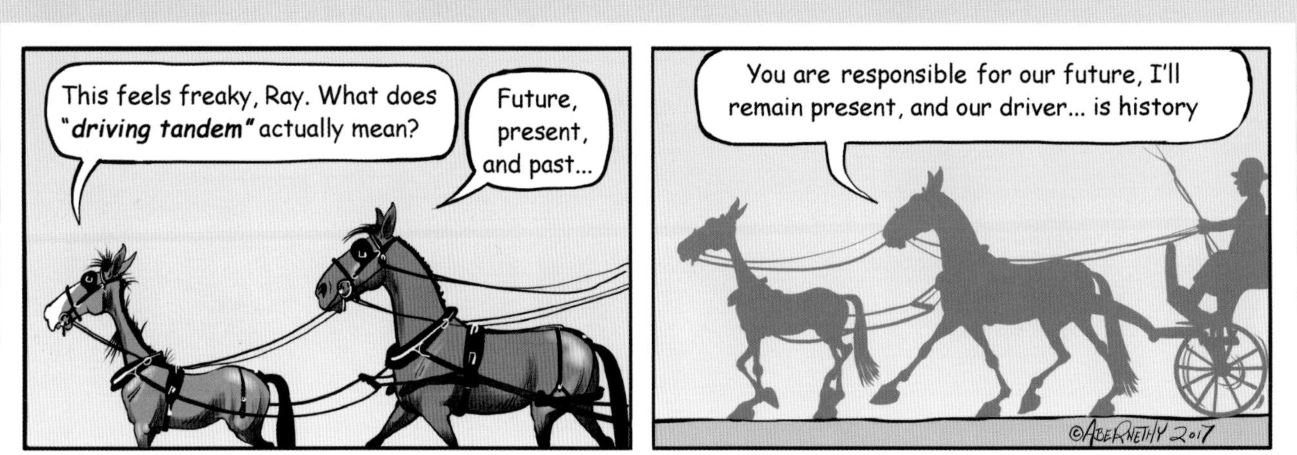
This feels freaky, Ray. What does "***driving tandem***" actually mean?
Future, present, and past...
You are responsible for our future, I'll remain present, and our driver... is history
©ABERNETHY 2017

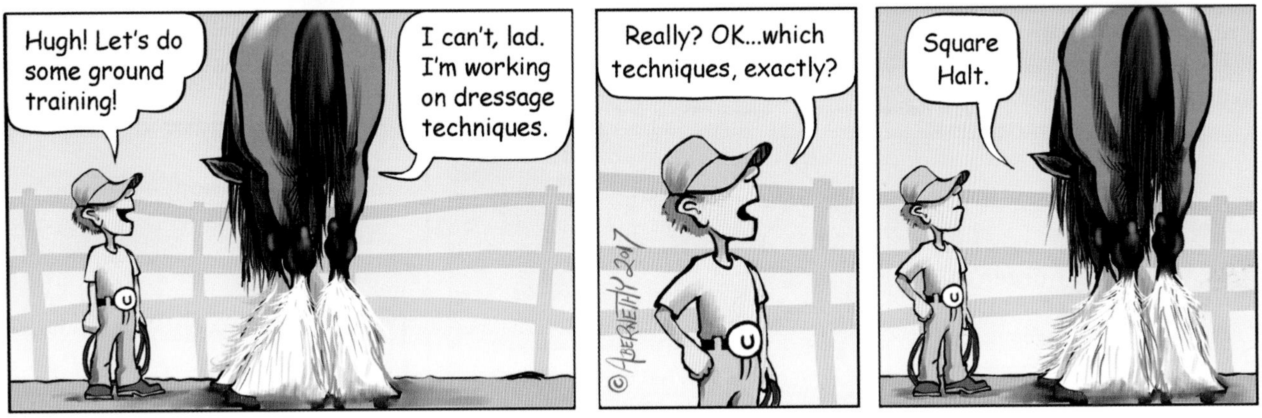
Hugh! Let's do some ground training!
I can't, lad. I'm working on dressage techniques.
Really? OK...which techniques, exactly?
©ABERNETHY 2017
Square Halt.

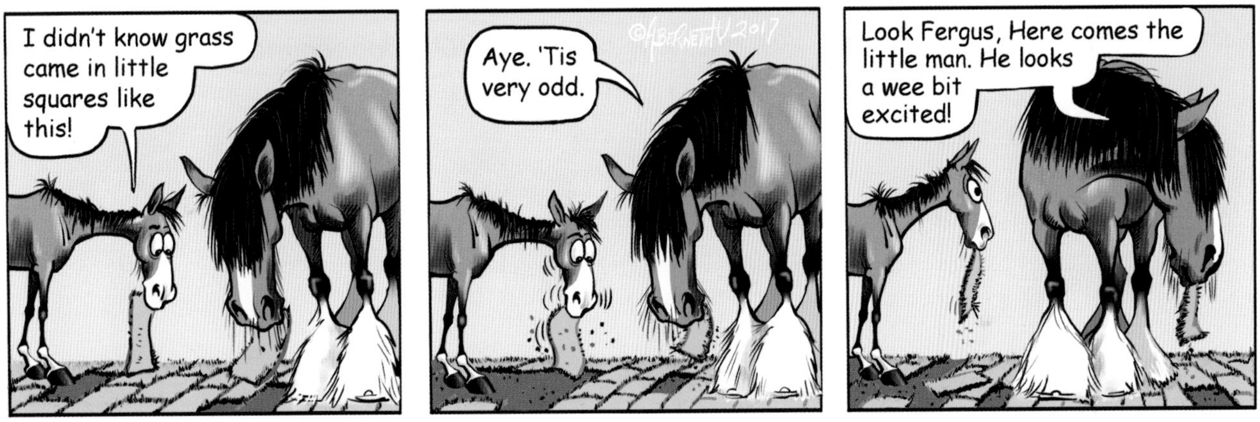
I didn't know grass came in little squares like this!
Aye. 'Tis very odd.
©ABERNETHY 2017
Look Fergus, Here comes the little man. He looks a wee bit excited!

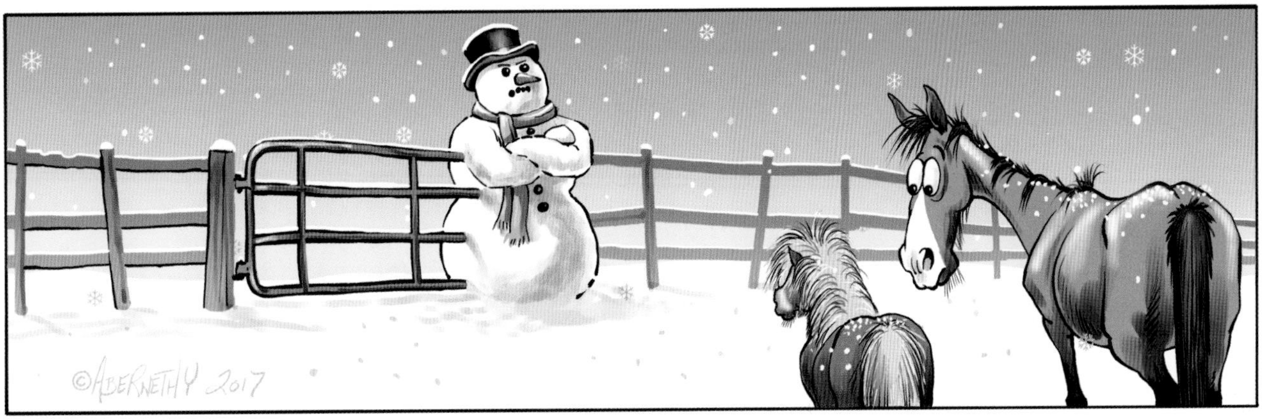
©ABERNETHY 2017

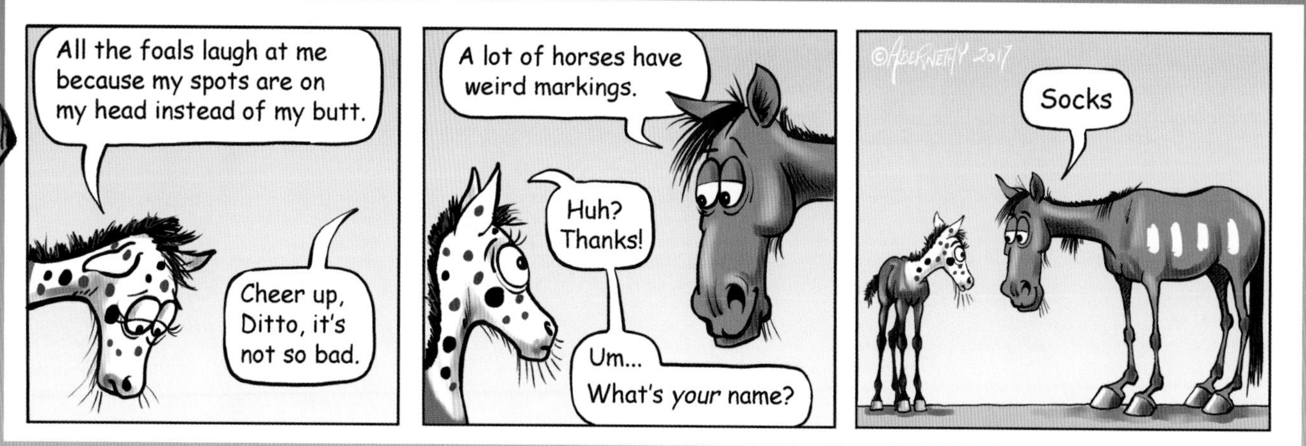
All the foals laugh at me because my spots are on my head instead of my butt.
Cheer up, Ditto, it's not so bad.
A lot of horses have weird markings.
Huh? Thanks!
Um...
What's *your* name?
©ABERNETHY 2017
Socks

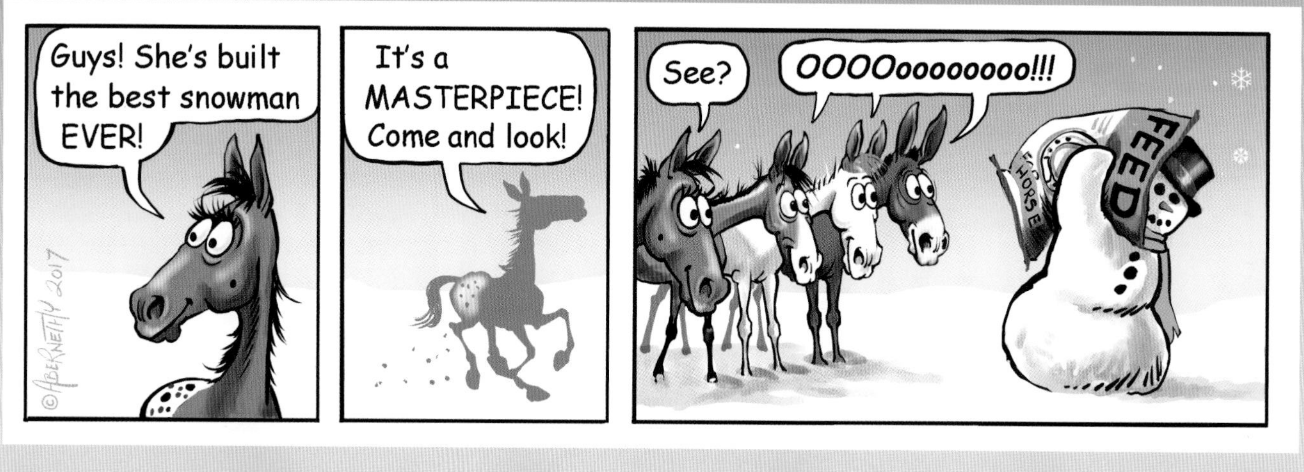
Guys! She's built the best snowman EVER!
©ABERNETHY 2017
It's a MASTERPIECE! Come and look!
See?
OOOOoooooooo!!!
FEED
HORSE

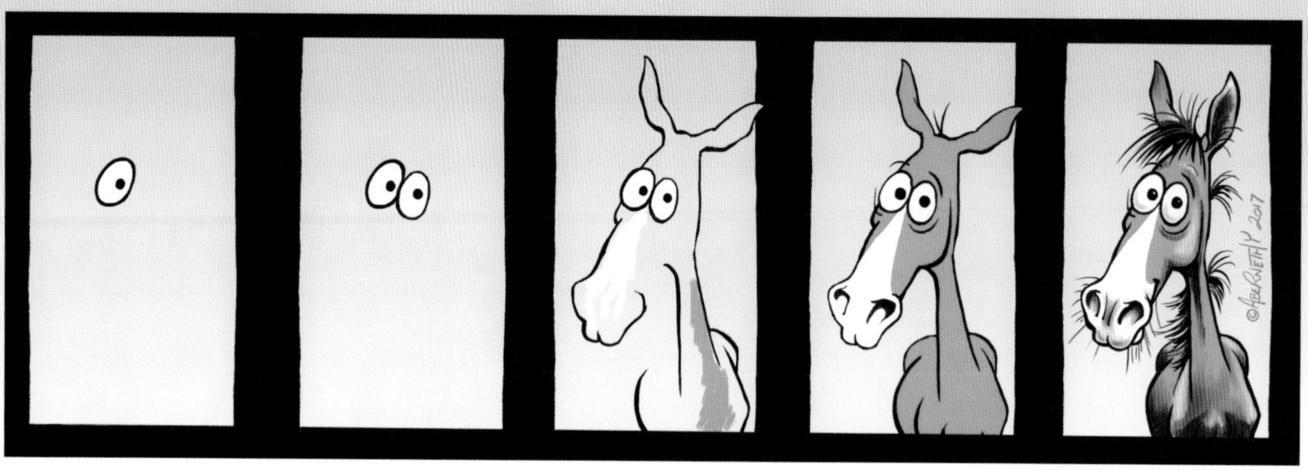
©ABERNETHY 2017

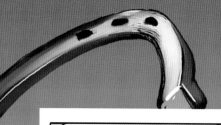

Today I am thankful for sweet hay. What are you thankful for?
Eighteen inches of stove pipe.
©Abernethy 2017

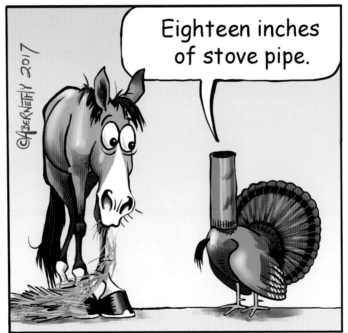

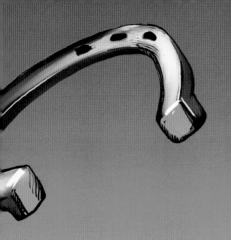

Fergus BY JEAN ABERNETHY

No. NO! Clevis! **NO!!**

I am *soooo* humiliated!

©Abernethy 2018

You've played every conceivable trick with that blanket, Fergus!

Couldn't you just **wear** it for one entire *night*?

What blanket?

©Abernethy 2018

79

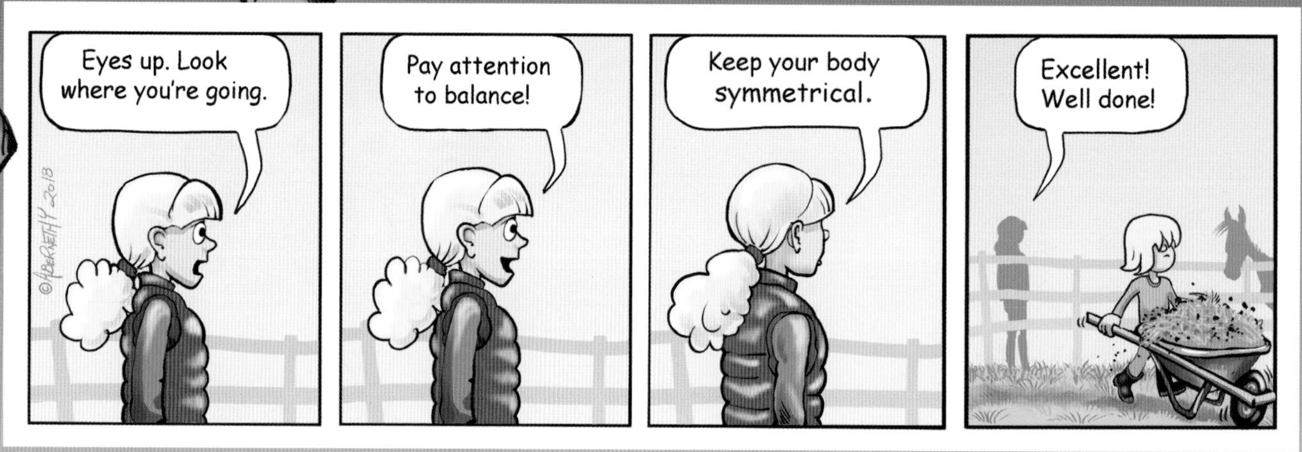
Eyes up. Look where you're going.
Pay attention to balance!
Keep your body symmetrical.
Excellent! Well done!
©ABERNETHY 2018

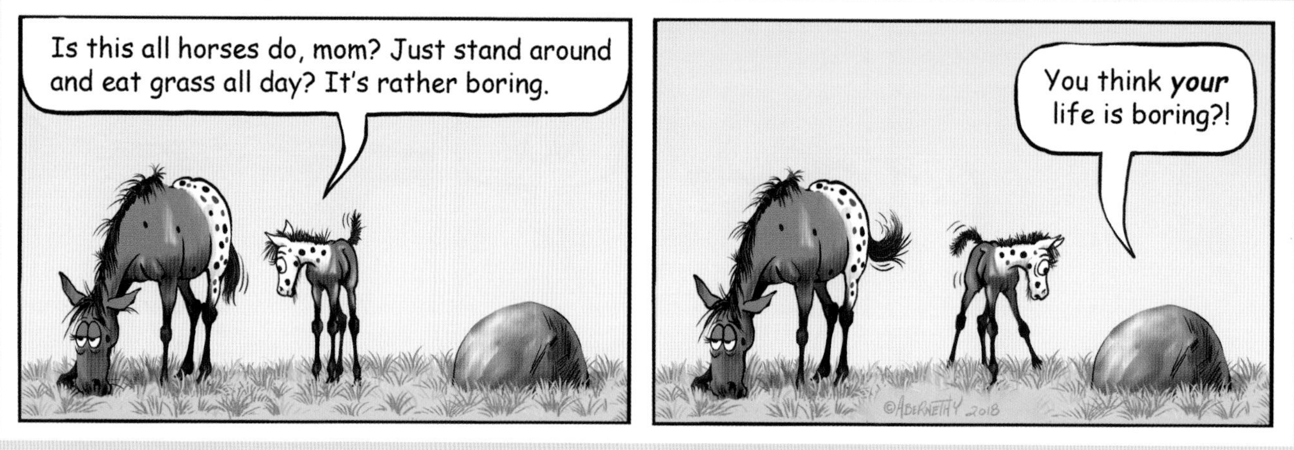
Is this all horses do, mom? Just stand around and eat grass all day? It's rather boring.
You think *your* life is boring?!
©ABERNETHY 2018

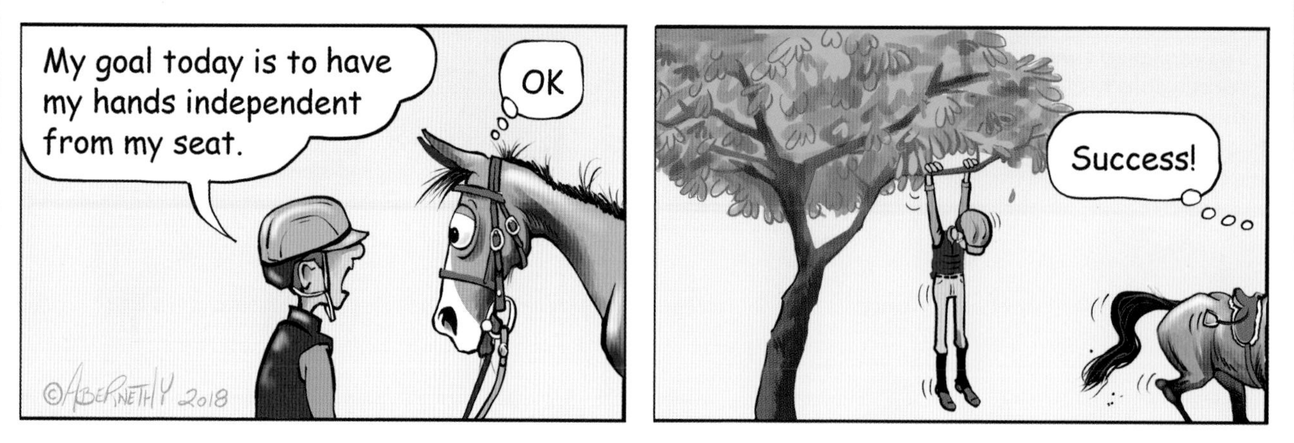
My goal today is to have my hands independent from my seat.
OK
Success!
©ABERNETHY 2018

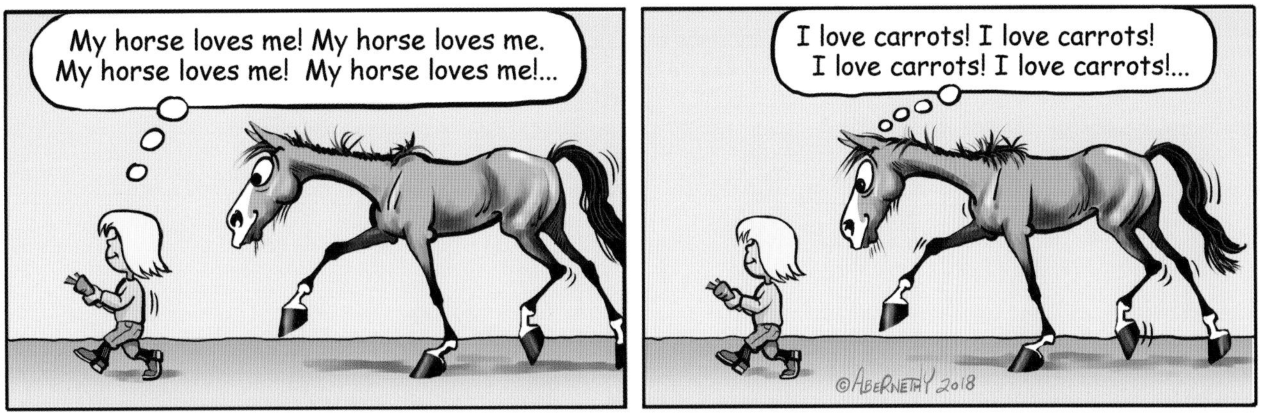
My horse loves me! My horse loves me.
My horse loves me! My horse loves me!...
I love carrots! I love carrots!
I love carrots! I love carrots!...
©ABERNETHY 2018

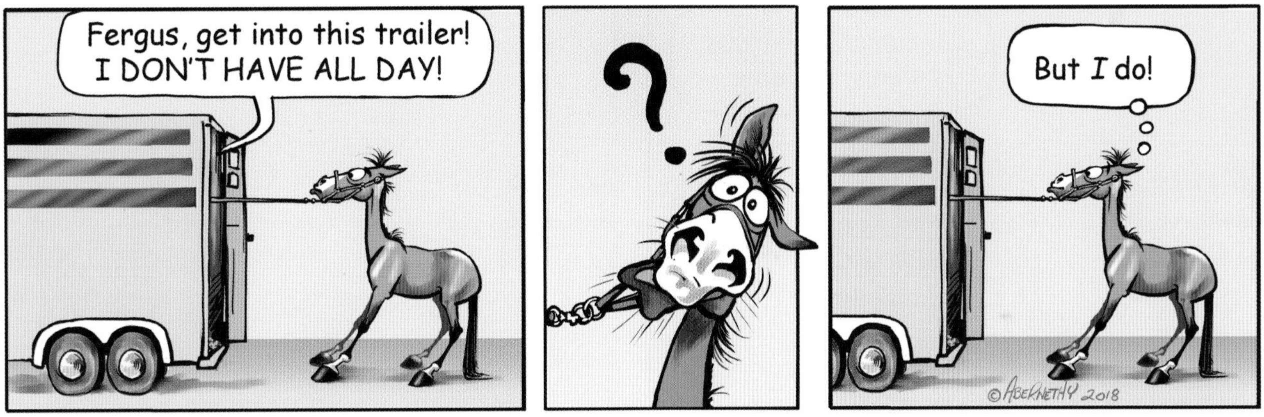
Fergus, get into this trailer!
I DON'T HAVE ALL DAY!
?
But *I* do!
©ABERNETHY 2018

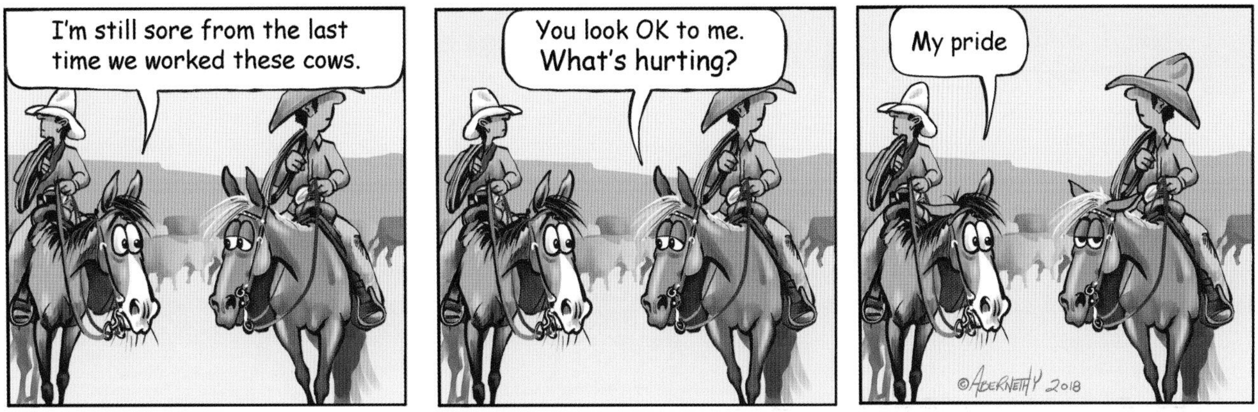
I'm still sore from the last time we worked these cows.
You look OK to me. What's hurting?
My pride
©ABERNETHY 2018

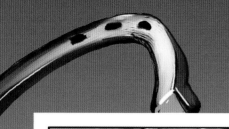

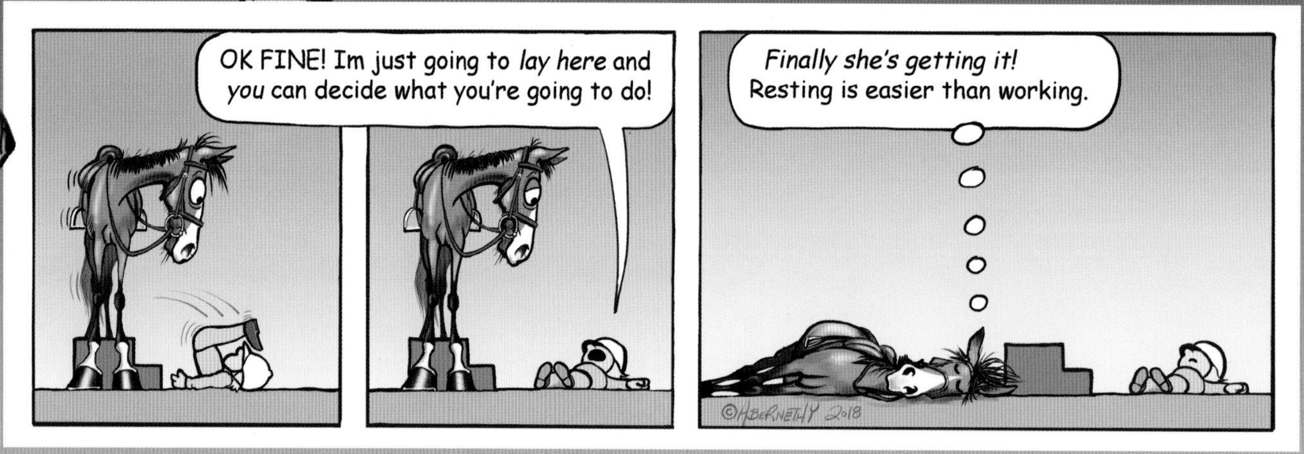
OK FINE! Im just going to *lay here* and *you* can decide what you're going to do!
Finally she's getting it! Resting is easier than working.
©ABERNETHY 2018

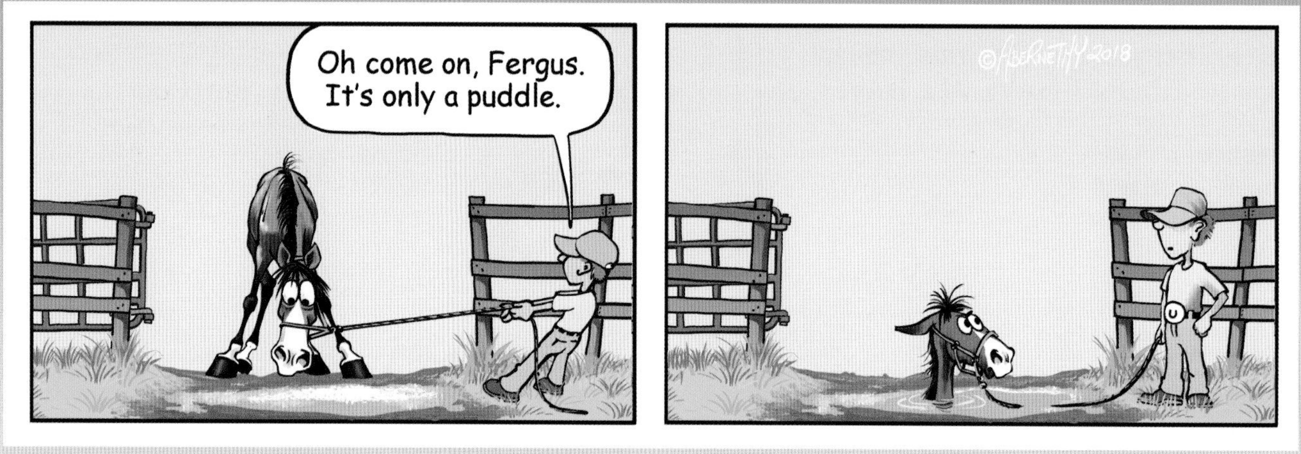
Oh come on, Fergus. It's only a puddle.
©ABERNETHY 2018

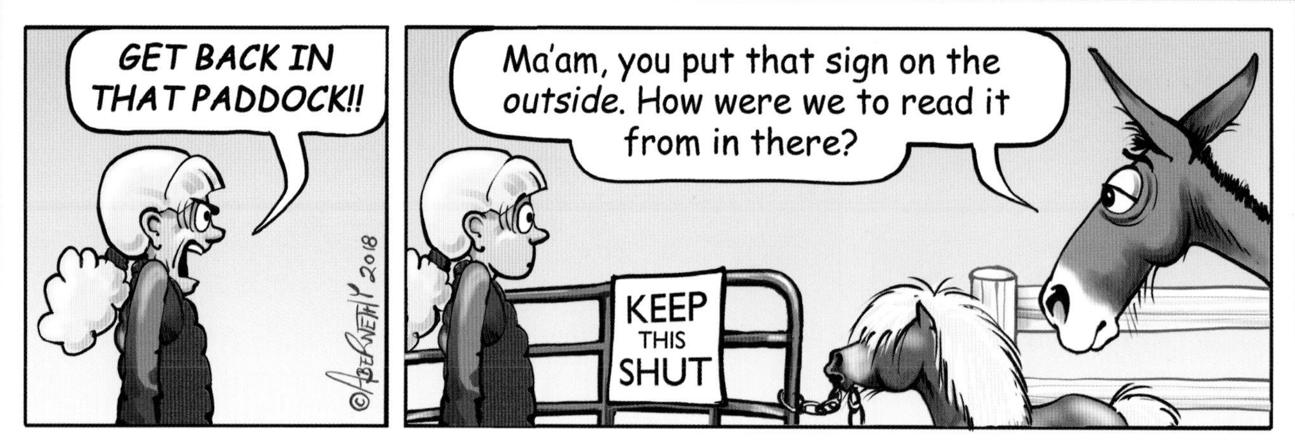
GET BACK IN THAT PADDOCK!!
©ABERNETHY 2018
Ma'am, you put that sign on the *outside*. How were we to read it from in there?
KEEP THIS SHUT

Hey guys, what's with the bright orange?
It's so that hunters won't shoot at us.
©Abernethy 2018
I don't think that's going to work, Steve.

She's suddenly riding better, Art. She's light, balanced, breathing deeply, and *very* focused!
©Abernethy 2018
That will only last a couple of weeks. She got new designer britches for Christmas.

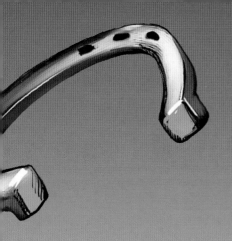

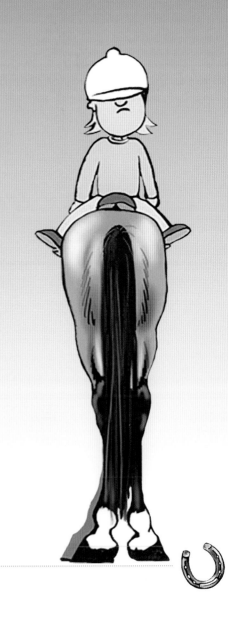

2019

Fergus BY JEAN ABERNETHY

I've been studying, Fergus. With your help...

...I can bring my horsemanship to a higher level.

Like this?

©ABERNETHY 2019

If you could give me one small nugget of wisdom, what would it be?

©Abernethy 2019

Wait.

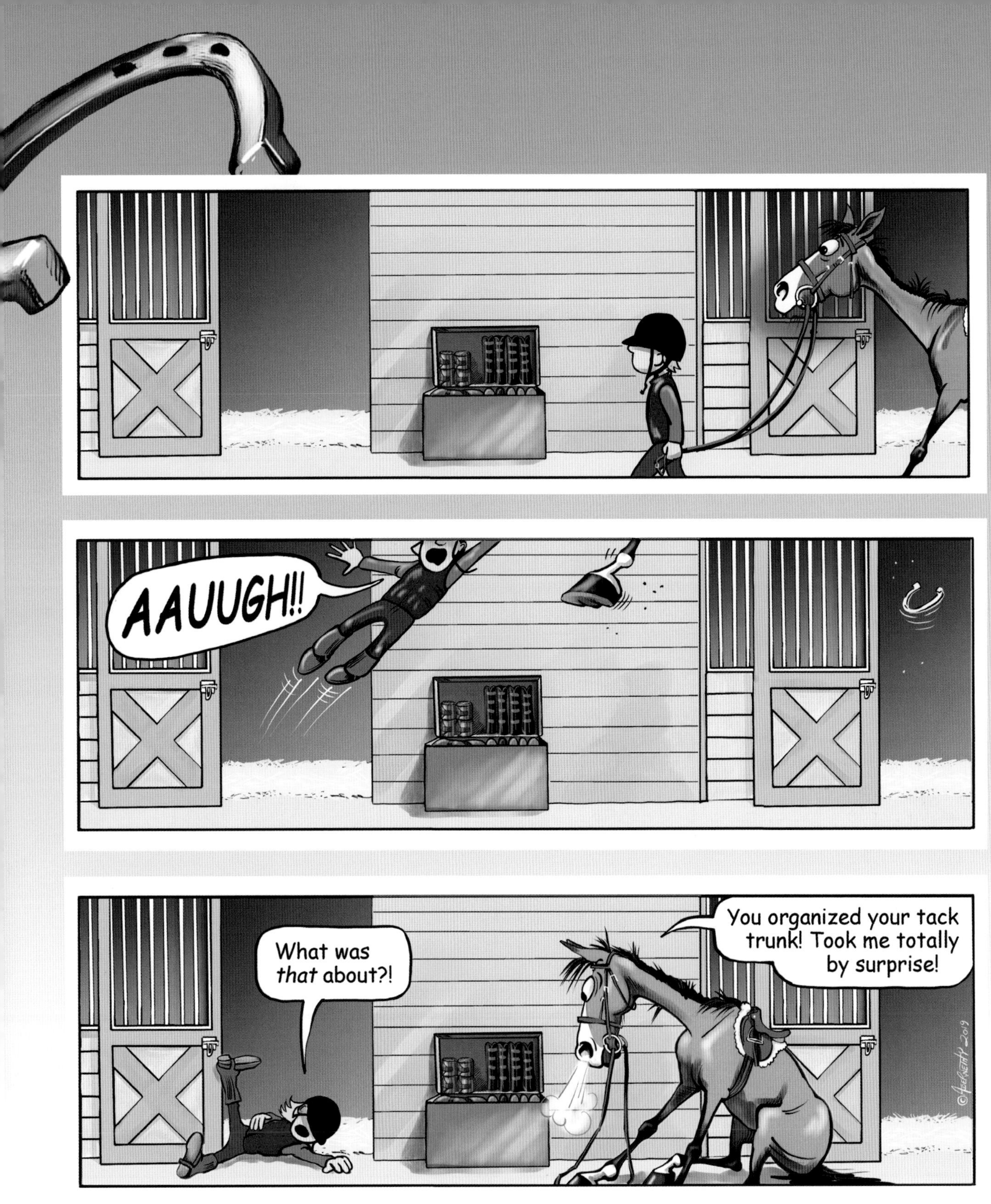
AAUUGH!!
What was *that* about?!
You organized your tack trunk! Took me totally by surprise!
©Abernethy 2019

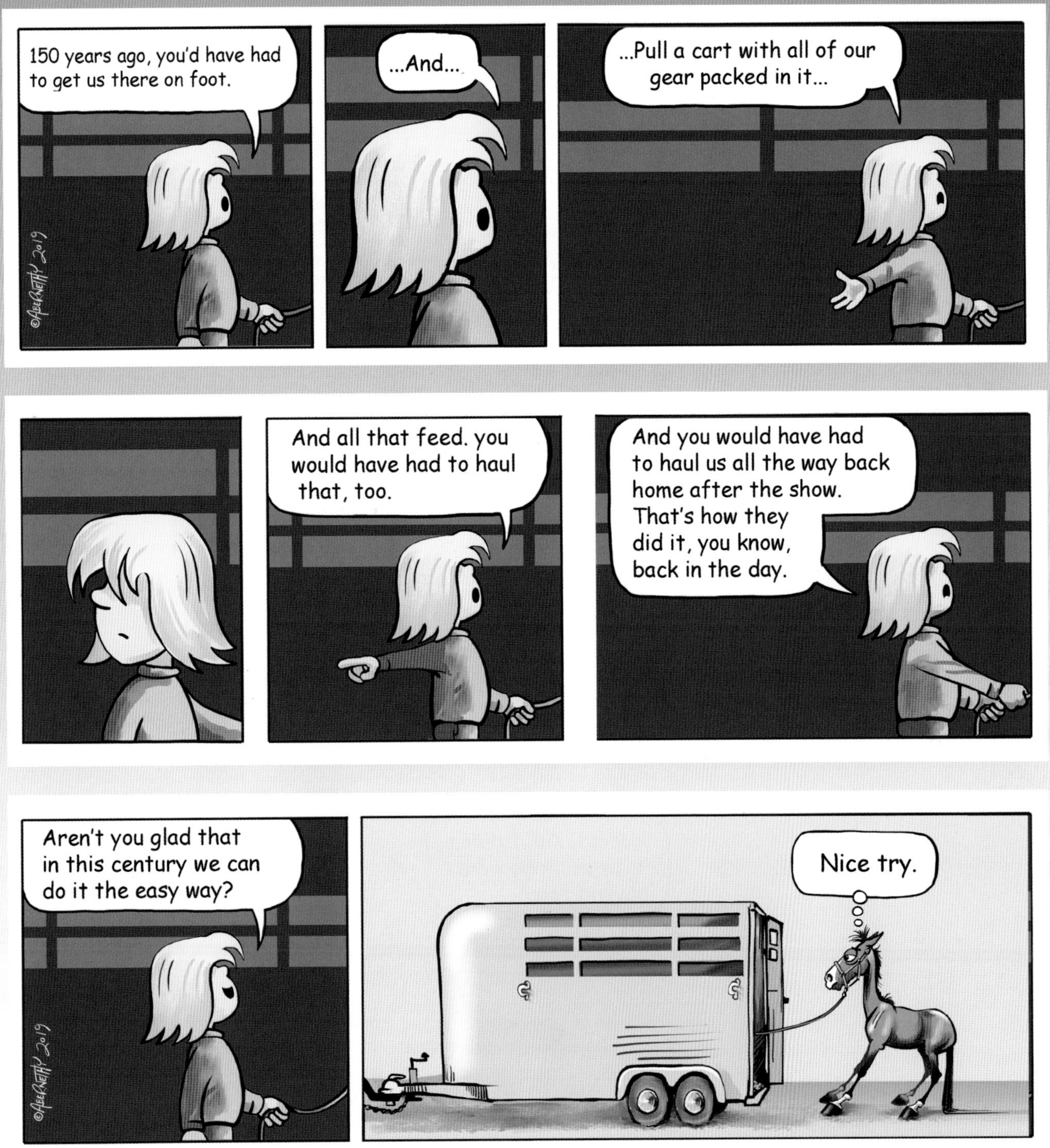
150 years ago, you'd have had to get us there on foot.
...And...
...Pull a cart with all of our gear packed in it...
And all that feed. you would have had to haul that, too.
And you would have had to haul us all the way back home after the show. That's how they did it, you know, back in the day.
Aren't you glad that in this century we can do it the easy way?
Nice try.

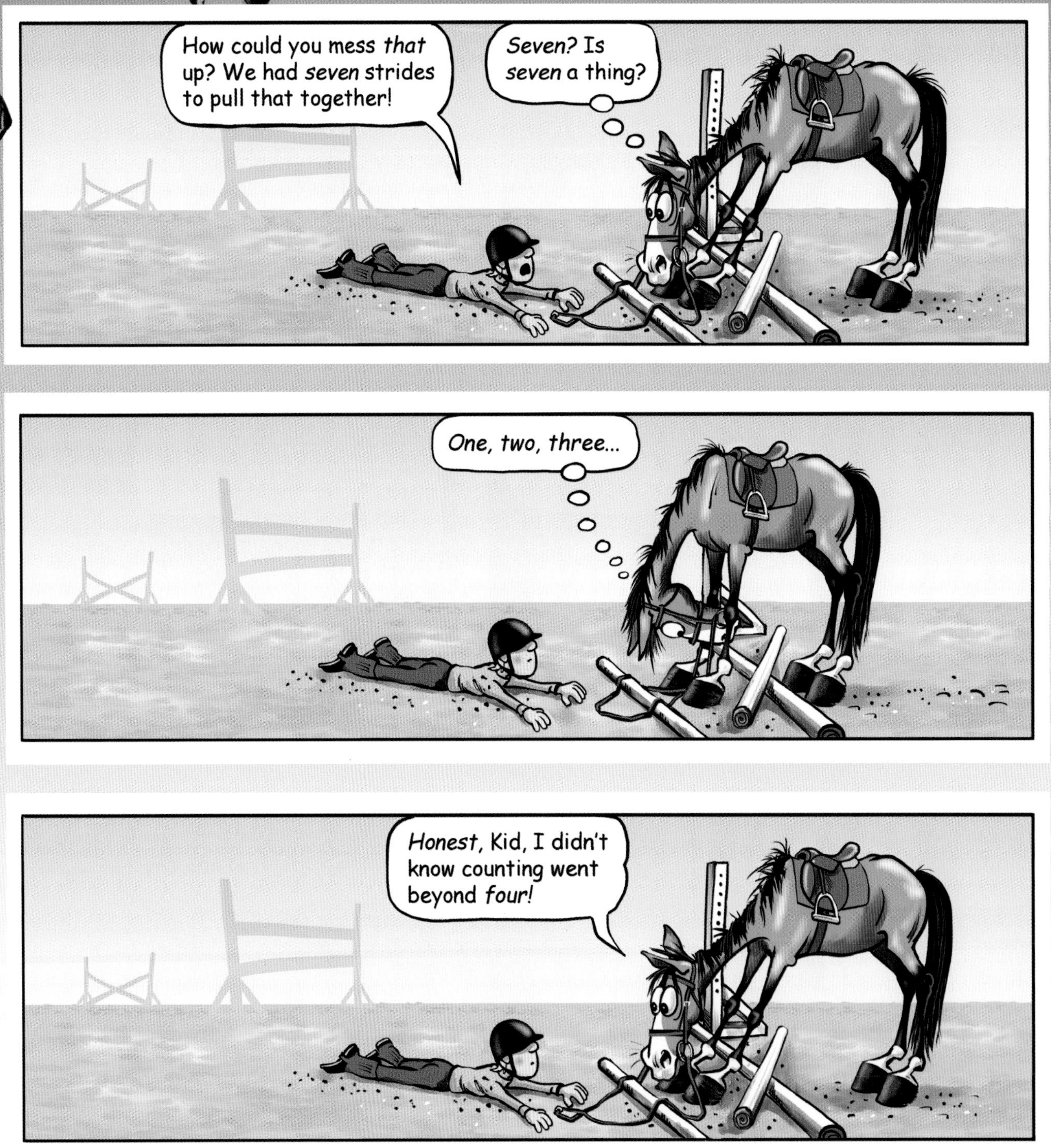
How could you mess *that* up? We had *seven* strides to pull that together!
Seven? Is *seven* a thing?
One, two, three...
Honest, Kid, I didn't know counting went beyond *four*!

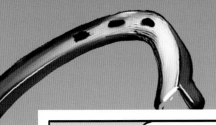

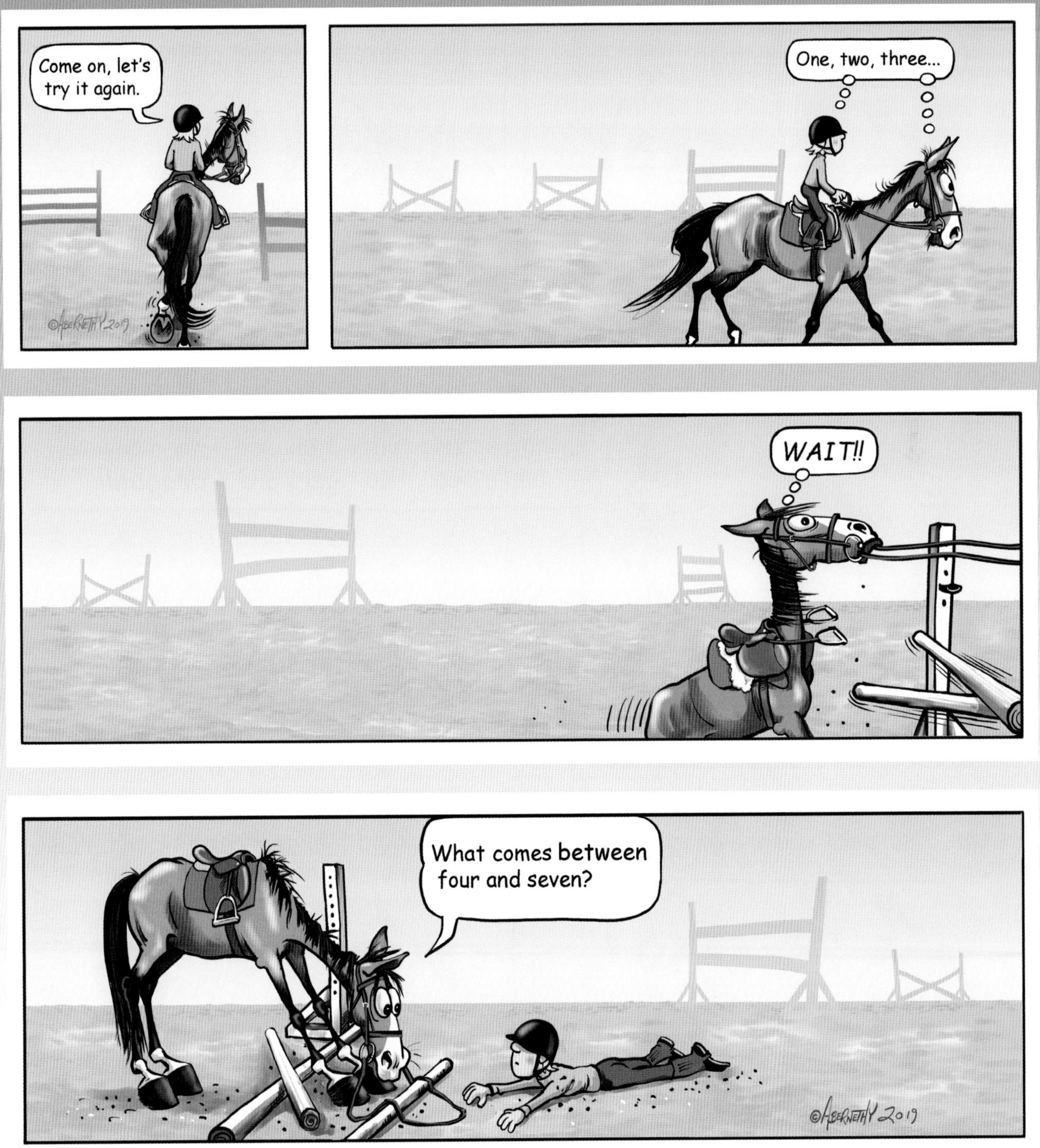
Come on, let's try it again.
One, two, three...
WAIT!!
What comes between four and seven?
©ABERNETHY 2019

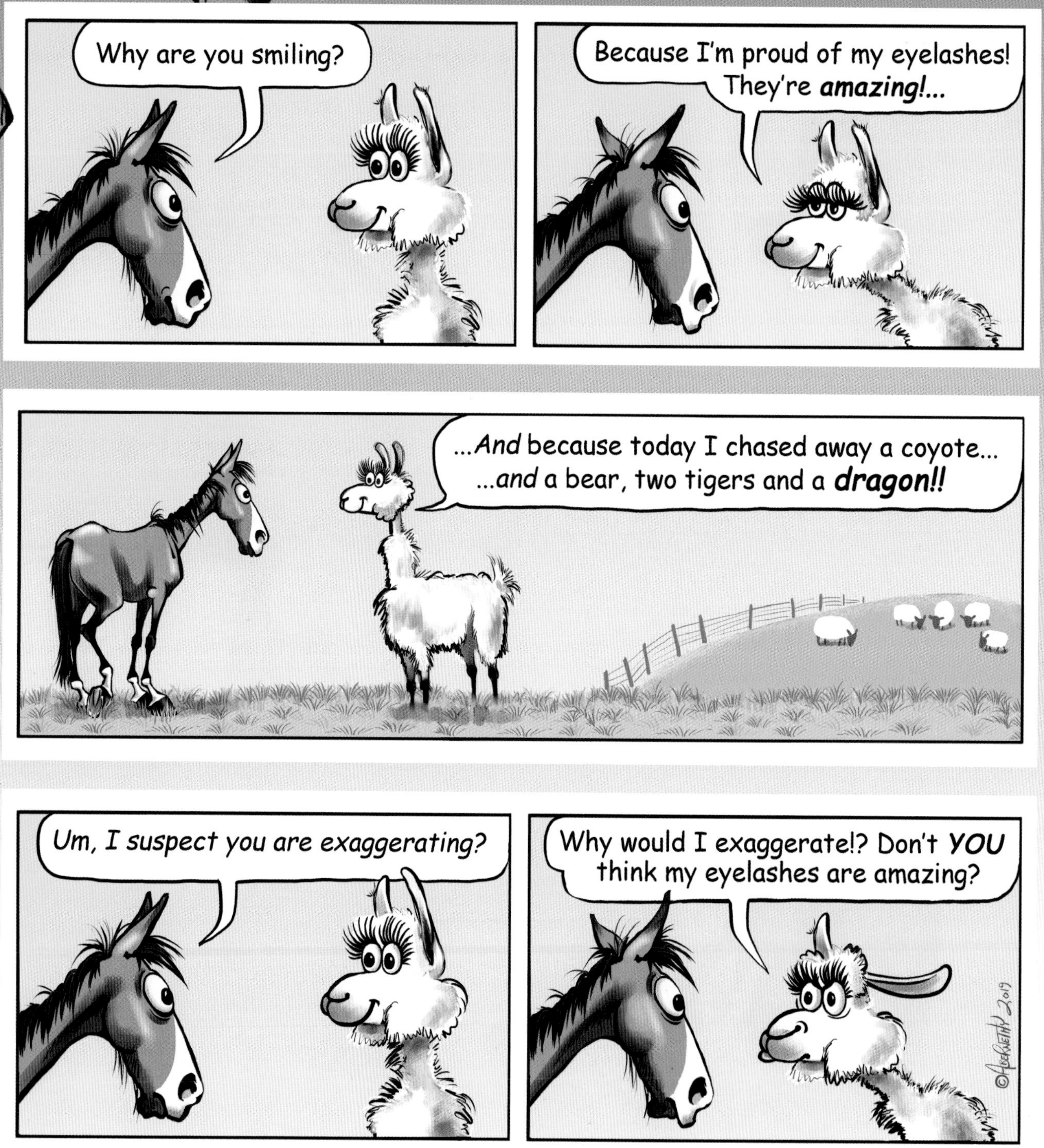
Why are you smiling?
Because I'm proud of my eyelashes! They're *amazing!...*
...And because today I chased away a coyote... *...and* a bear, two tigers and a ***dragon!!***
Um, I suspect you are exaggerating?
Why would I exaggerate!? Don't ***YOU*** think my eyelashes are amazing?

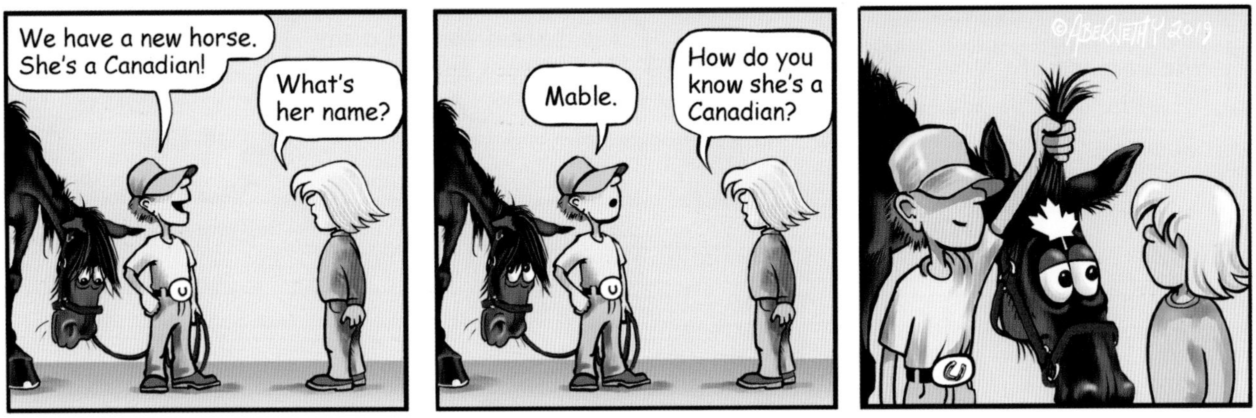
We have a new horse. She's a Canadian!
What's her name?
Mable.
How do you know she's a Canadian?
©ABERNETHY 2019

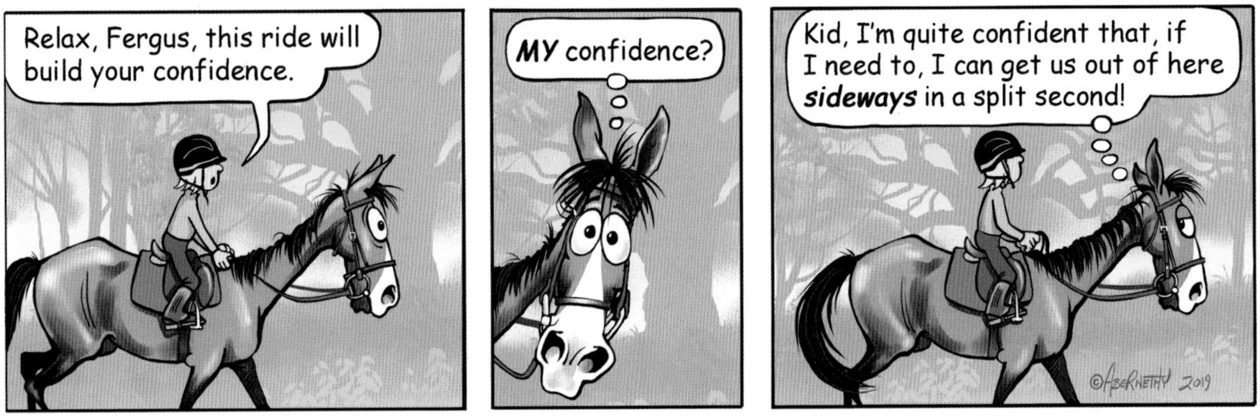
Relax, Fergus, this ride will build your confidence.
MY confidence?
Kid, I'm quite confident that, if I need to, I can get us out of here ***sideways*** in a split second!
©ABERNETHY 2019

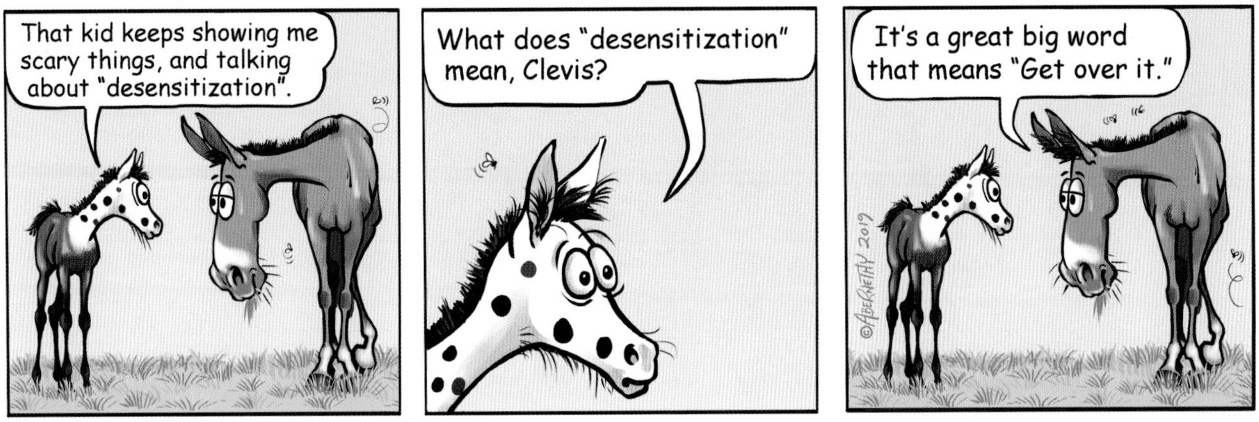
That kid keeps showing me scary things, and talking about "desensitization".
What does "desensitization" mean, Clevis?
It's a great big word that means "Get over it."
©ABERNETHY 2019

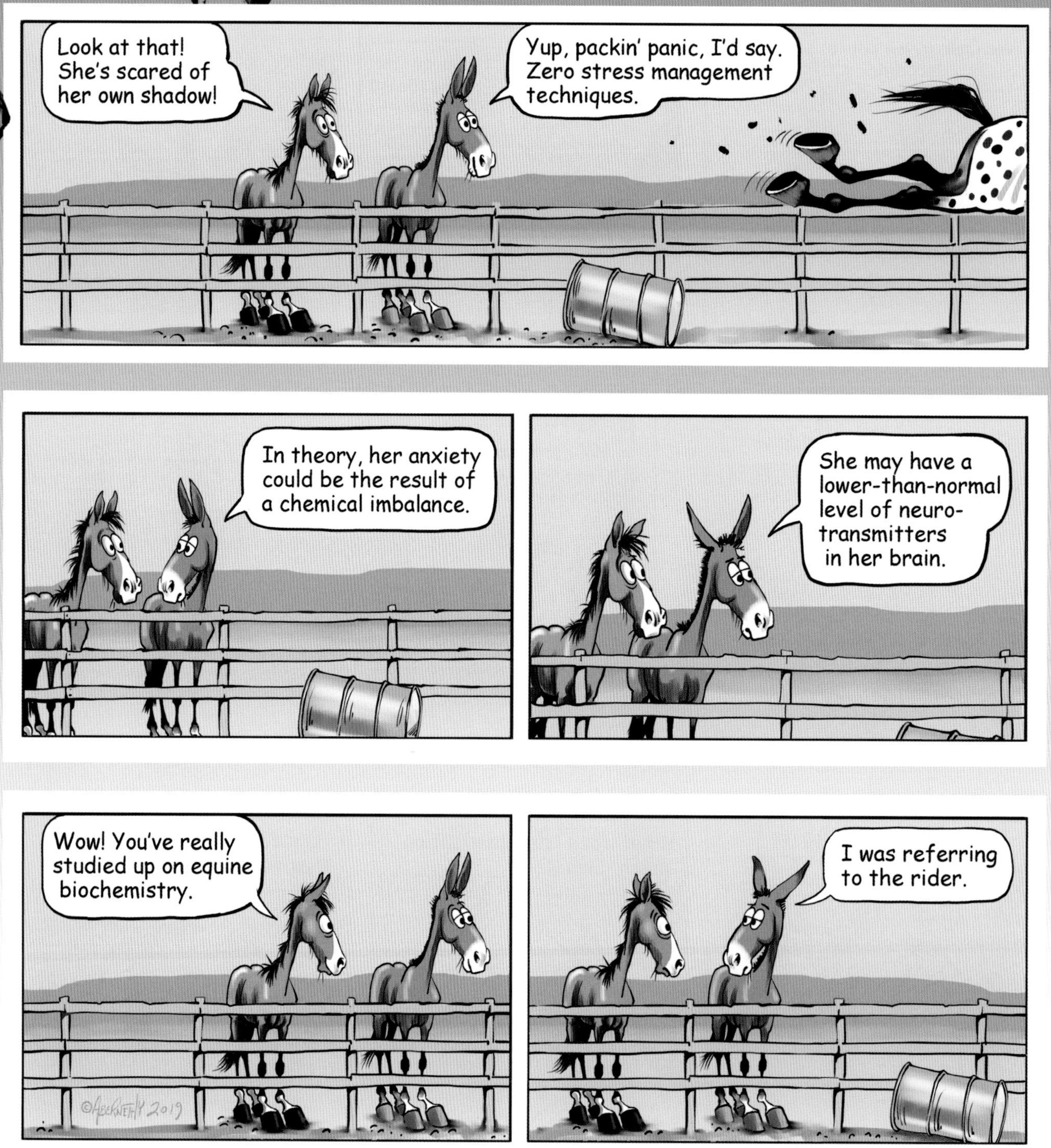
Look at that! She's scared of her own shadow!
Yup, packin' panic, I'd say. Zero stress management techniques.
In theory, her anxiety could be the result of a chemical imbalance.
She may have a lower-than-normal level of neuro-transmitters in her brain.
Wow! You've really studied up on equine biochemistry.
I was referring to the rider.
©Adckwerth 2019

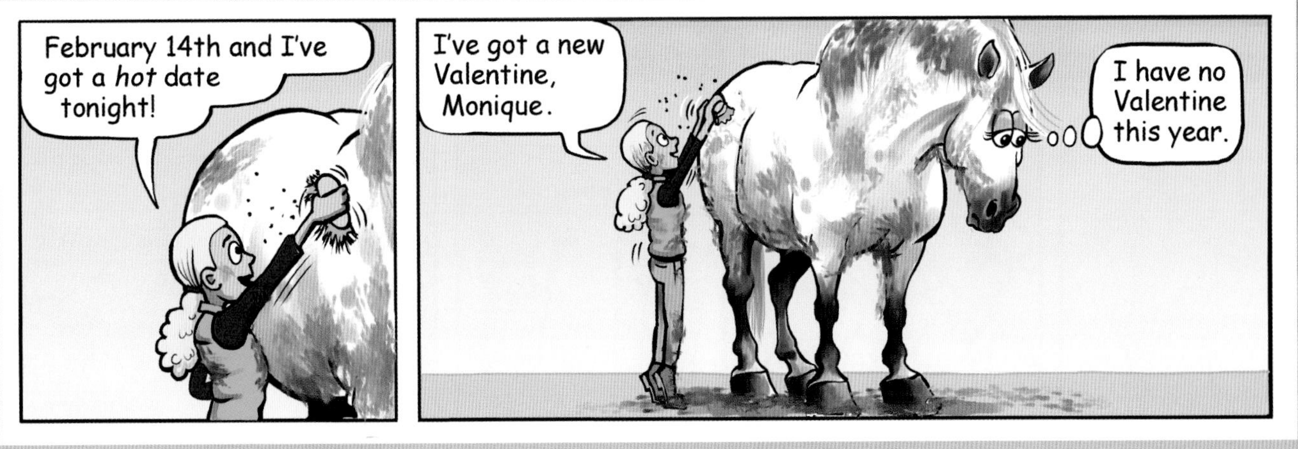
February 14th and I've got a *hot* date tonight!
I've got a new Valentine, Monique.
I have no Valentine this year.

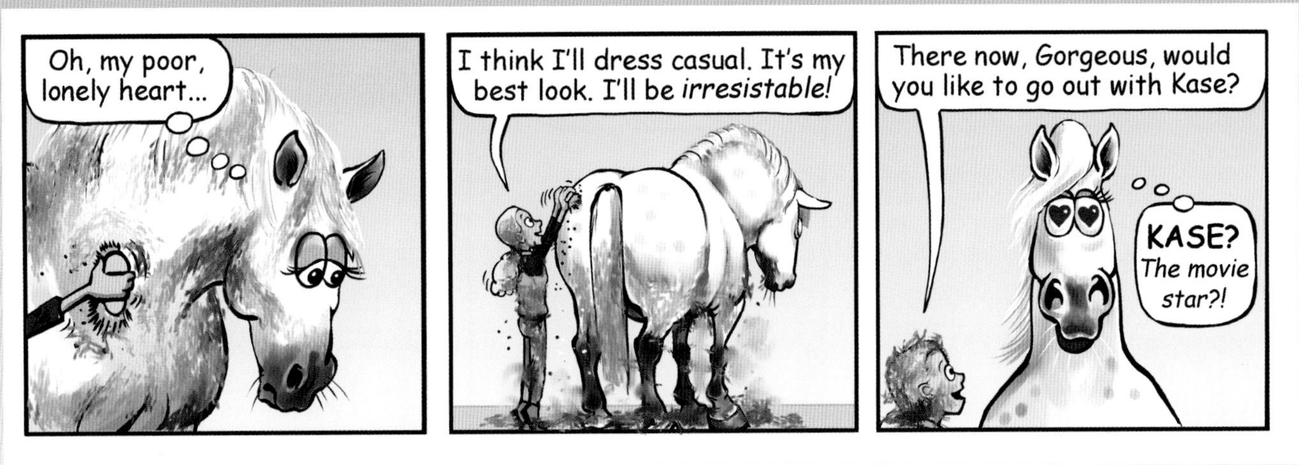
Oh, my poor, lonely heart...
I think I'll dress casual. It's my best look. I'll be *irresistable!*
There now, Gorgeous, would you like to go out with Kase?
KASE? *The movie star?!*

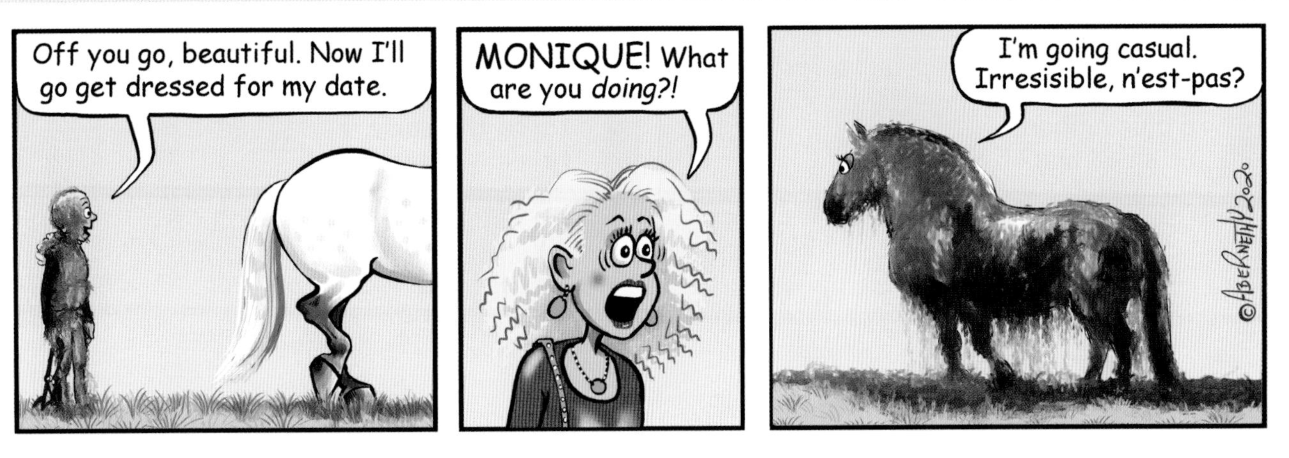
Off you go, beautiful. Now I'll go get dressed for my date.
MONIQUE! What are you *doing?!*
I'm going casual. Irresisible, n'est-pas?
©ABERNETHY 2020

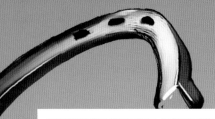

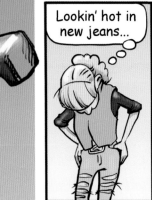

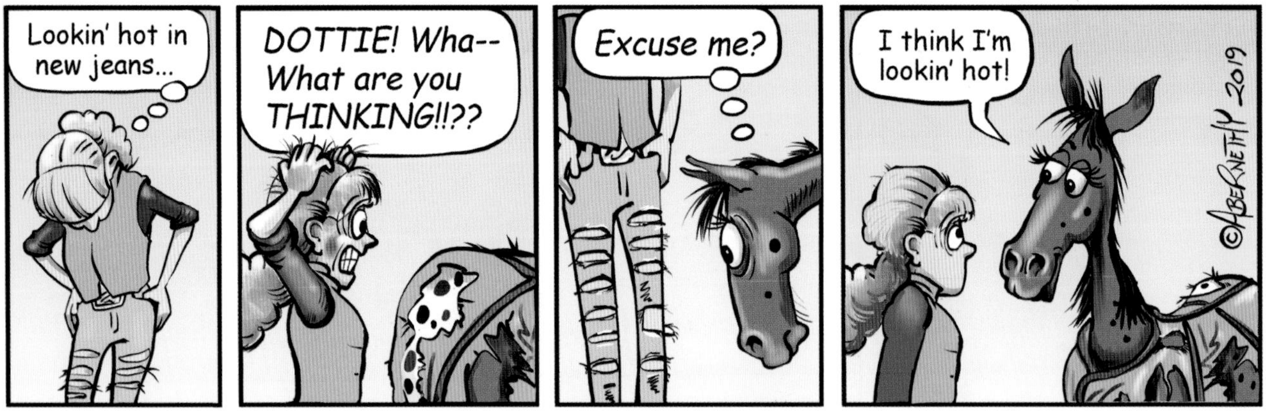
Lookin' hot in new jeans...
DOTTIE! Wha-- What are you THINKING!!??
Excuse me?
I think I'm lookin' hot!
©ABERNETHY 2019

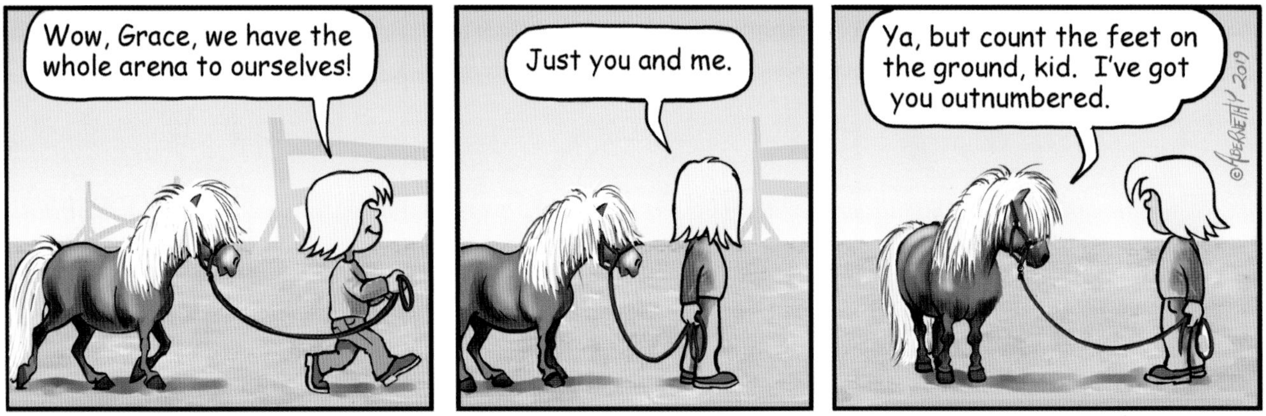
Wow, Grace, we have the whole arena to ourselves!
Just you and me.
Ya, but count the feet on the ground, kid. I've got you outnumbered.
©ABERNETHY 2019

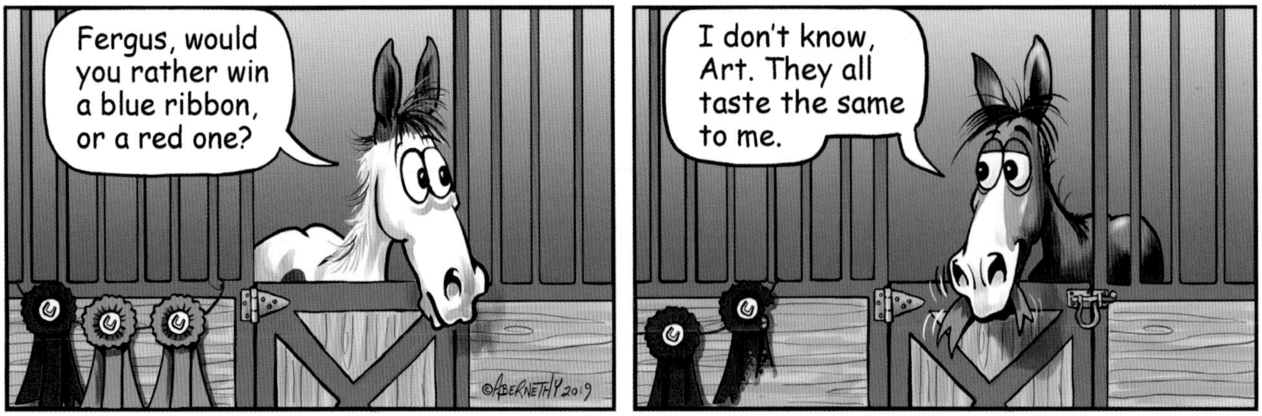
Fergus, would you rather win a blue ribbon, or a red one?
©ABERNETHY 2019
I don't know, Art. They all taste the same to me.

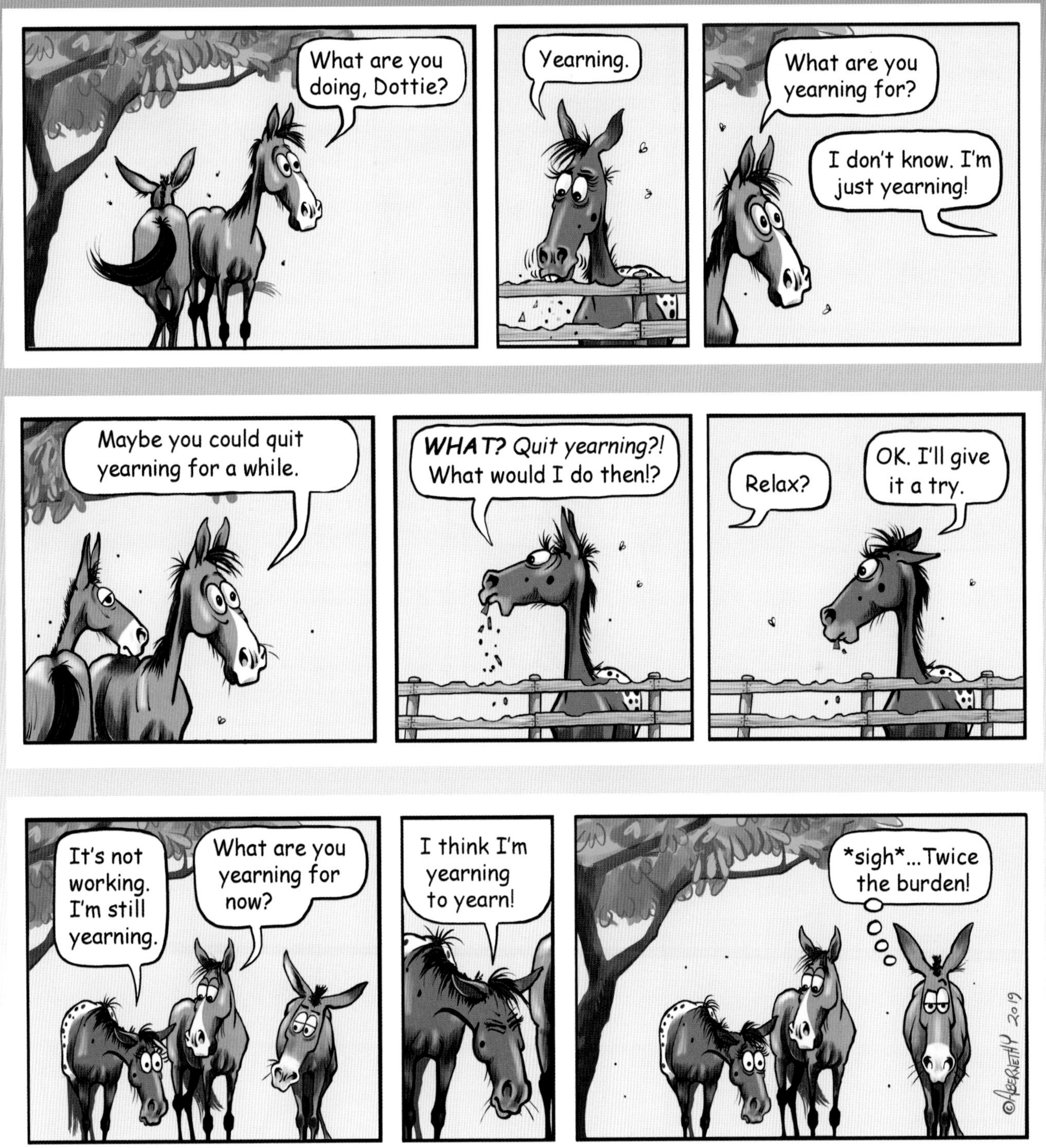
What are you doing, Dottie?
Yearning.
What are you yearning for?
I don't know. I'm just yearning!
Maybe you could quit yearning for a while.
WHAT? Quit yearning?! What would I do then!?
Relax?
OK. I'll give it a try.
It's not working. I'm still yearning.
What are you yearning for now?
I think I'm yearning to yearn!
sigh...Twice the burden!
©ABERNETHY 2019

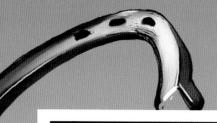

Can I have a drink from your bucket?

Sure.

What's your name?

Oh. Of course.

slurp... Slug.

I watched your last workout. You're **way** too tense stepping into a left lead.

Relax your neck. Think **ENERGY** right down your spine, and into your right hip.

Be more **SUPPLE!**

You don't have legs, you don't even have bones! How would you know all that!?

Dude, I'll **show** you.

Right lead...

...left lead. Got it?

You're so much more supple today, Fergus!

Coached by a slug.

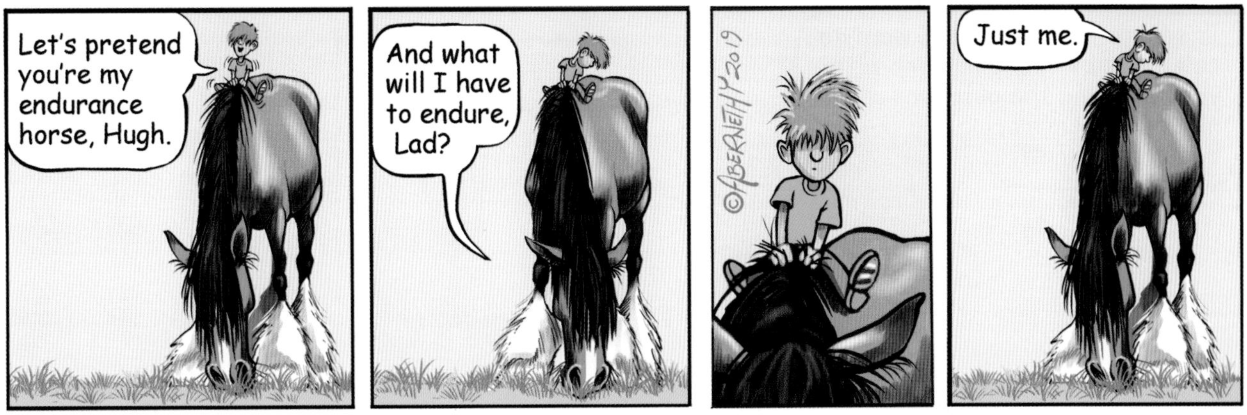
Let's pretend you're my endurance horse, Hugh.
And what will I have to endure, Lad?
©ABERNETHY 2019
Just me.

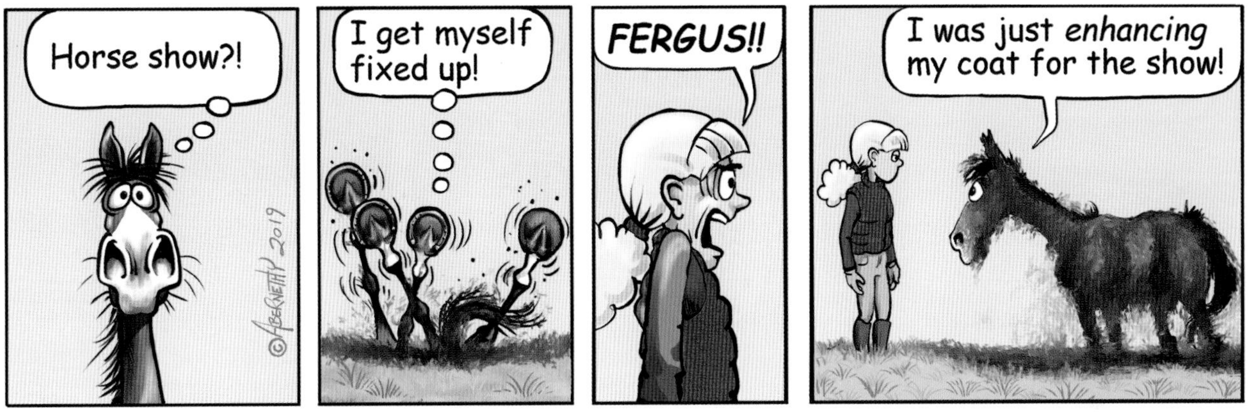
Horse show?!
©ABERNETHY 2019
I get myself fixed up!
FERGUS!!
I was just *enhancing* my coat for the show!

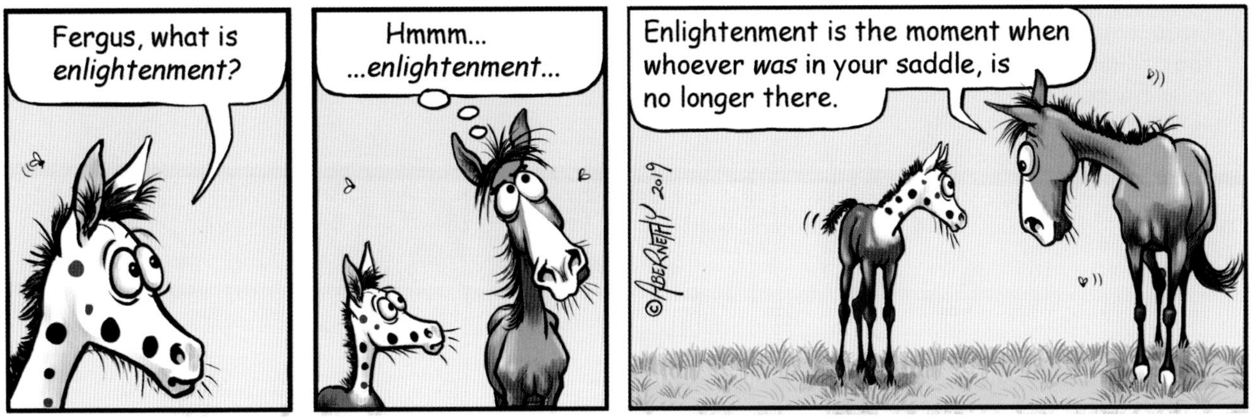
Fergus, what is *enlightenment?*
Hmmm... ...*enlightenment*...
Enlightenment is the moment when whoever *was* in your saddle, is no longer there.
©ABERNETHY 2019

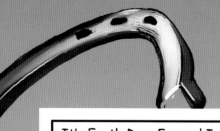

It's Earth Day, Fergus! I want to celebrate by spending time with you...enjoying the outdoors and nature and embracing our beautiful planet!

©ABERNETHY 2019

Well, OK, Kid.

Lie down

Grace, can you read?

Yes.

©ABERNETHY 2019

What does that say?

KE ITE SS T PHHU

KEEP THIS SHUT

It says, *This Way to the Good Stuff.*

'KEEP' THIS SHUT.

Dude, what's that thing on your forehead?

What thing?

Oh dear...um, next question...

©ABERNETHY 2019

...What's your name?

Pierce.

I love the dressage test!
OK Fergus, here come the tempi changes
Bring it *on!*
Tra-lee
tra-la
tra-lee
Tra-la
Tra- lee
Tra-la
la-la-dee-da...
...extended canter...
...square halt, and saaaa---LUTE!
Fergus, that was our ***WORST TEST EVER!!***
©ABERNETHY 2019
If you didn't want me to test you, why was it called a test?

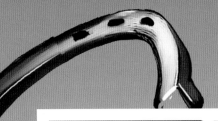

But I don't **want** to go down that road!

chsk chsk, walk on, Fergus!

FERGUS! Chsk chsk

Nope. Nope. Nope. Nope. Nope...

OK, dude, this isn't working. Time to get creative...

How do I get you to **want** to do this, Fergus?

Maybe with a teammate you'd be more motivated.

You mean like Ray? Oh yes, Ray is my good friend. Ray is my hero! Ray helps me stay centered.

I would be *oh so very motivated* working with Ray!

How about Pierce?"

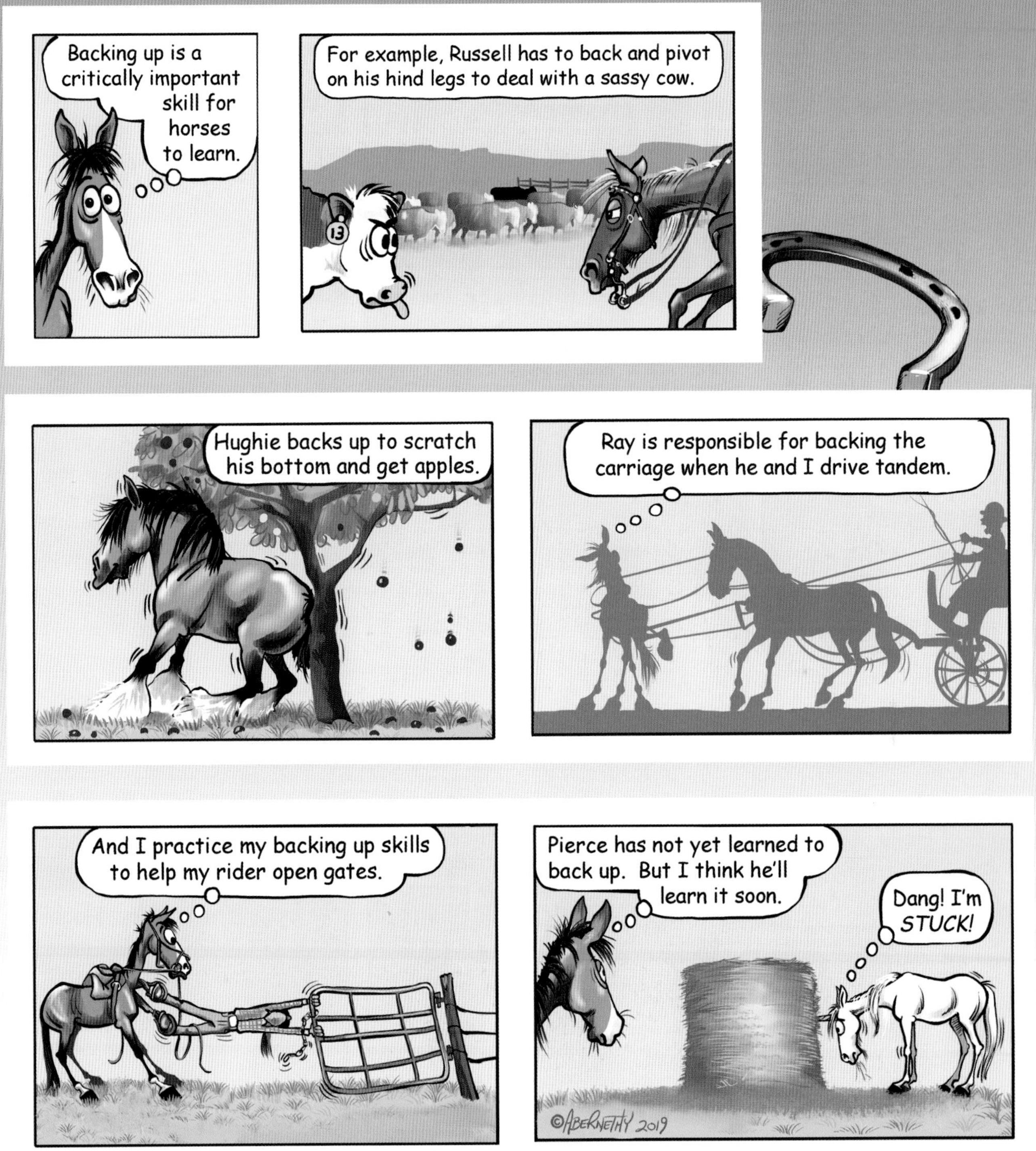
Backing up is a critically important skill for horses to learn.
For example, Russell has to back and pivot on his hind legs to deal with a sassy cow.
13
Hughie backs up to scratch his bottom and get apples.
Ray is responsible for backing the carriage when he and I drive tandem.
And I practice my backing up skills to help my rider open gates.
Pierce has not yet learned to back up. But I think he'll learn it soon.
Dang! I'm STUCK!
©ABERNETHY 2019

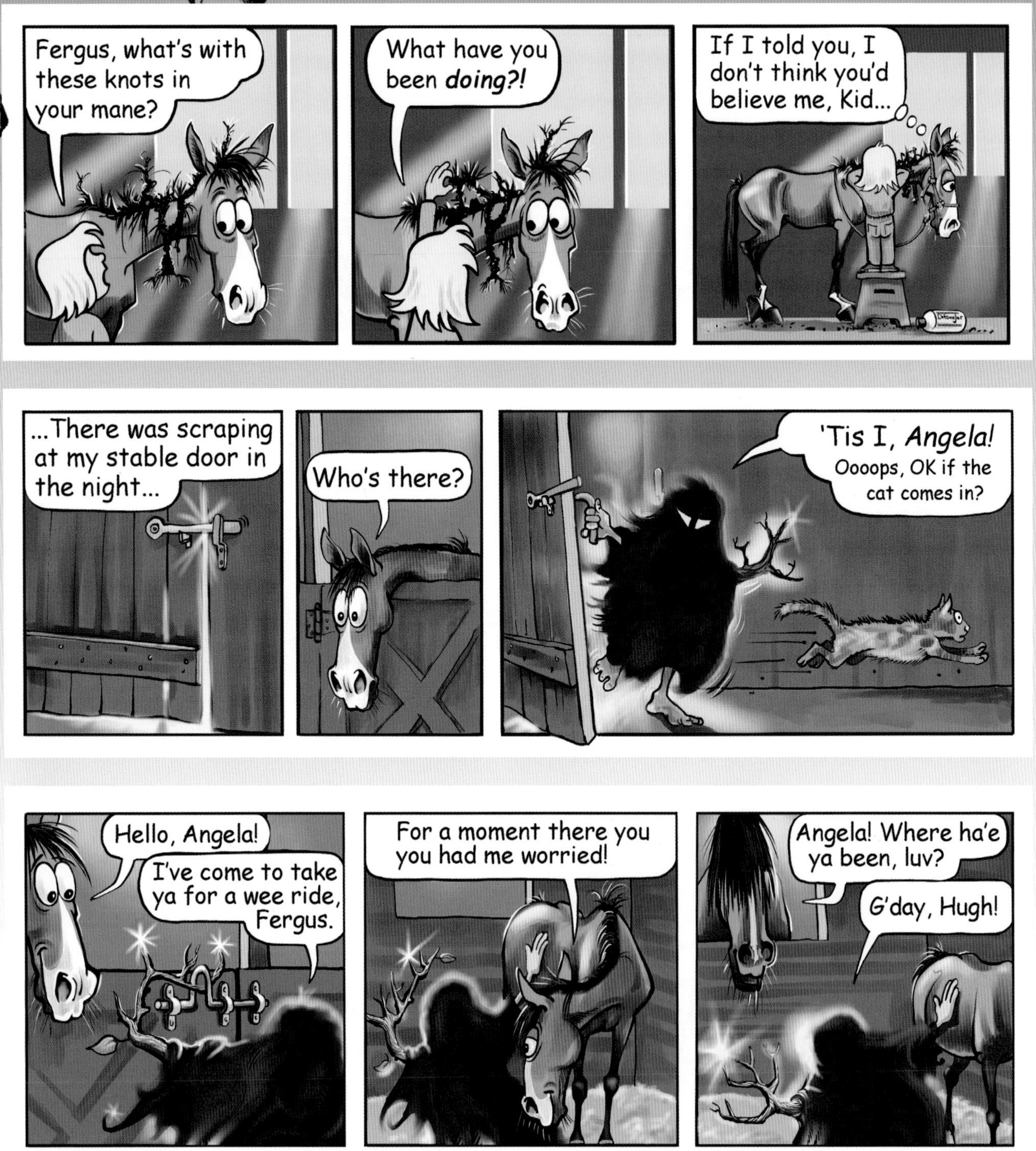
Fergus, what's with these knots in your mane?
What have you been *doing?!*
If I told you, I don't think you'd believe me, Kid...
...There was scraping at my stable door in the night...
Who's there?
'Tis I, *Angela!*
Oooops, OK if the cat comes in?
Hello, Angela!
I've come to take ya for a wee ride, Fergus.
For a moment there you you had me worried!
Angela! Where ha'e ya been, luv?
G'day, Hugh!

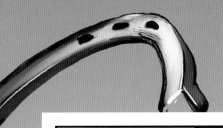

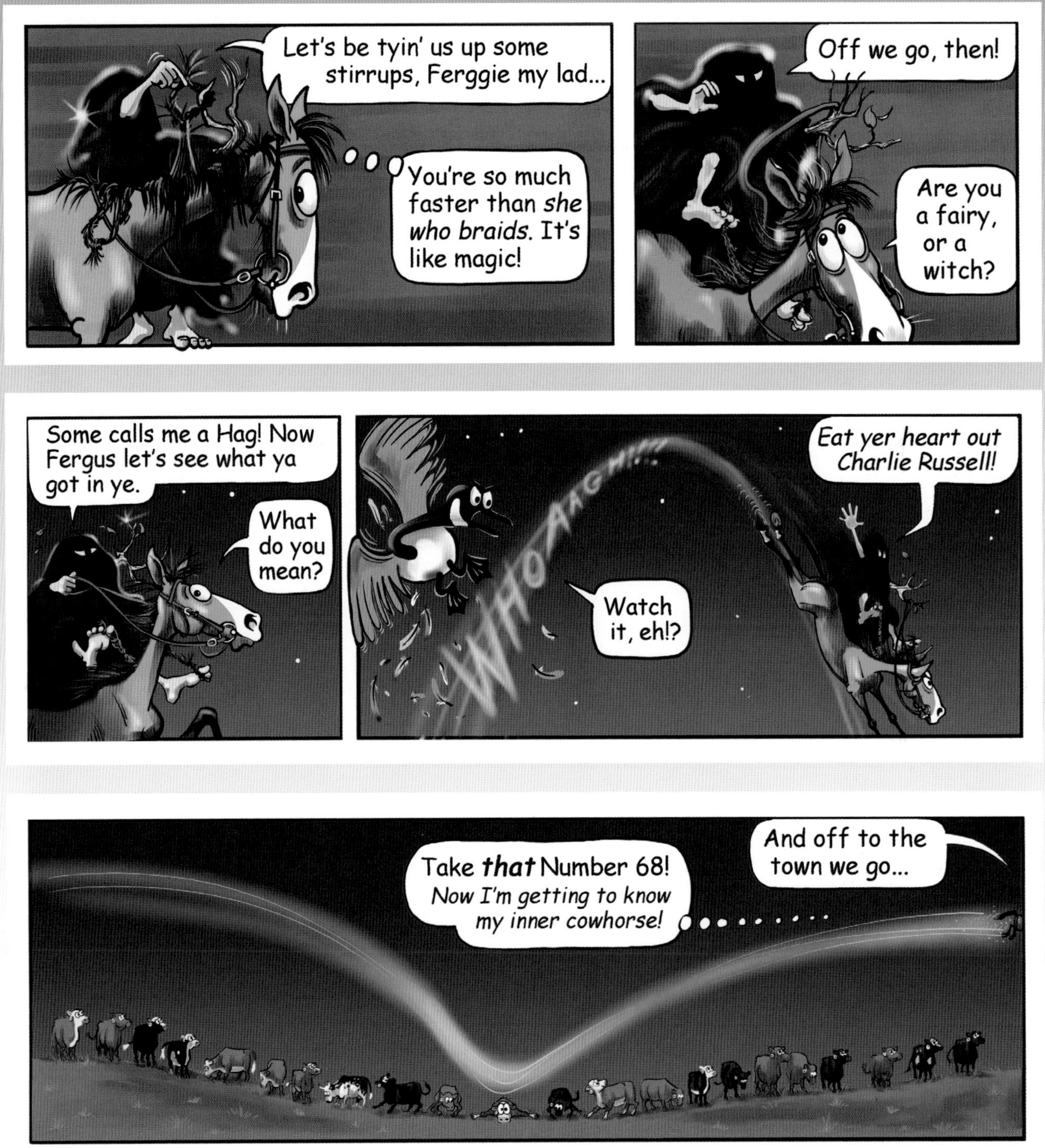

Let's be tyin' us up some stirrups, Ferggie my lad...
You're so much faster than *she who braids*. It's like magic!
Off we go, then!
Are you a fairy, or a witch?
Some calls me a Hag! Now Fergus let's see what ya got in ye.
What do you mean?
WHOAAGH!!!
Watch it, eh!?
Eat yer heart out Charlie Russell!
Take ***that*** Number 68!
Now I'm getting to know my inner cowhorse!
And off to the town we go...

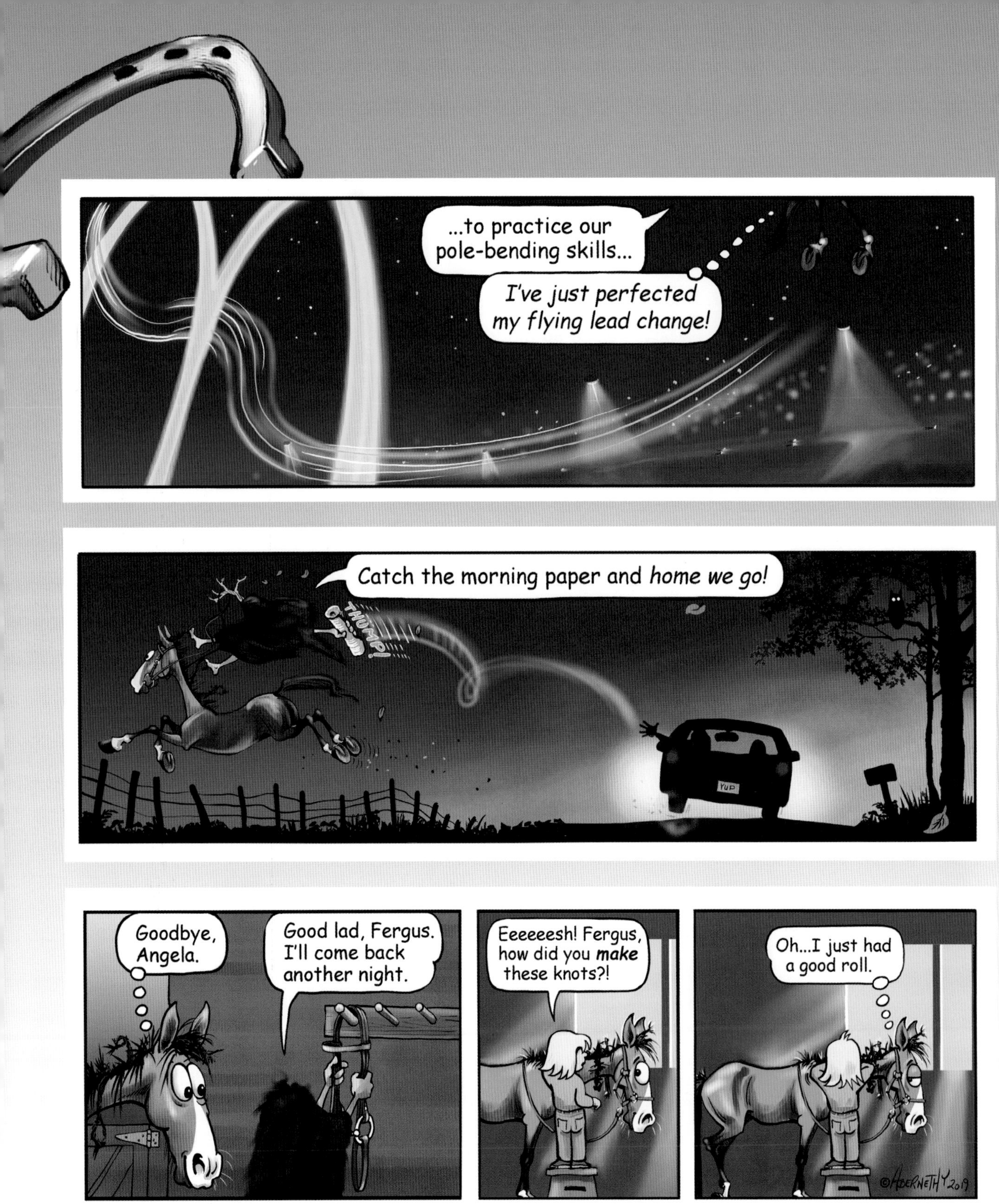

...to practice our pole-bending skills...
I've just perfected my flying lead change!
Catch the morning paper and home we go!
THUMP!
YUP
Goodbye, Angela.
Good lad, Fergus. I'll come back another night.
Eeeeeesh! Fergus, how did you make these knots?!
Oh...I just had a good roll.
©ABERNETHY 2019

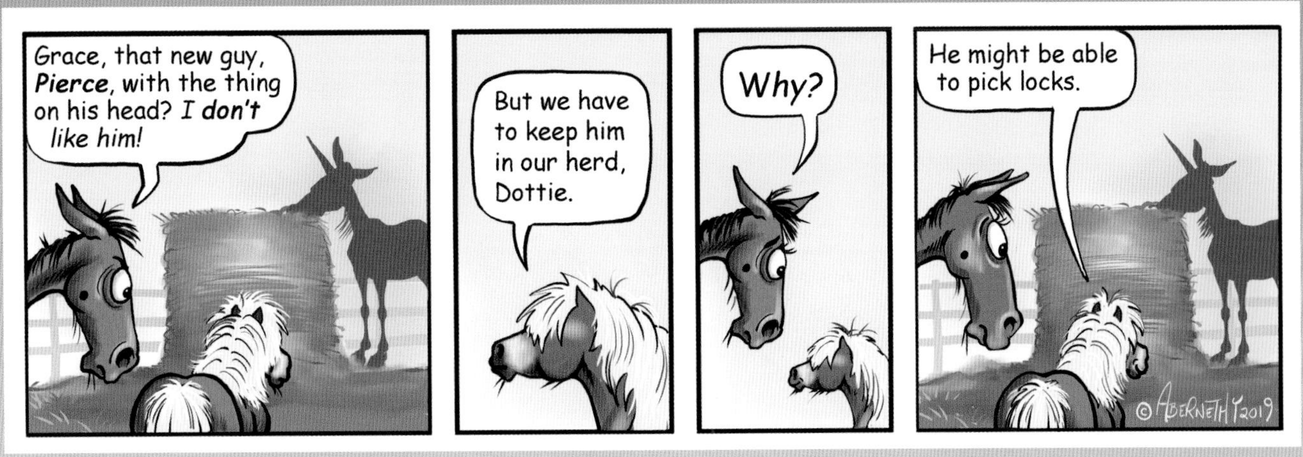
Grace, that new guy, **Pierce**, with the thing on his head? *I **don't** like him!*
But we have to keep him in our herd, Dottie.
Why?
He might be able to pick locks.
©ABERNETHY 2019

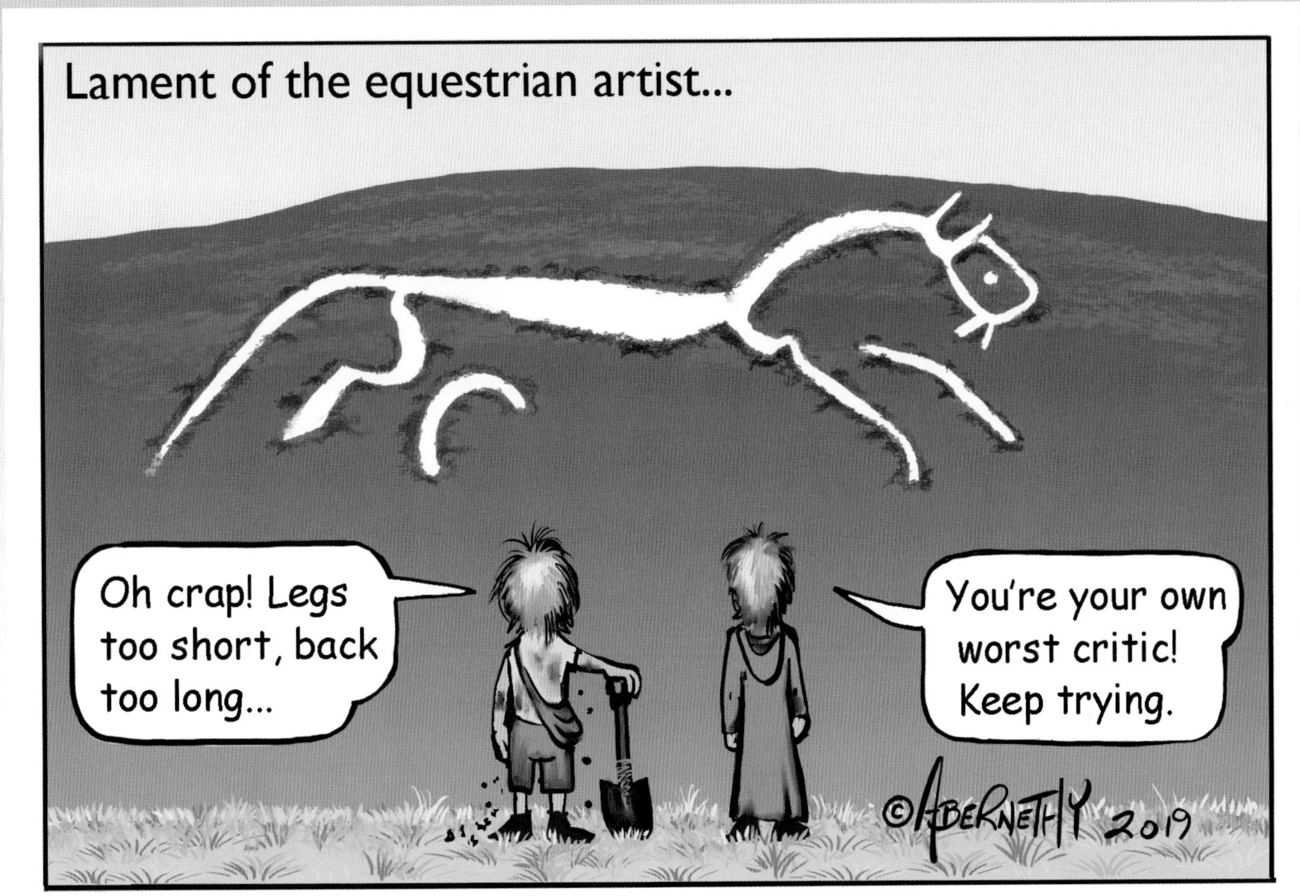
Lament of the equestrian artist...
Oh crap! Legs too short, back too long...
You're your own worst critic! Keep trying.
©ABERNETHY 2019

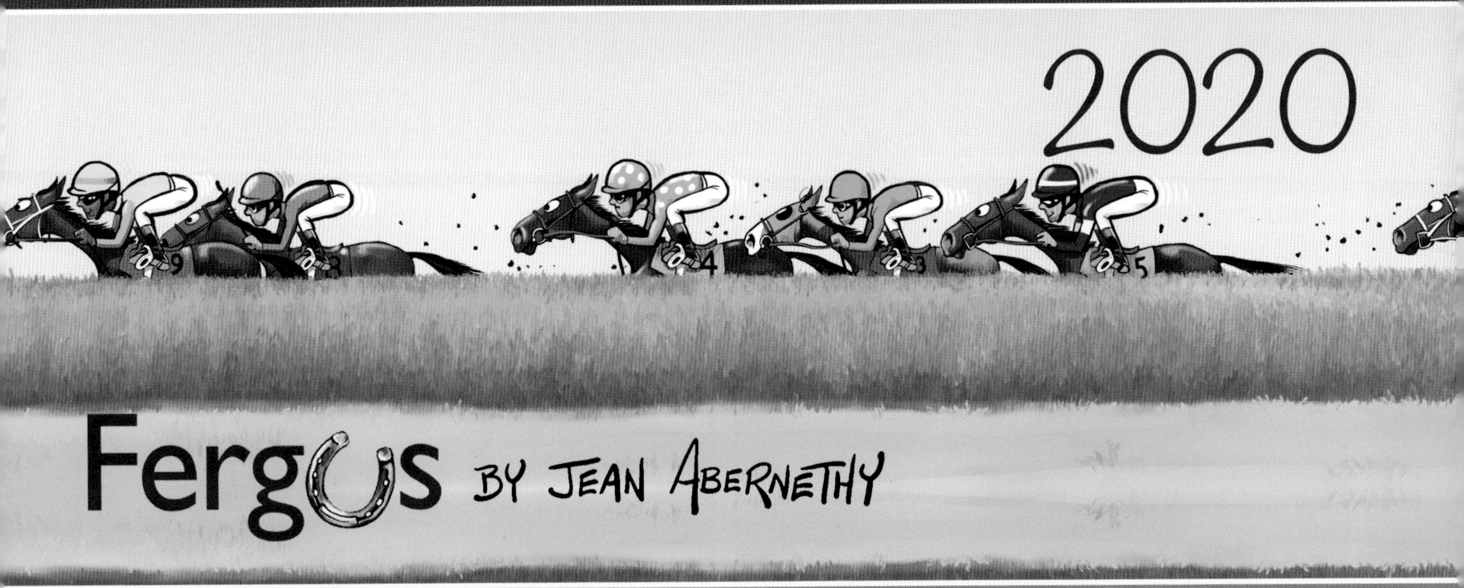
2020
Fergus BY JEAN ABERNETHY

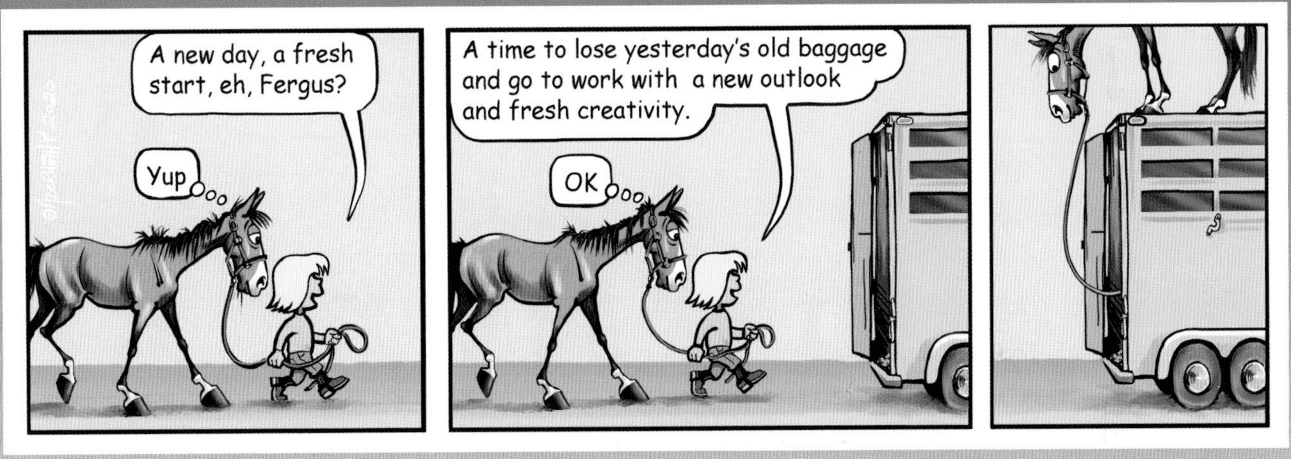
A new day, a fresh start, eh, Fergus?
Yup
A time to lose yesterday's old baggage and go to work with a new outlook and fresh creativity.
OK

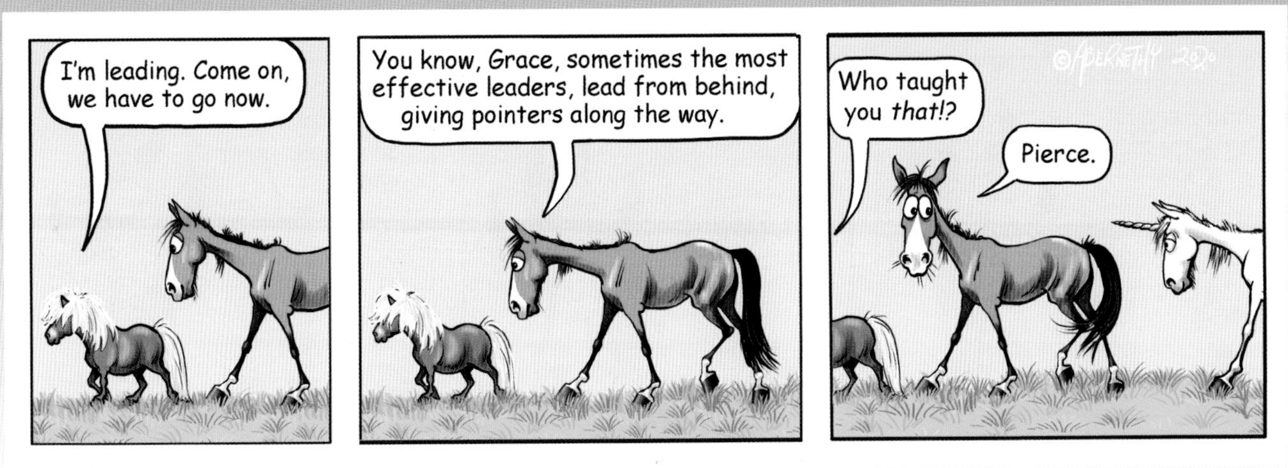
I'm leading. Come on, we have to go now.
You know, Grace, sometimes the most effective leaders, lead from behind, giving pointers along the way.
Who taught you *that!?*
Pierce.

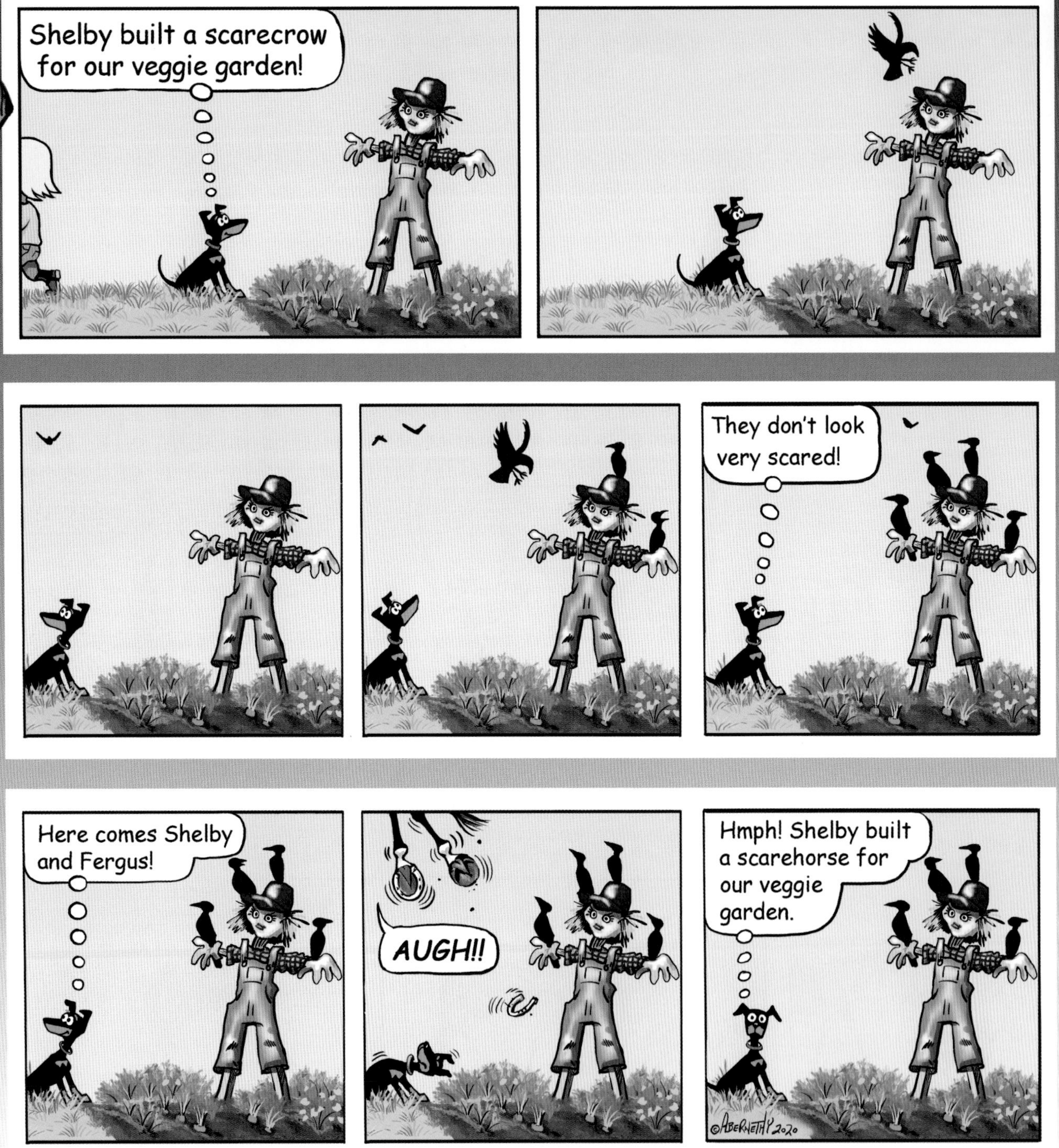
Shelby built a scarecrow for our veggie garden!
They don't look very scared!
Here comes Shelby and Fergus!
AUGH!!
Hmph! Shelby built a scarehorse for our veggie garden.
©ABERNETHY 2020

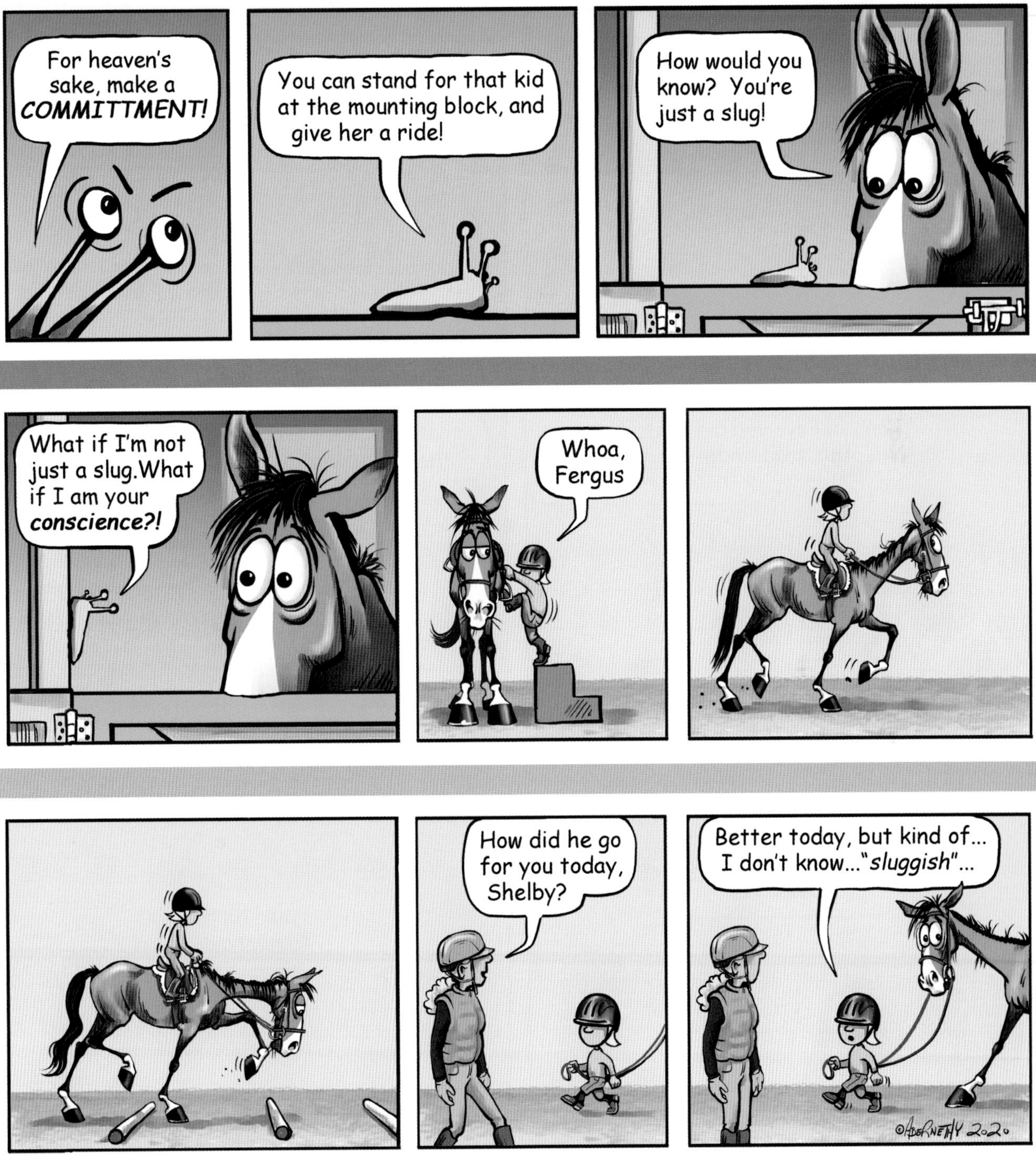
For heaven's sake, make a *COMMITTMENT!*
You can stand for that kid at the mounting block, and give her a ride!
How would you know? You're just a slug!
What if I'm not just a slug. What if I am your *conscience?!*
Whoa, Fergus
How did he go for you today, Shelby?
Better today, but kind of... I don't know..."*sluggish*"...
©ABERNETHY 2020

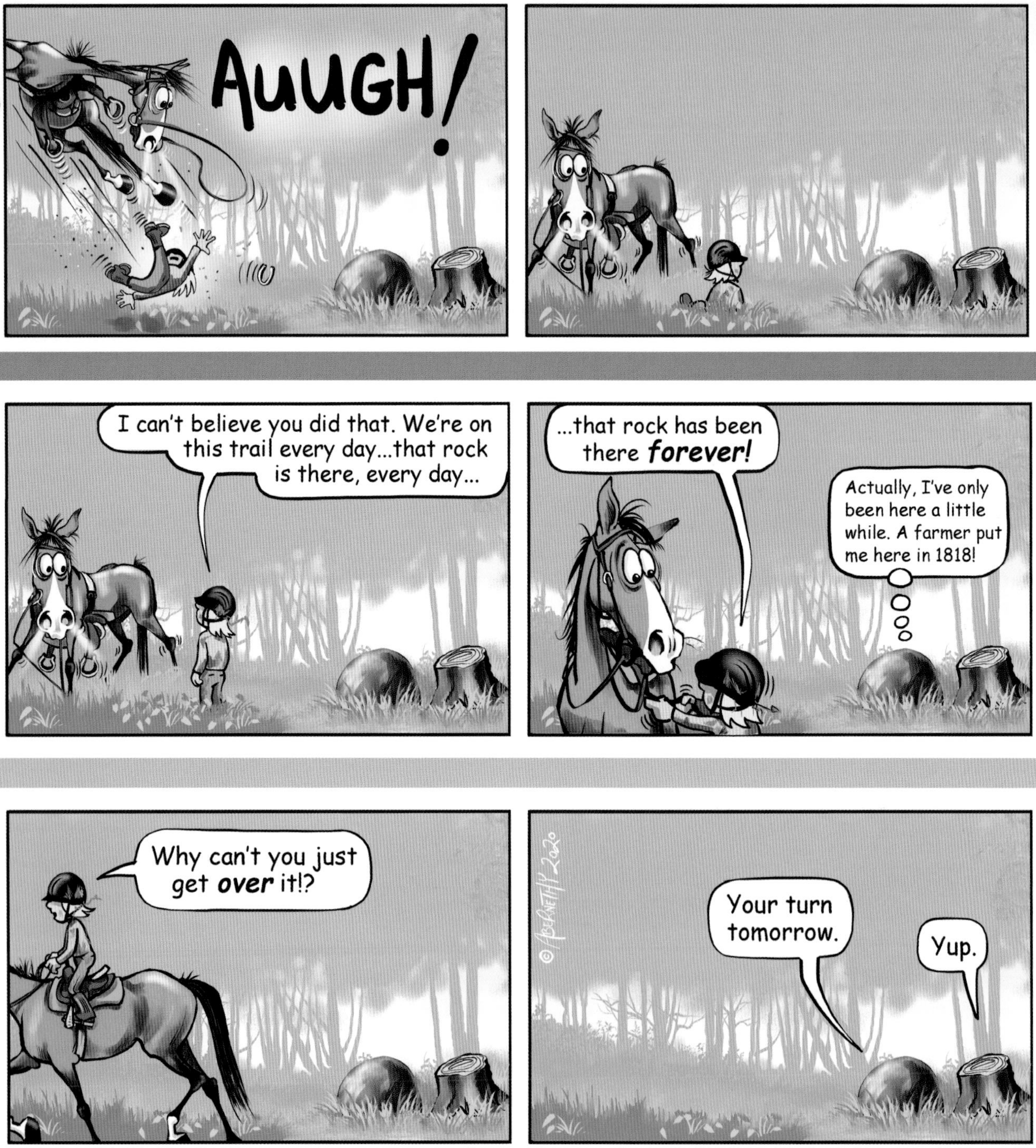
AUUGH!
I can't believe you did that. We're on this trail every day...that rock is there, every day...
...that rock has been there *forever!*
Actually, I've only been here a little while. A farmer put me here in 1818!
Why can't you just get *over* it!?
© Abernethy 2020
Your turn tomorrow.
Yup.

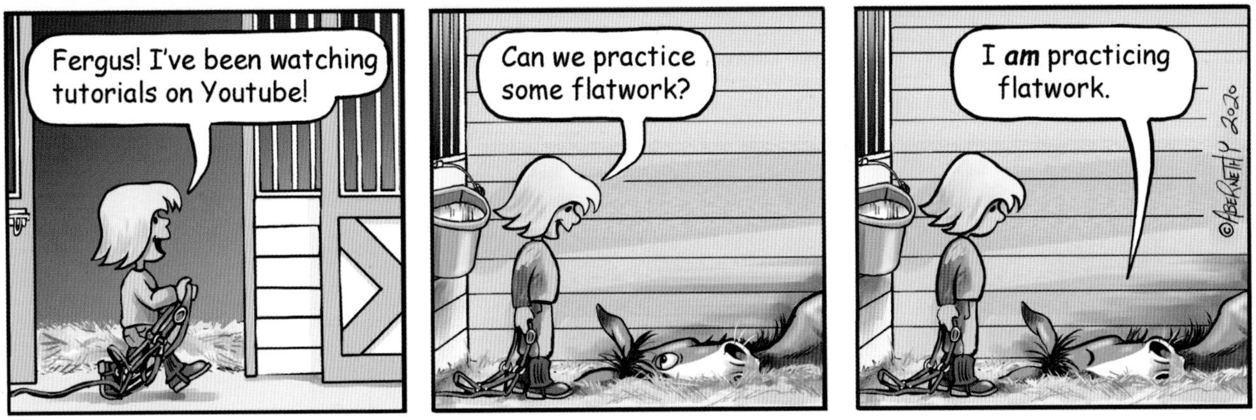
Fergus! I've been watching tutorials on Youtube!
Can we practice some flatwork?
I *am* practicing flatwork.
©ABERNETHY 2020

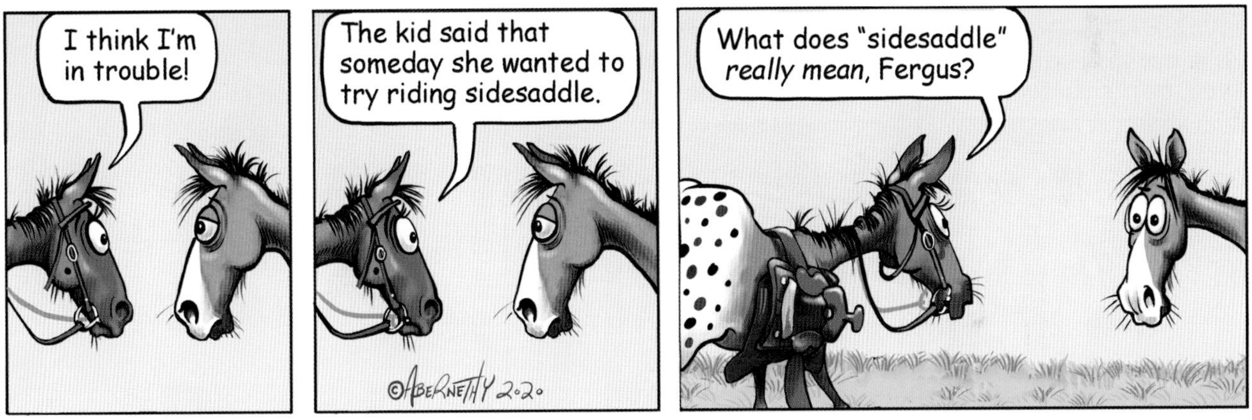
I think I'm in trouble!
The kid said that someday she wanted to try riding sidesaddle.
©ABERNETHY 2020
What does "sidesaddle" *really mean*, Fergus?

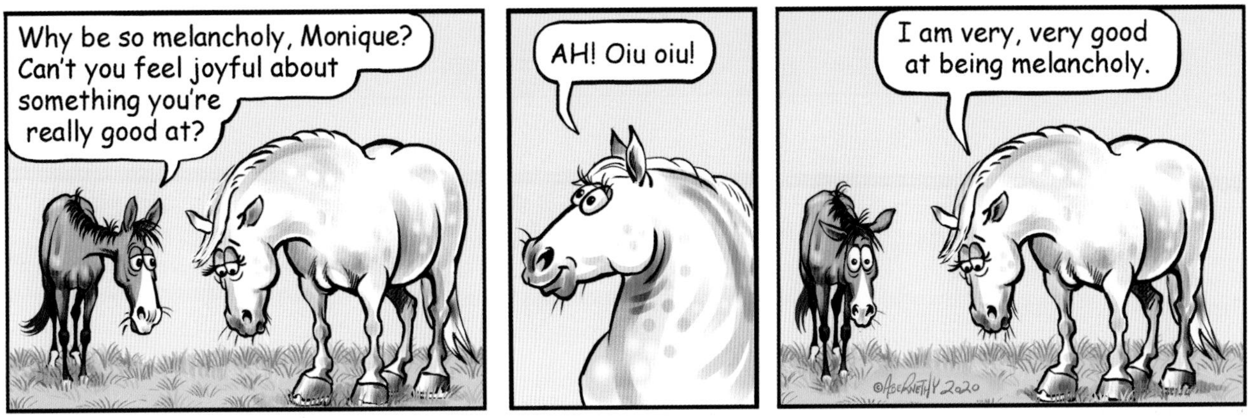
Why be so melancholy, Monique? Can't you feel joyful about something you're really good at?
AH! Oiu oiu!
I am very, very good at being melancholy.
©ABERNETHY 2020

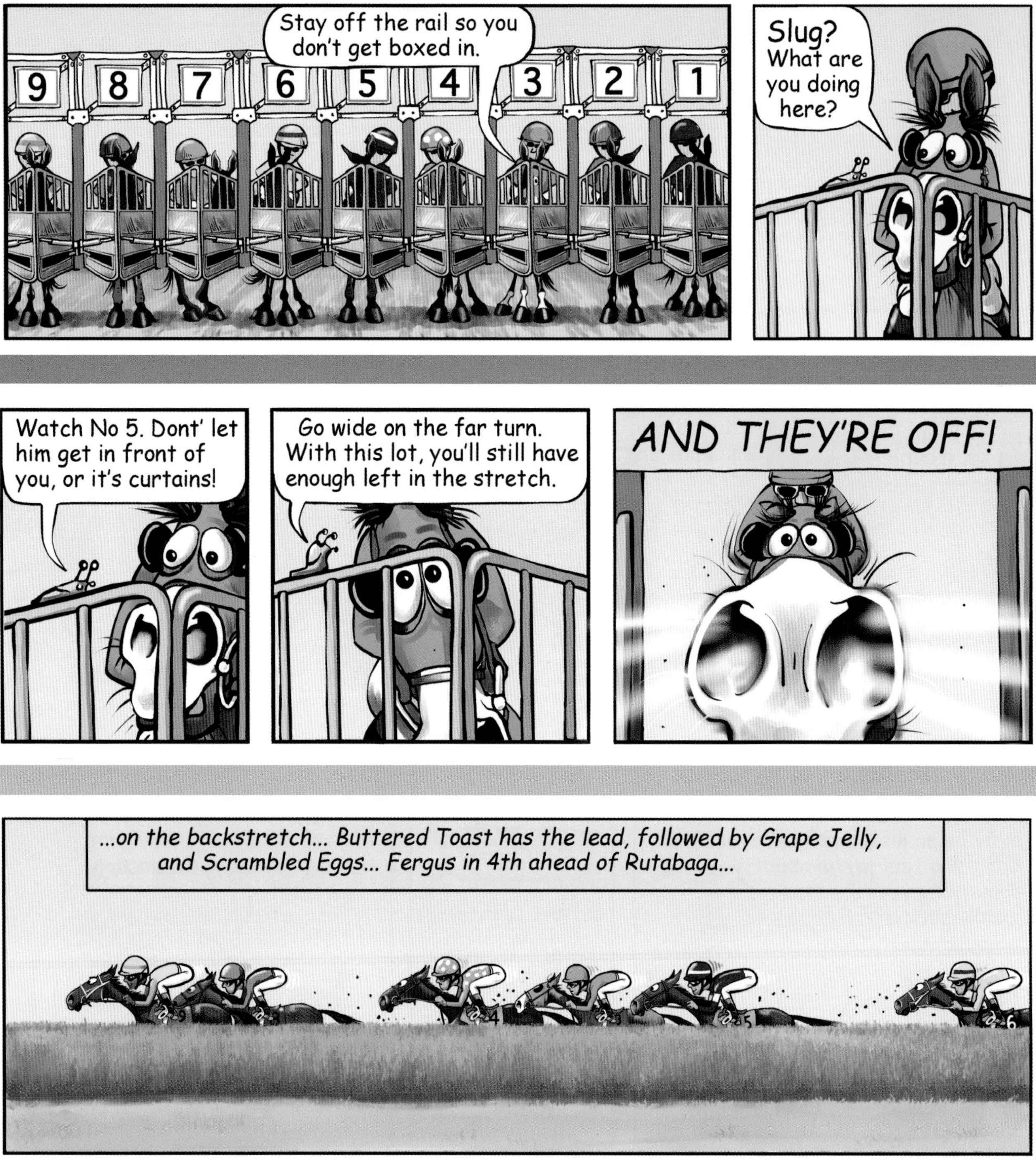
9 8 7 6 5 4 3 2 1
Stay off the rail so you don't get boxed in.
Slug? What are you doing here?
Watch No 5. Dont' let him get in front of you, or it's curtains!
Go wide on the far turn. With this lot, you'll still have enough left in the stretch.
AND THEY'RE OFF!
...on the backstretch... Buttered Toast has the lead, followed by Grape Jelly, and Scrambled Eggs... Fergus in 4th ahead of Rutabaga...

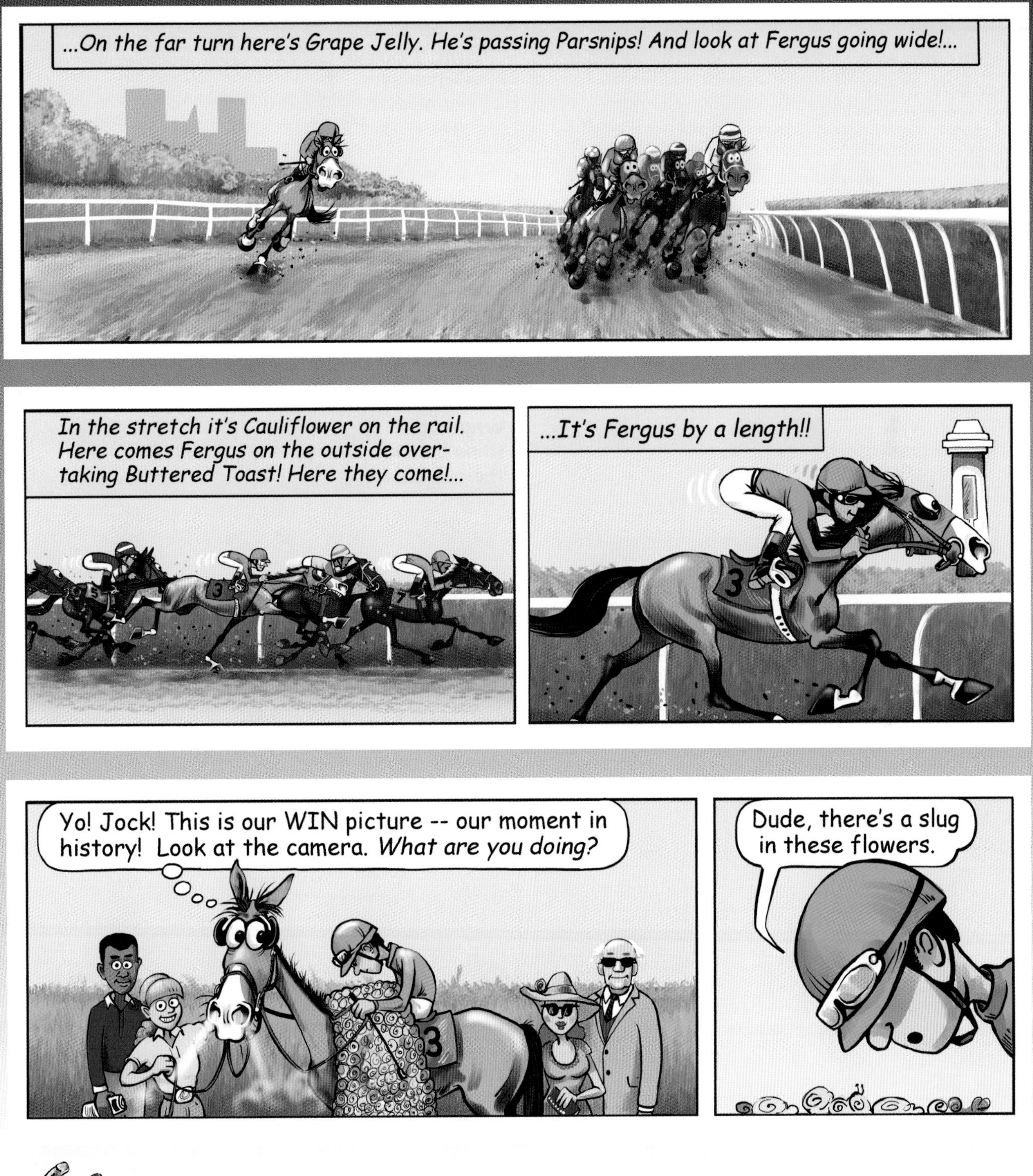
...On the far turn here's Grape Jelly. He's passing Parsnips! And look at Fergus going wide!...
In the stretch it's Cauliflower on the rail. Here comes Fergus on the outside over-taking Buttered Toast! Here they come!...
...It's Fergus by a length!!
Yo! Jock! This is our WIN picture -- our moment in history! Look at the camera. *What are you doing?*
Dude, there's a slug in these flowers.

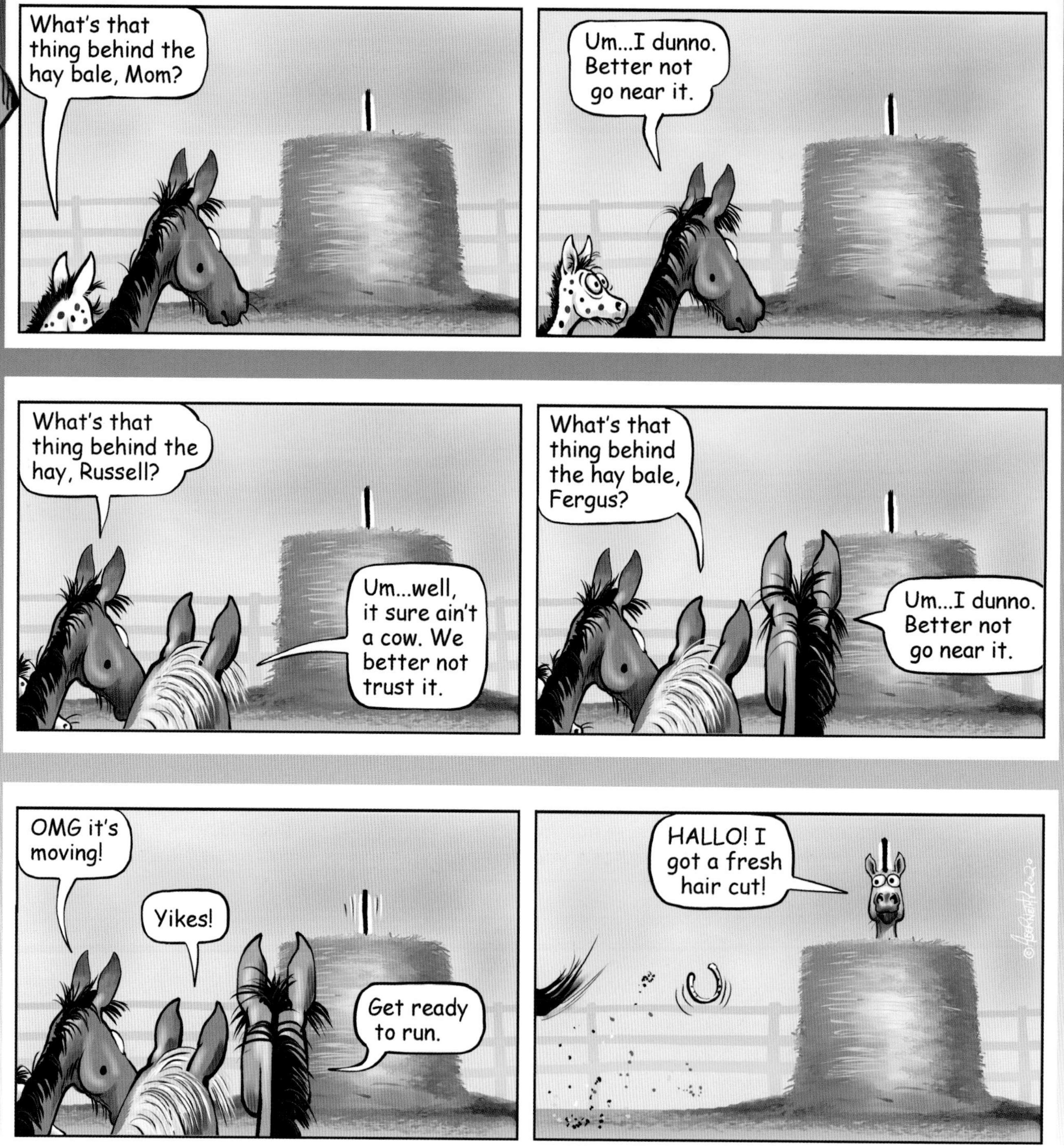
What's that thing behind the hay bale, Mom?
Um...I dunno. Better not go near it.
What's that thing behind the hay, Russell?
Um...well, it sure ain't a cow. We better not trust it.
What's that thing behind the hay bale, Fergus?
Um...I dunno. Better not go near it.
OMG it's moving!
Yikes!
Get ready to run.
HALLO! I got a fresh hair cut!

I can't believe you just followed me into this trailer.
Well, today there wasn't a problem.
There has **never** been a problem! What have I done differently?!
Why wouldn't you follow me into the trailer yesterday?
Yesterday there was a problem.
What was yesterday's problem?
Yesterday I didn't *want* to get onto the trailer.
©ABERNETHY 2020

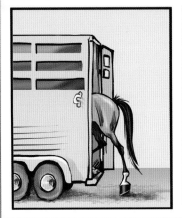

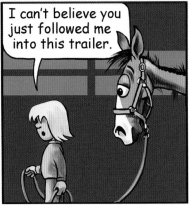

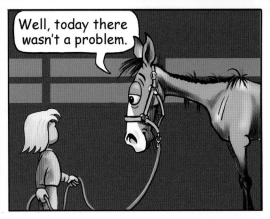

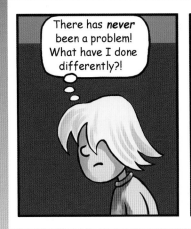

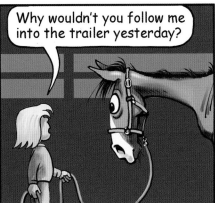

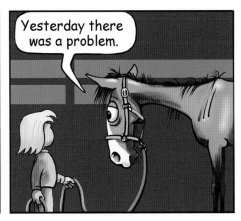

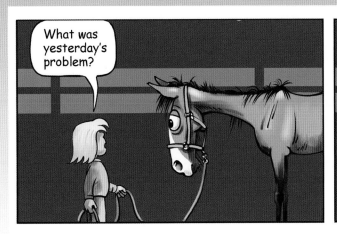

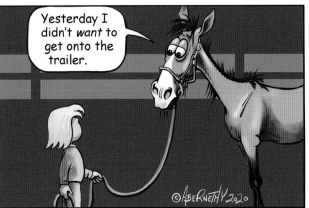

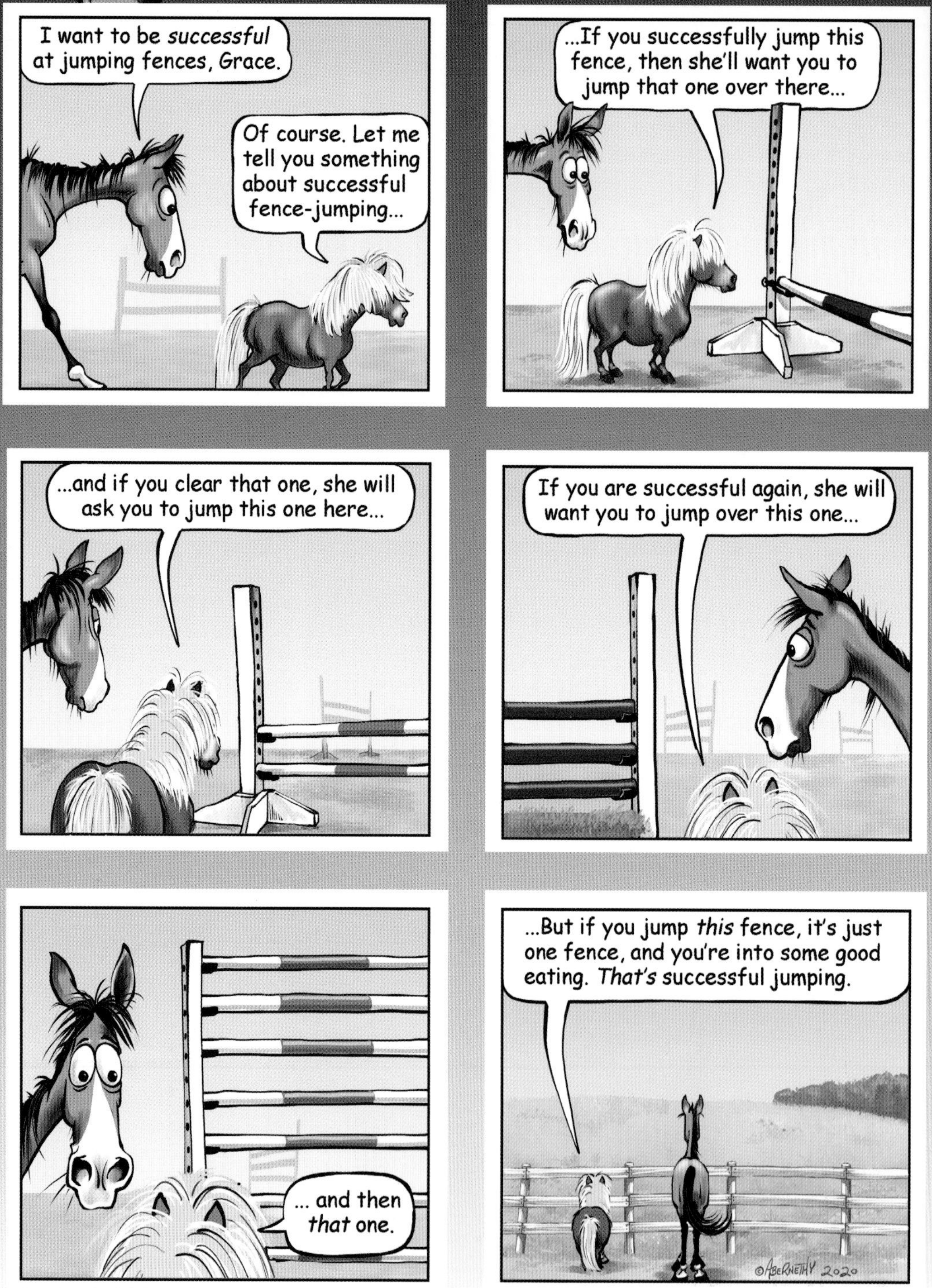
I want to be *successful* at jumping fences, Grace.
Of course. Let me tell you something about successful fence-jumping...
...If you successfully jump this fence, then she'll want you to jump that one over there...
...and if you clear that one, she will ask you to jump this one here...
If you are successful again, she will want you to jump over this one...
... and then *that* one.
...But if you jump *this* fence, it's just one fence, and you're into some good eating. *That's* successful jumping.
©ABERNETHY 2020

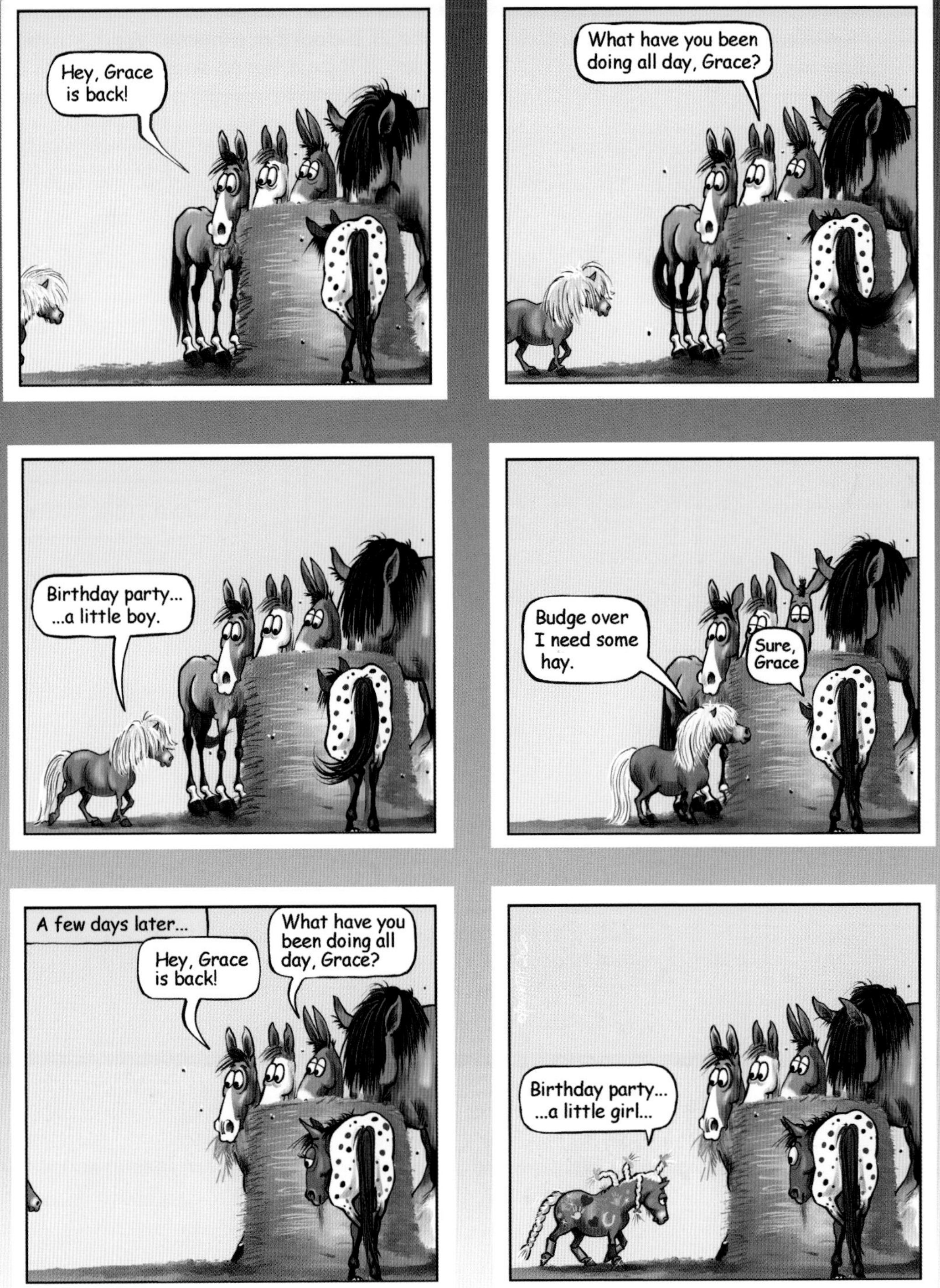
Hey, Grace is back!
What have you been doing all day, Grace?
Birthday party... ...a little boy.
Budge over I need some hay.
Sure, Grace
A few days later...
Hey, Grace is back!
What have you been doing all day, Grace?
Birthday party... ...a little girl...

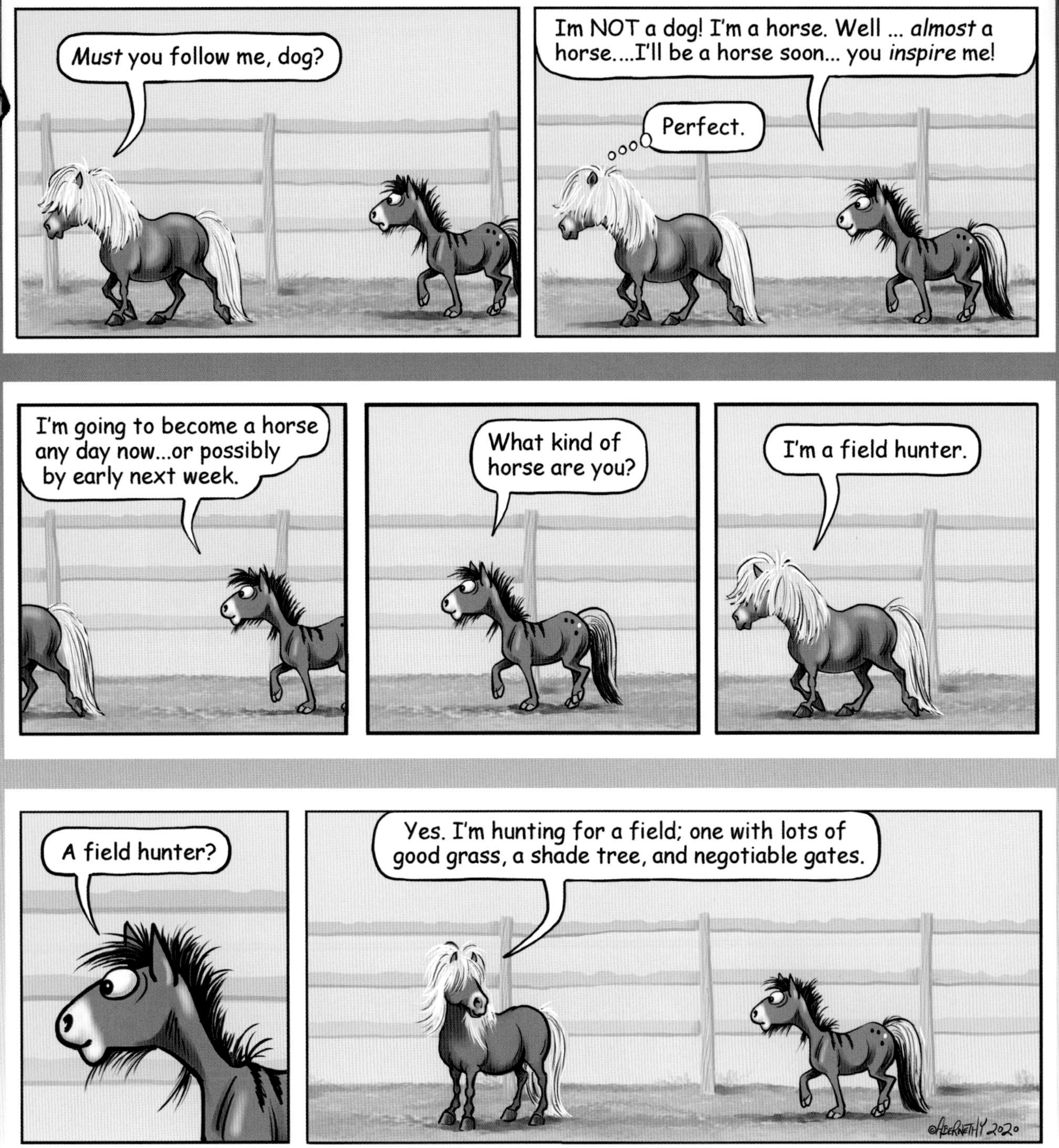

Must you follow me, dog?
Im NOT a dog! I'm a horse. Well ... *almost* a horse....I'll be a horse soon... you *inspire* me!
Perfect.
I'm going to become a horse any day now...or possibly by early next week.
What kind of horse are you?
I'm a field hunter.
A field hunter?
Yes. I'm hunting for a field; one with lots of good grass, a shade tree, and negotiable gates.
©ABERNETHY 2020

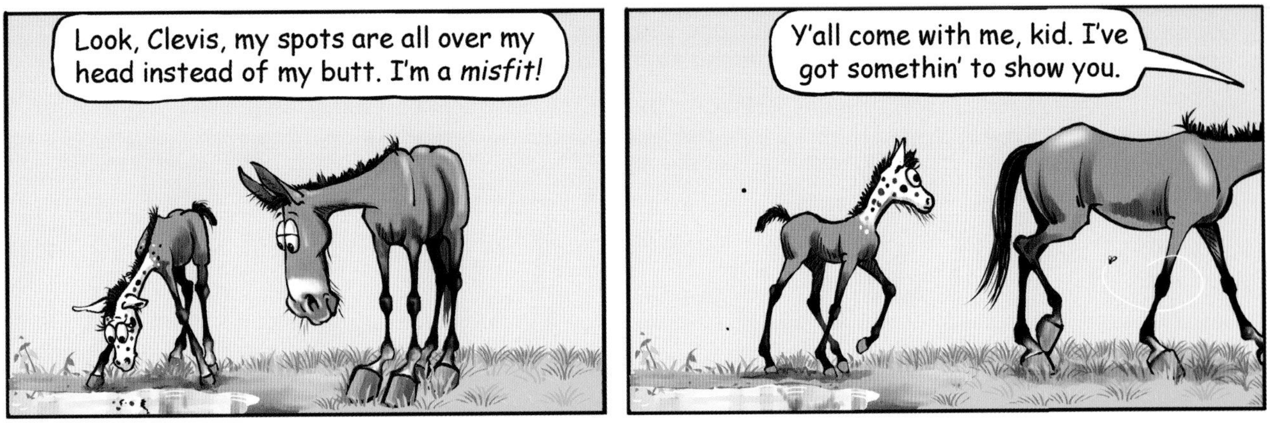
Look, Clevis, my spots are all over my head instead of my butt. I'm a *misfit!*
Y'all come with me, kid. I've got somethin' to show you.

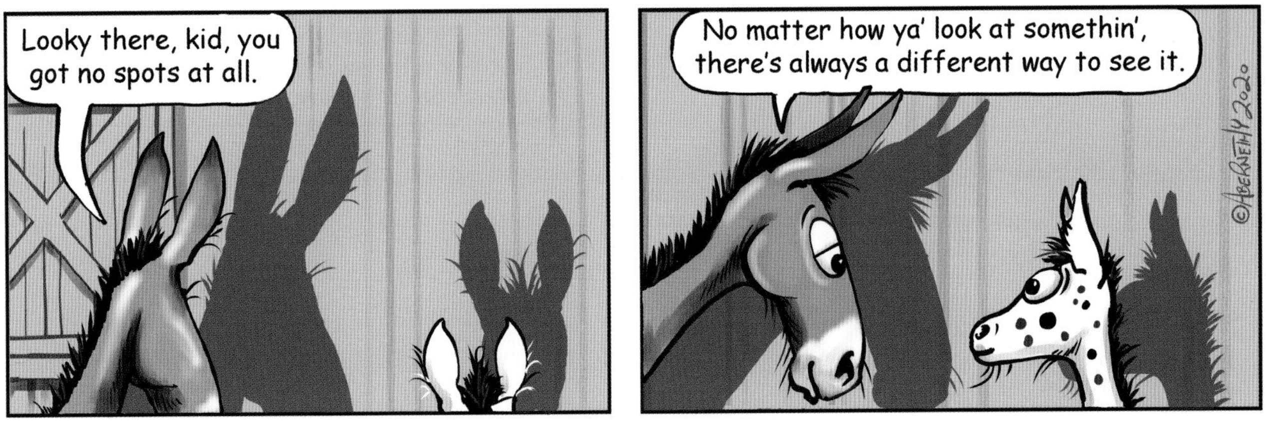
Looky there, kid, you got no spots at all.
No matter how ya' look at somethin', there's always a different way to see it.
©Abernethy 2020

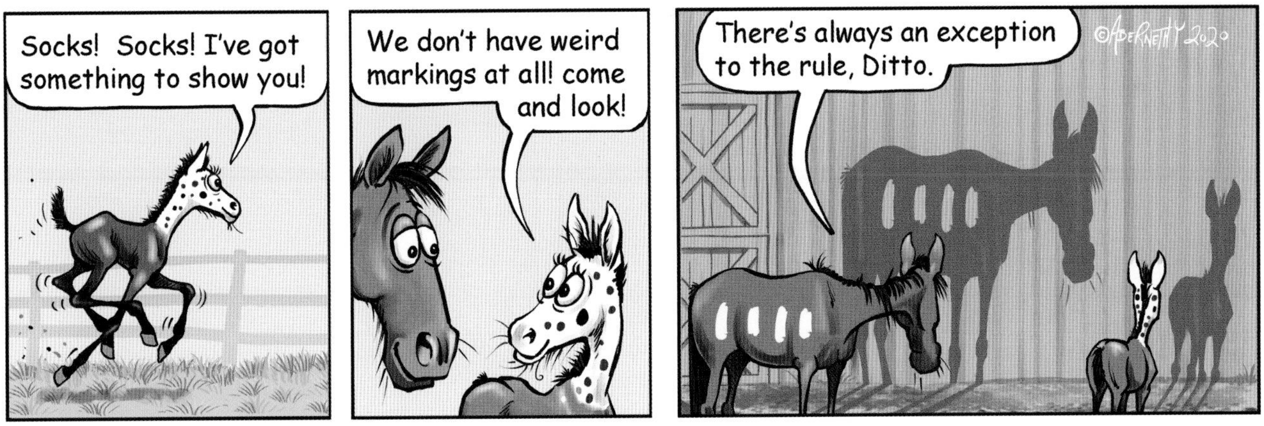
Socks! Socks! I've got something to show you!
We don't have weird markings at all! come and look!
There's always an exception to the rule, Ditto.
©Abernethy 2020

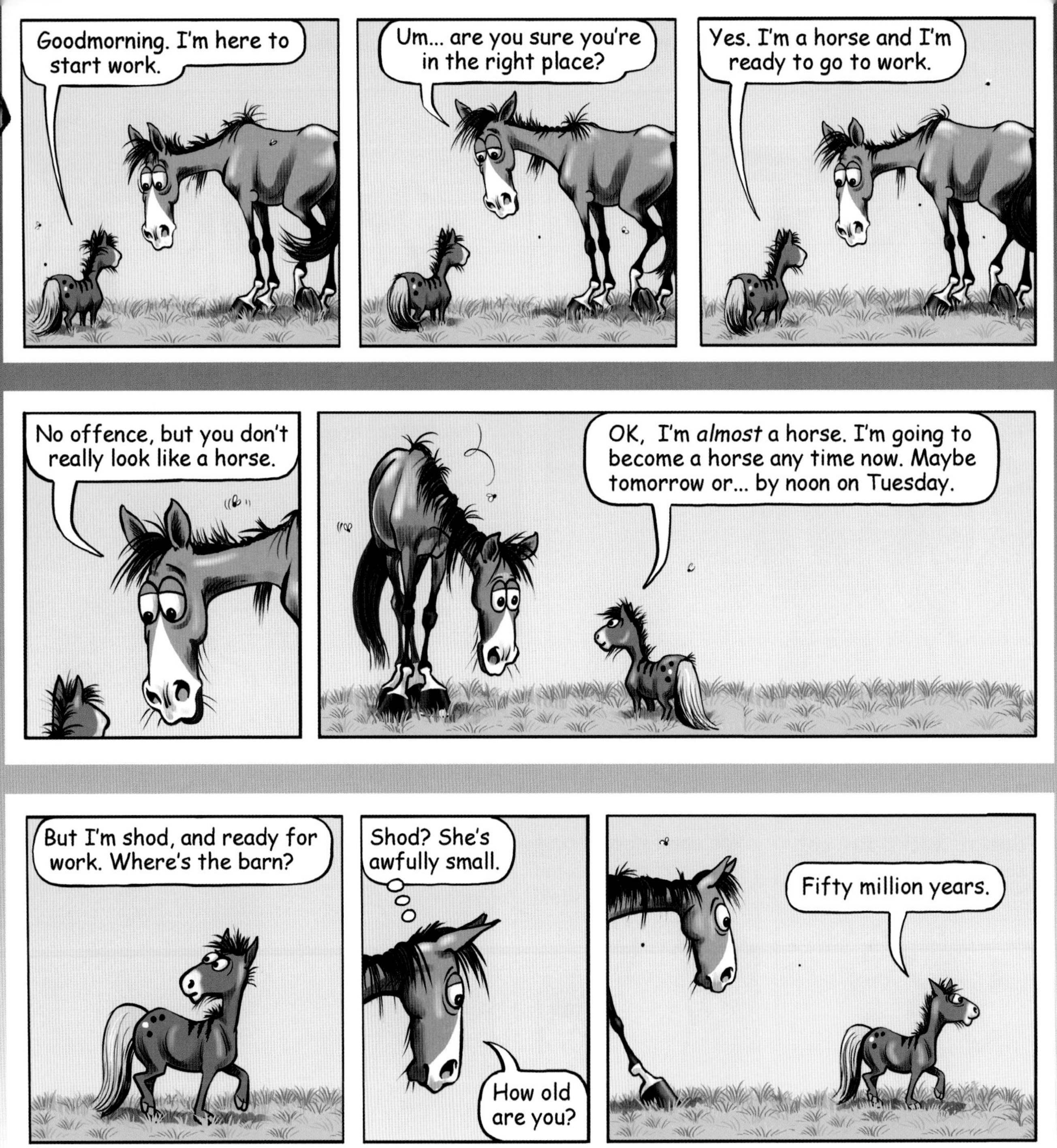
Goodmorning. I'm here to start work.
Um... are you sure you're in the right place?
Yes. I'm a horse and I'm ready to go to work.
No offence, but you don't really look like a horse.
OK, I'm *almost* a horse. I'm going to become a horse any time now. Maybe tomorrow or... by noon on Tuesday.
But I'm shod, and ready for work. Where's the barn?
Shod? She's awfully small.
How old are you?
Fifty million years.

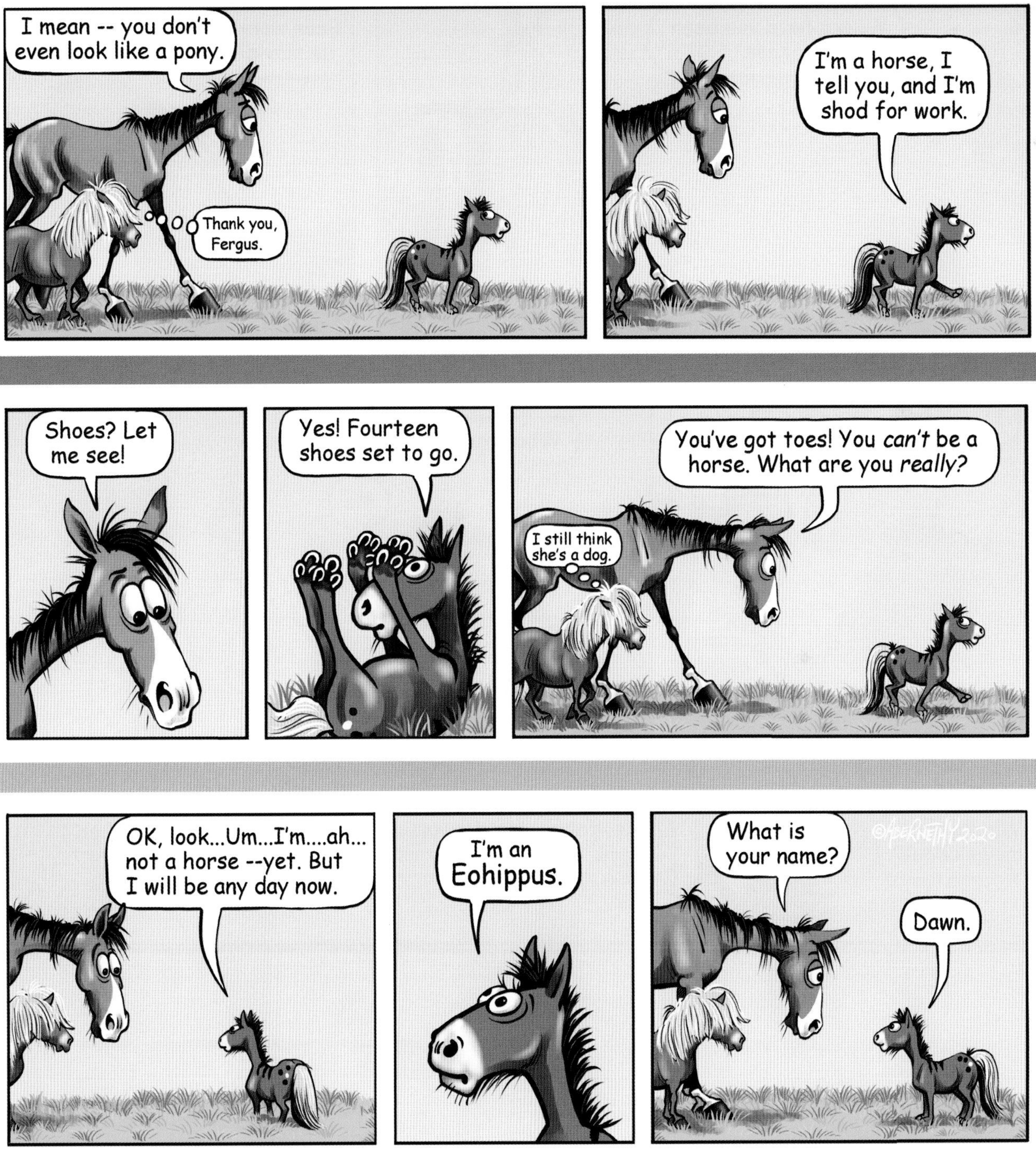
I mean -- you don't even look like a pony.
Thank you, Fergus.
I'm a horse, I tell you, and I'm shod for work.
Shoes? Let me see!
Yes! Fourteen shoes set to go.
I still think she's a dog.
You've got toes! You *can't* be a horse. What are you *really?*
OK, look...Um...I'm....ah... not a horse --yet. But I will be any day now.
I'm an Eohippus.
What is your name?
Dawn.

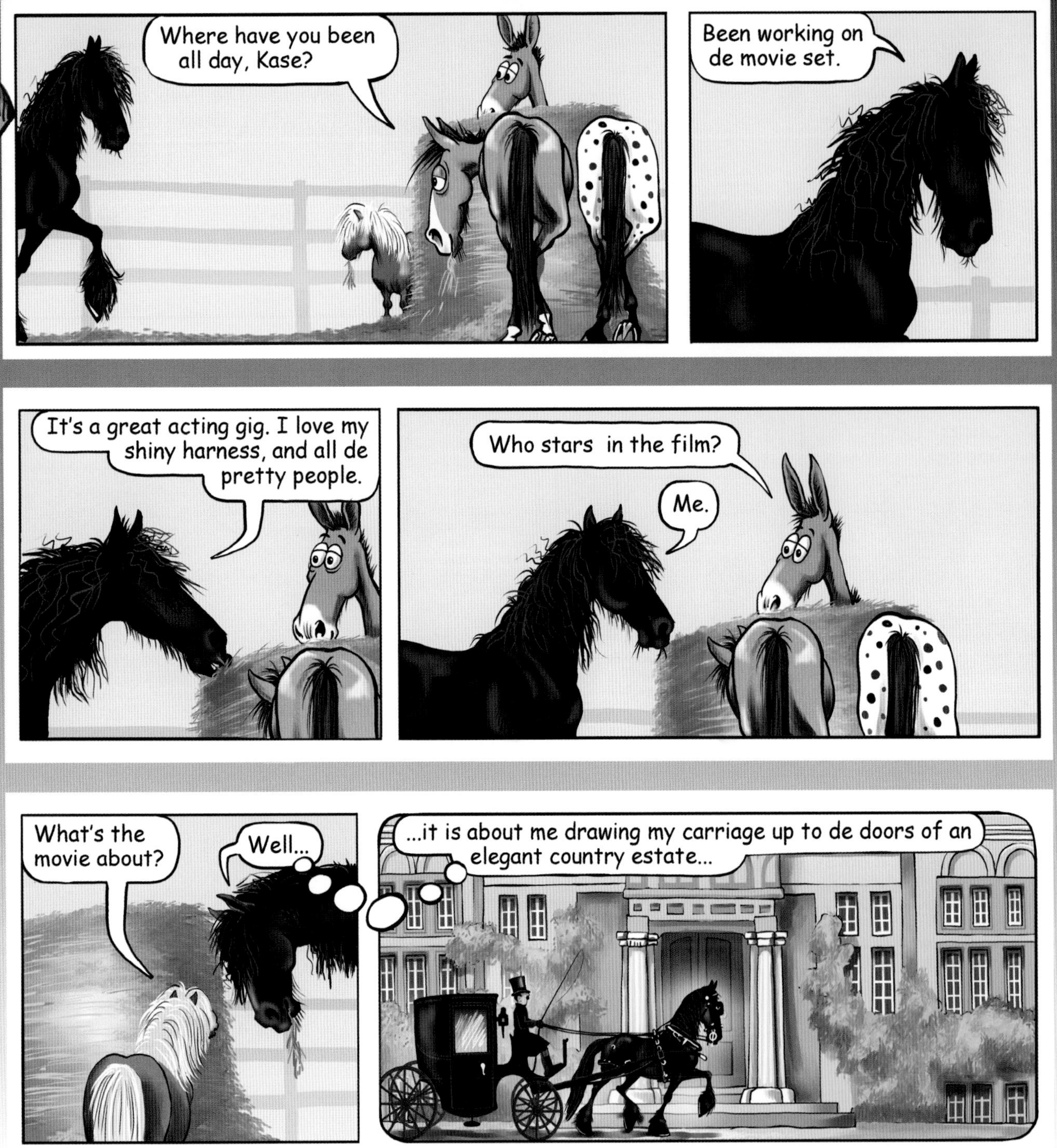
Where have you been all day, Kase?
Been working on de movie set.
It's a great acting gig. I love my shiny harness, and all de pretty people.
Who stars in the film?
Me.
What's the movie about?
Well...
...it is about me drawing my carriage up to de doors of an elegant country estate...

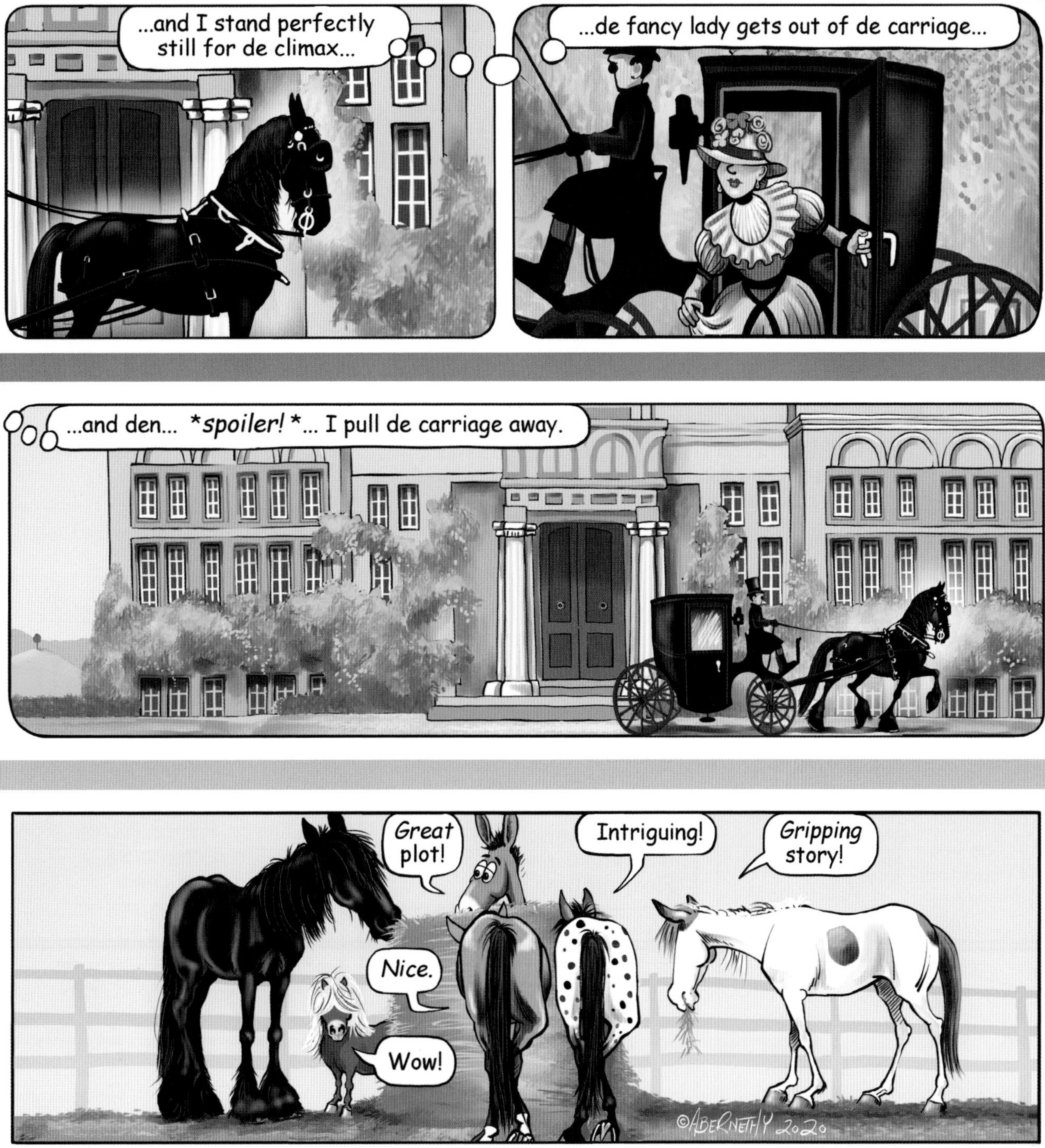
...and I stand perfectly still for de climax...
...de fancy lady gets out of de carriage...
...and den... *spoiler!*... I pull de carriage away.
Great plot!
Intriguing!
Gripping story!
Nice.
Wow!
©ABERNETHY 2020

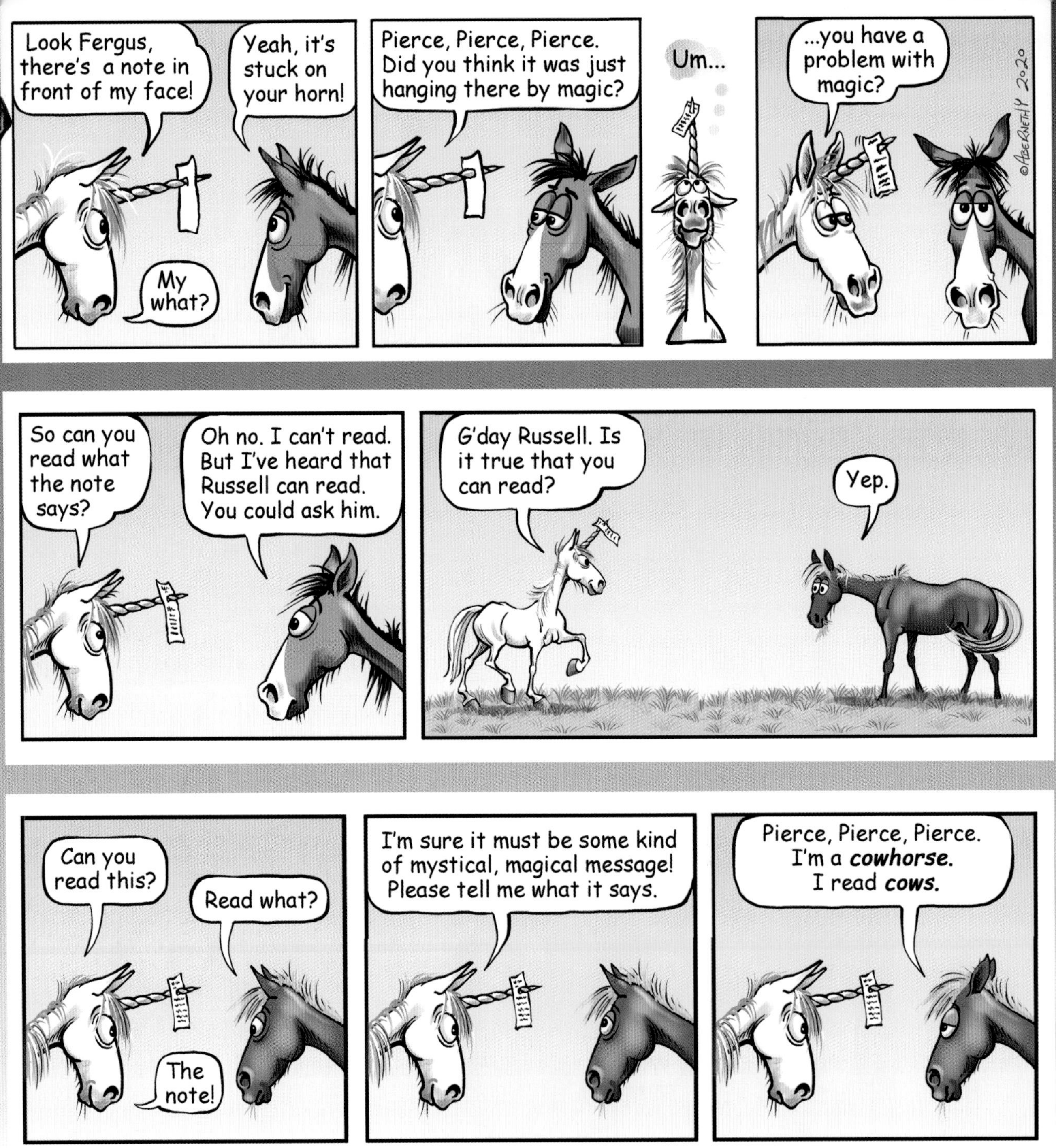
Look Fergus, there's a note in front of my face!
Yeah, it's stuck on your horn!
My what?
Pierce, Pierce, Pierce. Did you think it was just hanging there by magic?
Um...
...you have a problem with magic?
©ABERNETHY 2020
So can you read what the note says?
Oh no. I can't read. But I've heard that Russell can read. You could ask him.
G'day Russell. Is it true that you can read?
Yep.
Can you read this?
Read what?
The note!
I'm sure it must be some kind of mystical, magical message! Please tell me what it says.
Pierce, Pierce, Pierce. I'm a **cowhorse.** I read **cows.**

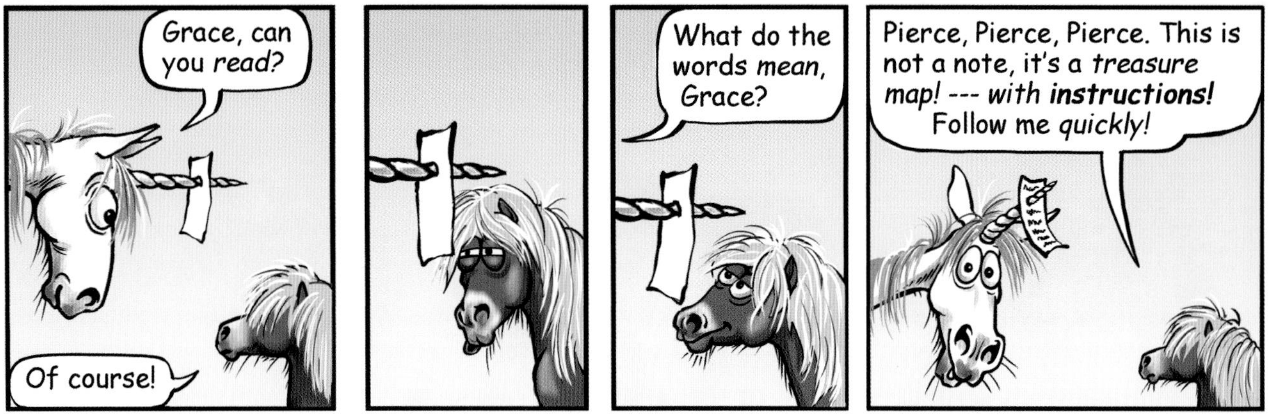
Grace, can you *read?*
Of course!
What do the words *mean,* Grace?
Pierce, Pierce, Pierce. This is not a note, it's a *treasure map!* --- *with* **instructions!** Follow me *quickly!*

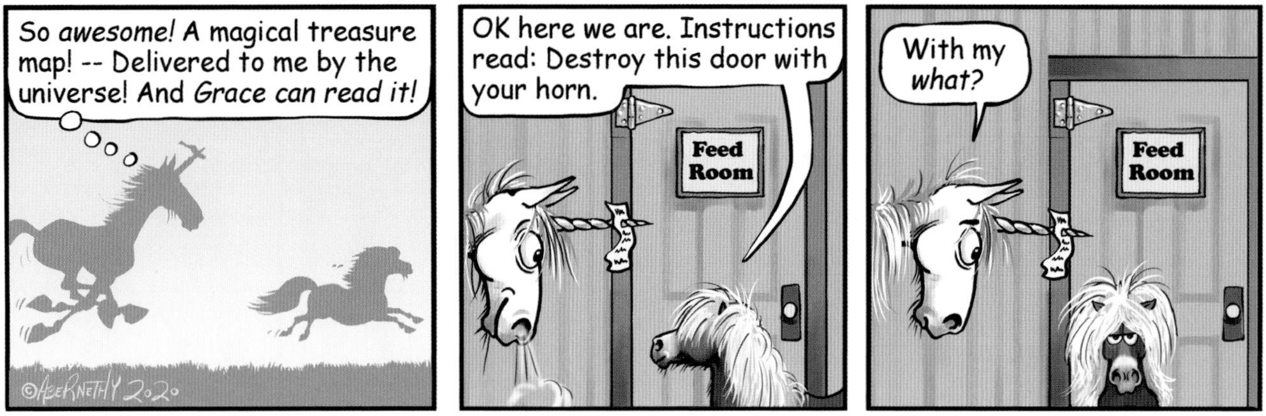
So *awesome!* A magical treasure map! -- Delivered to me by the universe! And *Grace can read it!*
©ABERNETHY 2020
OK here we are. Instructions read: Destroy this door with your horn.
Feed Room
With my *what?*
Feed Room

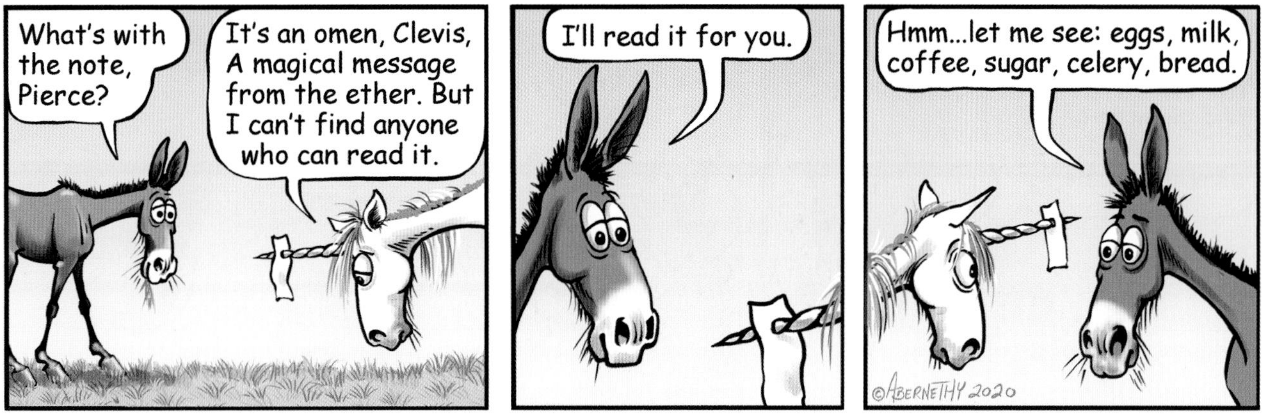
What's with the note, Pierce?
It's an omen, Clevis, A magical message from the ether. But I can't find anyone who can read it.
I'll read it for you.
Hmm...let me see: eggs, milk, coffee, sugar, celery, bread.
©ABERNETHY 2020

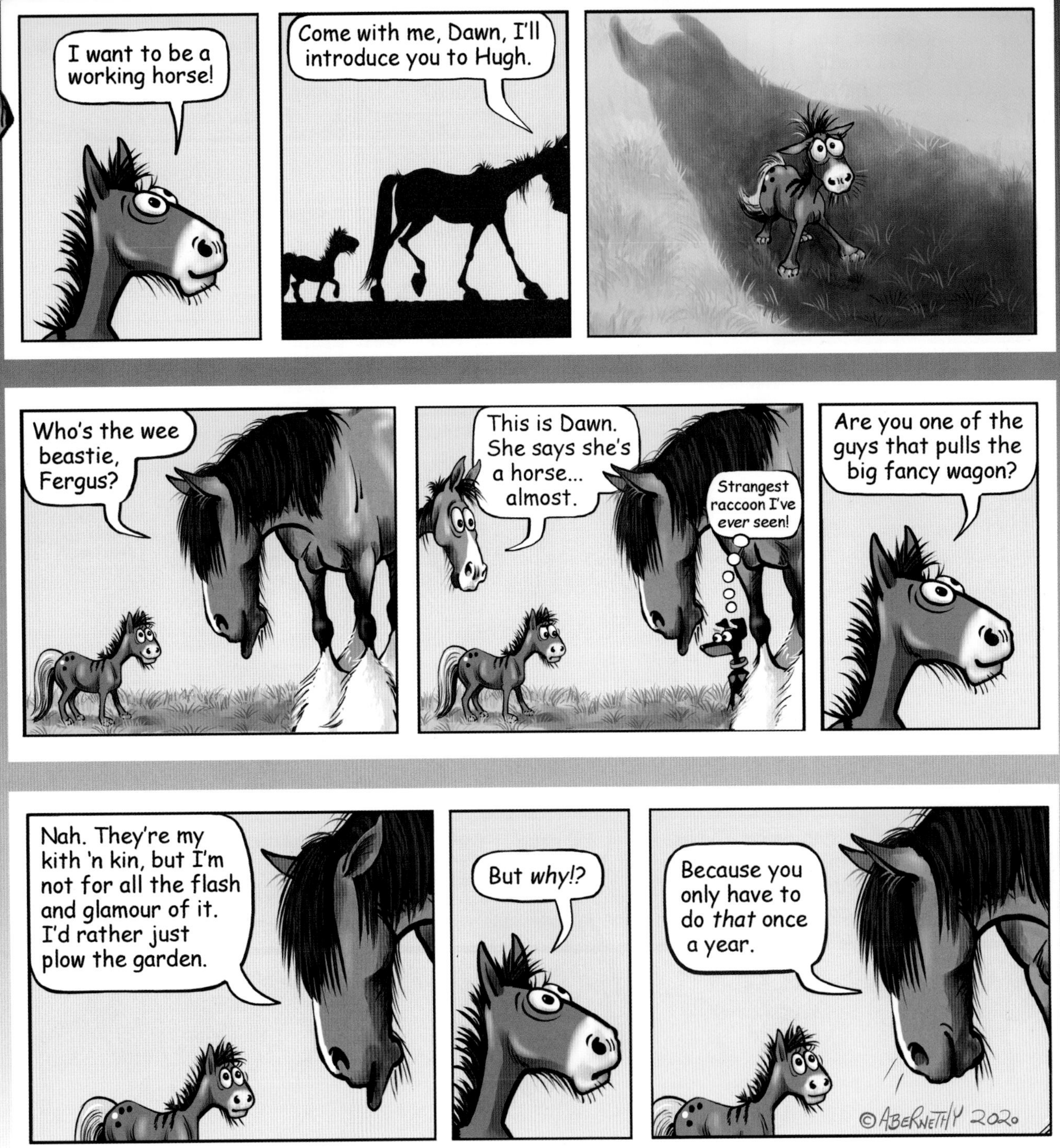
I want to be a working horse!
Come with me, Dawn, I'll introduce you to Hugh.
Who's the wee beastie, Fergus?
This is Dawn. She says she's a horse... almost.
Strangest raccoon I've ever seen!
Are you one of the guys that pulls the big fancy wagon?
Nah. They're my kith 'n kin, but I'm not for all the flash and glamour of it. I'd rather just plow the garden.
But *why!?*
Because you only have to do *that* once a year.
©ABERNETHY 2020

When Fergus gets nervous I like to distract him with comical thoughts.

Remember that hilarious fainting goat we saw yesterday, Fergus?

Fergus?...

...it takes his mind off his anxiety.

How could you mess up a hunter class so badly?!

Well, there's one thing you never explained to me.

What was that?

What, exactly, were we hunting for?

The Human Condition

There were a few times, Fergus, when I felt we couldn't hide away in our funny, fanciful realm, ignoring world events. In 2015 following the Charlie Bido massacre that put the world into shock, I introduced Monique.

Why do humans fight and kill each other, Fergus?
I don't know, Monique.
But how can we comfort them?
Like we always have. Do your work generously. And when your people are sad, let them put their arms around your neck, and their face into your mane. That helps them more than you might think.
©ABERNETHY 2015
Merci. Je le ferai.

The comic bore three little stripes of the French flag, and received a powerful response from our social media viewers.

When 50 Muslims were killed in a mass shooting in New Zealand a few years later, we swapped out the flag and posted the comic again.

Fergus, you've taught me that sometimes a touch of sentiment is as powerful as a good laugh. As we grapple with the human condition, you and your friends can remind us to give thanks to horses and all creatures who help us keep our balance.

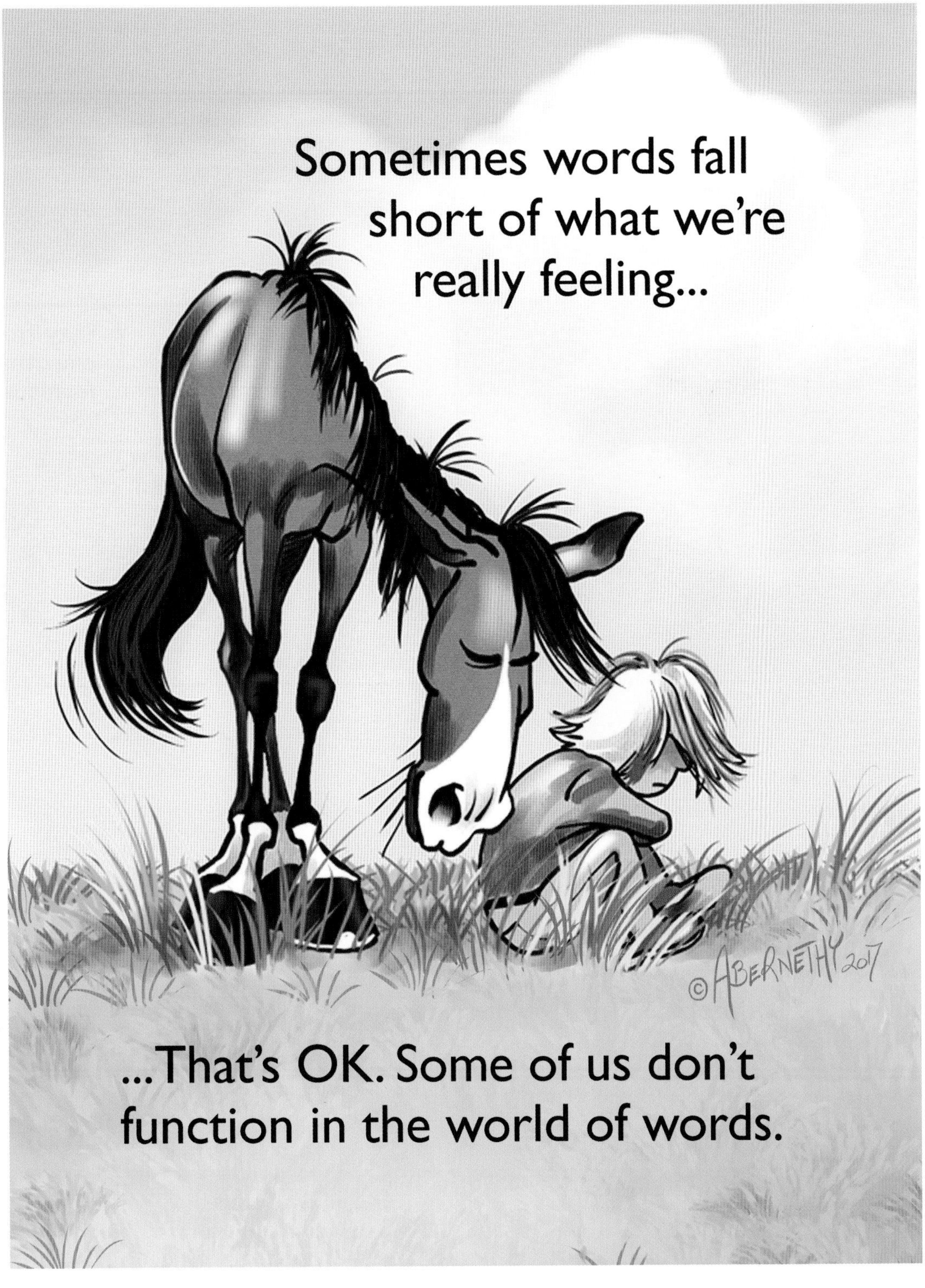
Sometimes words fall short of what we're really feeling...
©ABERNETHY 2017
...That's OK. Some of us don't function in the world of words.

You and Monique noticed our sadness as we humans watched Australia burn in January of 2020.

Qu'est-ce qui les rend tristes dans leur téléphone, Fergus?
Why do they look in their phones and feel sad, Fergus?
They feel empathy, Monique.
©ABERNETHY 2020

And when the Covid-19 pandemic swept around the world, you came through for us again, Fergus.

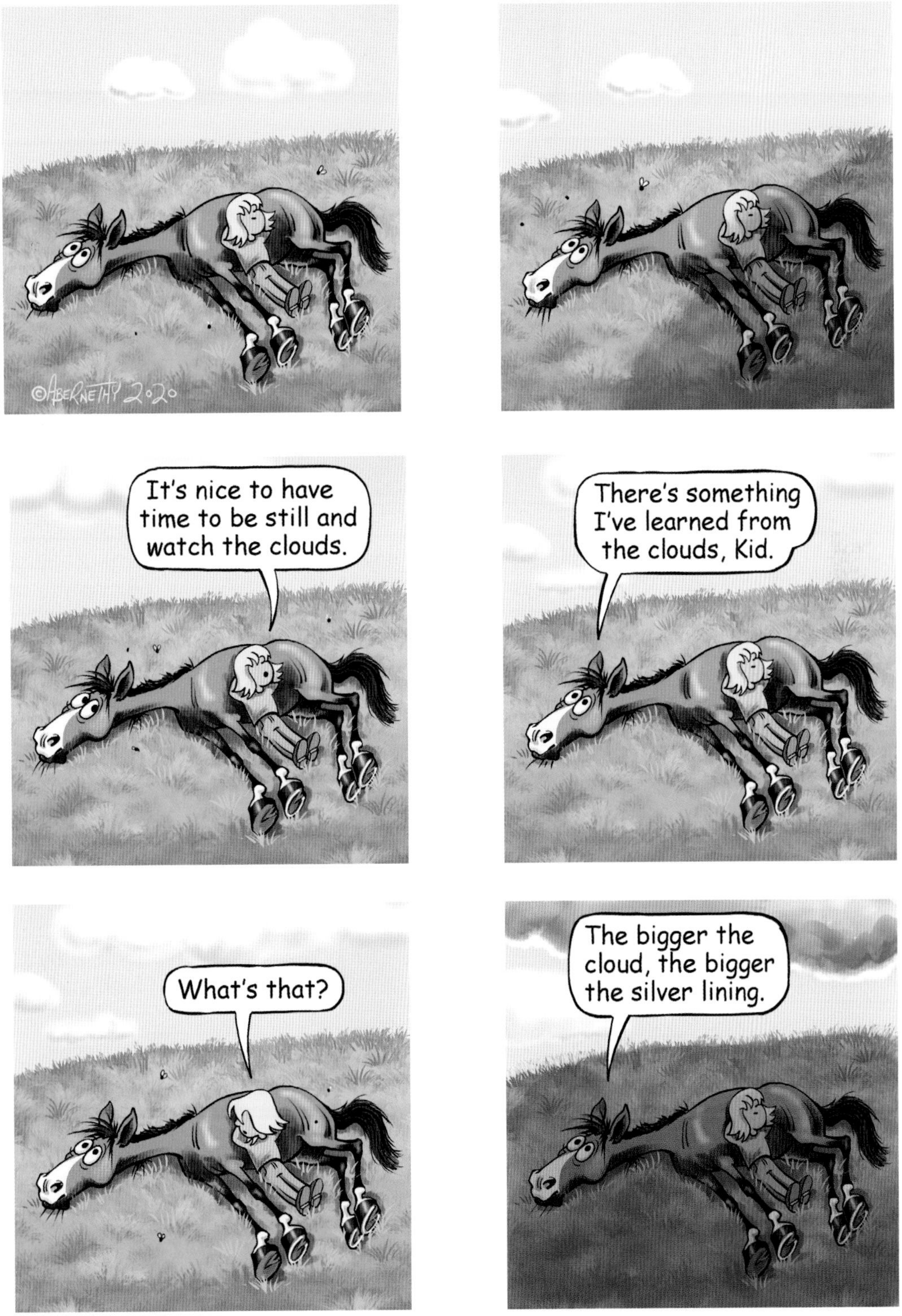
©ABERNETHY 2020
It's nice to have time to be still and watch the clouds.
There's something I've learned from the clouds, Kid.
What's that?
The bigger the cloud, the bigger the silver lining.

So... What's Next?

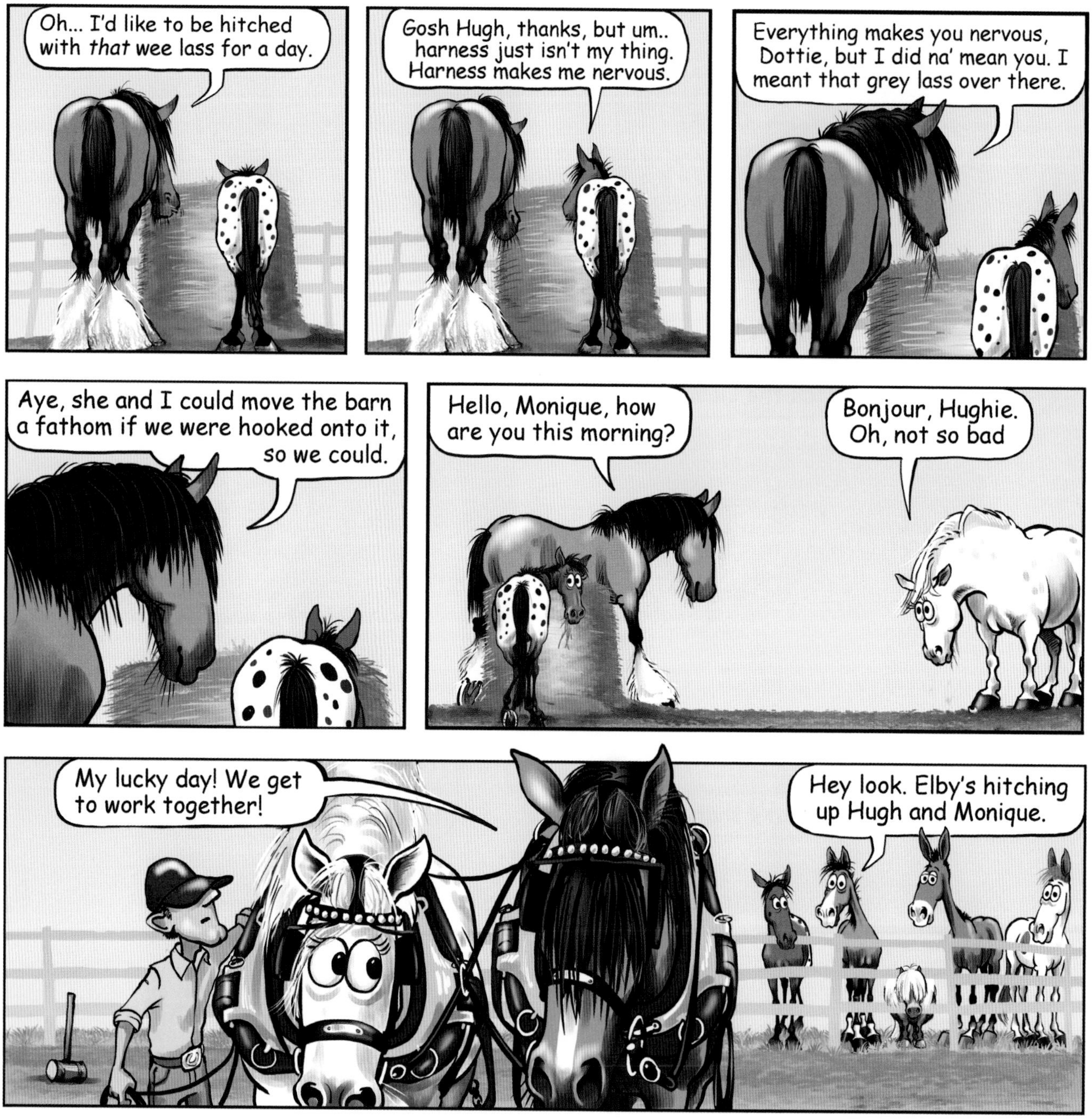
Oh... I'd like to be hitched with *that* wee lass for a day.
Gosh Hugh, thanks, but um.. harness just isn't my thing. Harness makes me nervous.
Everything makes you nervous, Dottie, but I did na' mean you. I meant that grey lass over there.
Aye, she and I could move the barn a fathom if we were hooked onto it, so we could.
Hello, Monique, how are you this morning?
Bonjour, Hughie. Oh, not so bad
My lucky day! We get to work together!
Hey look. Elby's hitching up Hugh and Monique.

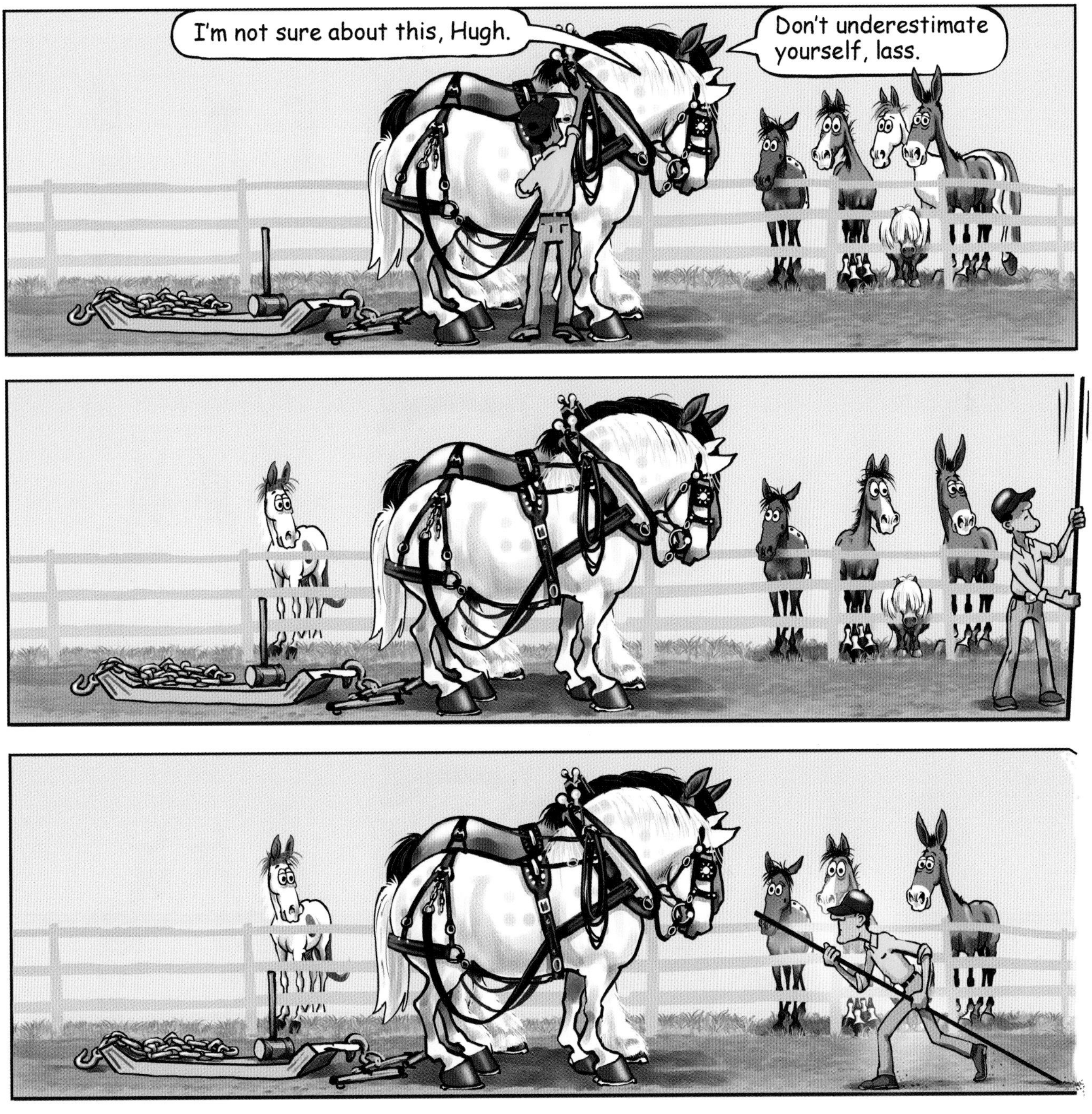
I'm not sure about this, Hugh.
Don't underestimate yourself, lass.

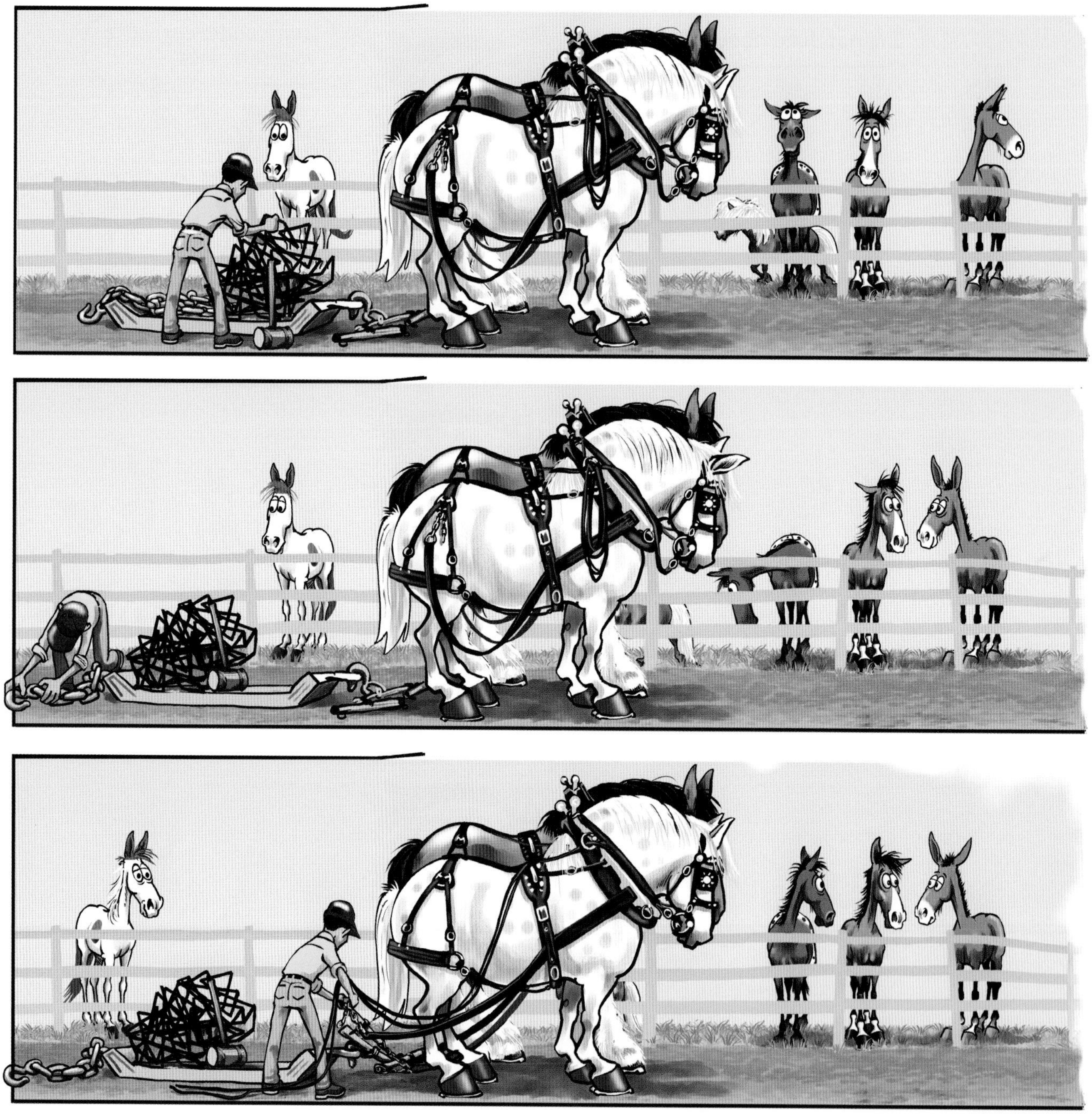

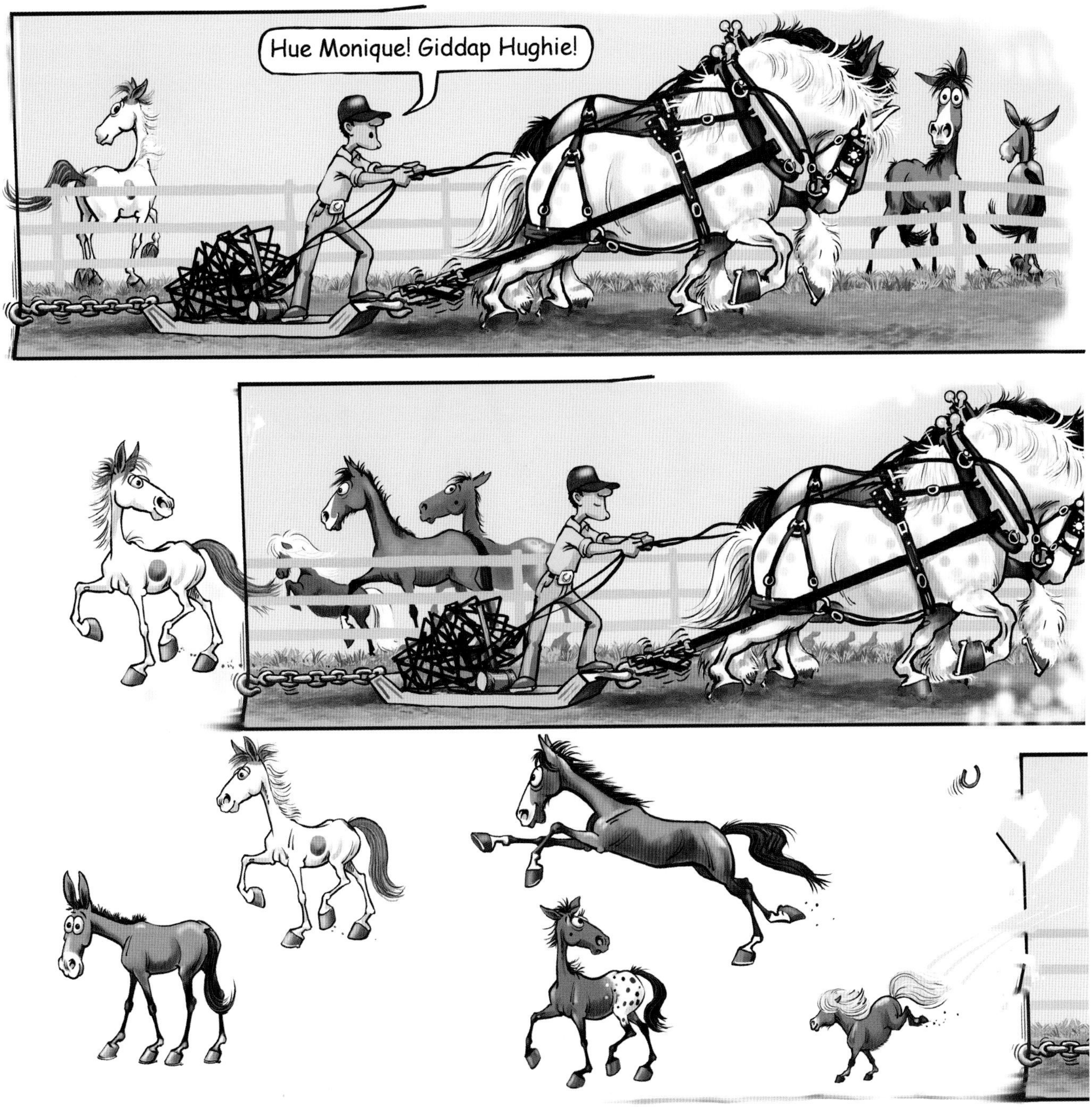
Hue Monique! Giddap Hughie!

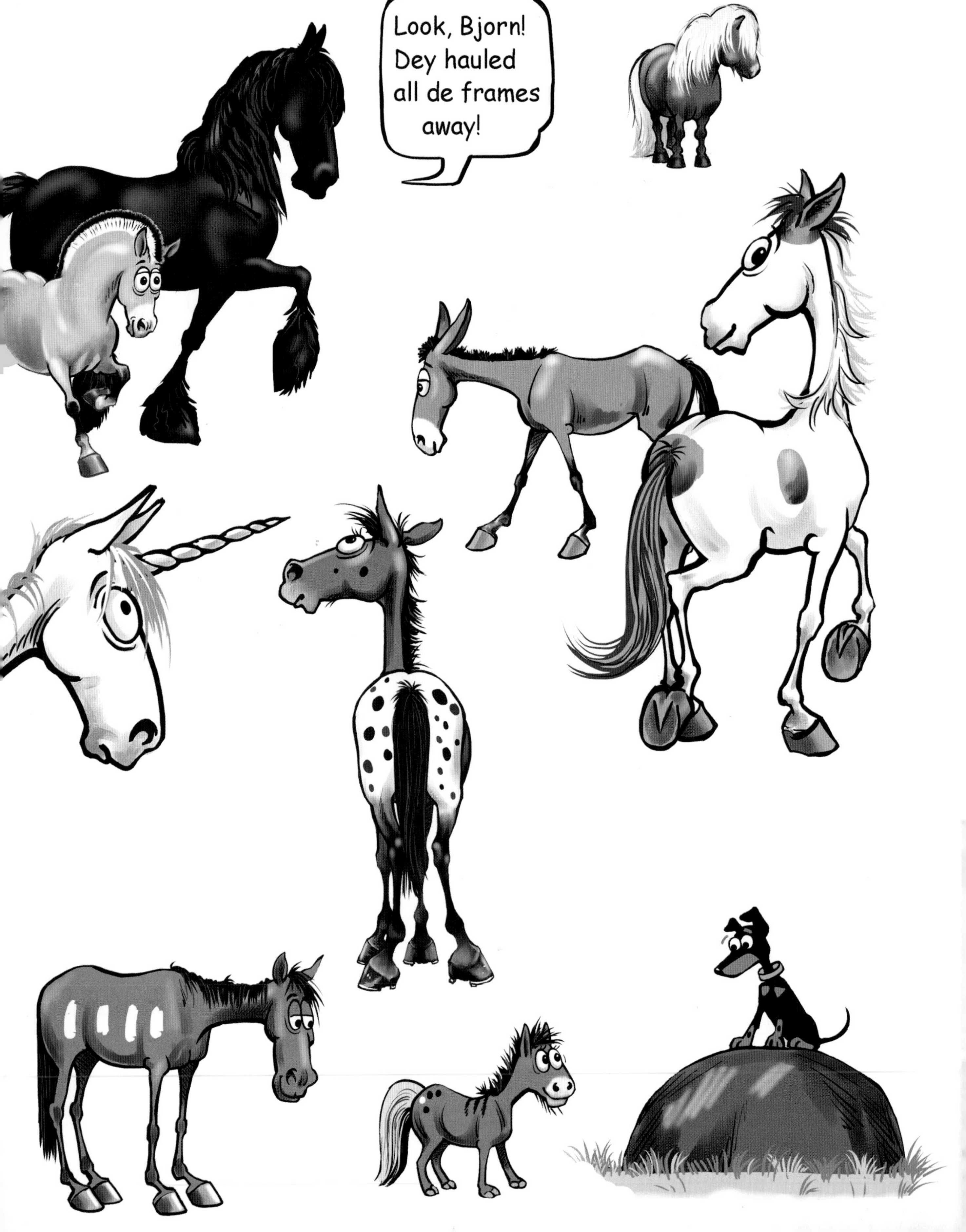
Look, Bjorn! Dey hauled all de frames away!

It's been a grand 20 years, Fergus.
Now...

...Where do you want
to go from here?

Your friend,

jean

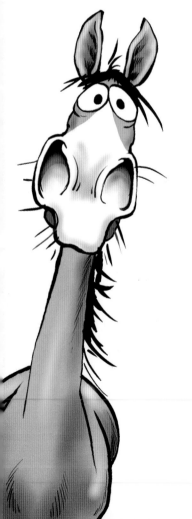

Let's Stay Friends!

www.fergusthehorse.com

 FergusTheHorse

 @fergus_the_horse

 Fergus The Horse